DATE DUE

A CHILD ANALYSIS WITH ANNA FREUD

A
Child Analysis
with
Anna Freud

PETER HELLER

Translated by
Salomé Burckhardt and Mary Weigand
and revised by the Author

International Universities Press, Inc.
Madison   Connecticut

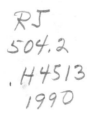

The first version of the major portions of this book appeared in German, with a commentary by the coeditor, Günther Bittner, as *Eine Kinderanalyse bei Anna Freud (1929–1932)*, published by Königshausen & Neumann, Würzburg, 1983.

Library of Congress Cataloging In Publication Data

Heller, Peter, 1920–
    [Kinderanalyse bei Anna Freud (1929–1932). English]
    A child analysis with Anna Freud / Peter Heller ; translated by
Salome Burckhardt and Mary Weigand and revised by the author.
      p. cm.
    Translation of: Eine Kinderanalyse bei Anna Freud (1929–1932)
    Includes index.
    ISBN 0-8236-0835-2
    1. Freud, Anna, 1895–   . 2. Heller, Peter, 1920–   . 3. Child
analysis—Case studies. 4. Psychotherapy patients—Biography.
I. Freud, Anna, 1895–   . II. Title.
RJ504.2.H4513 1990
618.92′8914—dc20   89-2146
                                                        CIP

Manufactured in the United States of America

CONTENTS

ACKNOWLEDGMENTS

Work on this book has been supported by grants from the State University of New York at Buffalo, the S.U.N.Y. Research Foundation, and a Guggenheim Fellowship.

PREFACE

Rudolf Ekstein, Ph.D.

Some time ago I received a book, published in the German language, and for me it was a treasure chest of years past, a return to Vienna, my city of origin, and to my beginnings as a student of psychoanalysis. I am referring to *Eine Kinderanalyse bei Anna Freud (1929–1932), (A Child Analysis with Anna Freud)*, by Peter Heller, published with an instructive and valuable commentary by Günther Bittner to which I am indebted for my comments. For me this book was a rediscovery, a return to the past, and it also gave me the pleasure of resuming an old relationship, my contact with Professor Peter Heller. I had met him years ago, back in Vienna, when I was a university student moving toward my Ph.D. in philosophy and psychology, while Peter Heller moved toward the end of high school, the mastery of the Gymnasium. Since my training was in psychoanalytic pedagogy, I had been asked to become Peter Heller's tutor, his *Hauslehrer*. The Viennese psychoanalyst, Willi Hoffer, introduced me to the Heller family. I knew at that time Peter had been analyzed, or perhaps was still in analysis, but I do not recall exactly if I knew that his child analysis was conducted by Miss Freud. I had some idea Thesi Bergmann, also a psychoanalytic pedagogue, was the governess of the young boy, and for quite a number of years a mother substitute after his father's divorce.

We met here many years later, both of us having achieved successful careers in America, and I began to gain insight into that analysis, as seen reflected in Anna Freud's notes, Peter's many drawings, the stories, the poetry, the letters now again in his possession.

I have now read the German version of Peter Heller's commentaries as well as the excellent English translation and have been given the privilege of writing the preface and thus trying to make this time alive to American readers and others who will see this book in its English translation.

Peter's father, Hans Heller, recently wrote an autobiography of his own entitled *Zwischen zwei Welten (Between Two Worlds)*, referring to the move from the German language, our mother tongue, to the acquired English language and to our new homes after the escape from occupied Austria to England and America; the moves back and forth between two homes, between two languages, different cultures, and different ways of thinking and living.

I should like to try to make that past, the origin of child analysis and its development alive and current for later generations of pedagogues and teachers, psychiatrists and psychoanalysts, and others concerned with the field of mental health. Peter's father, Hans Heller, was born in Austria, near Vienna. He was a few years older than I and at the end of his autobiography he wants to break the silence of years past. He thinks of his autobiography as perhaps the last occasion to say what should be said. He speaks of nearing the end of his life, but not reaching his goals and he wonders whether there is such a thing as *the* goal one can reach. He thinks of life as a relay race, a relay race through time. The message goes from father to son, from father to son—through all eternity. "Take the baton and go on, run on, boy. . . ."

I look at the material Anna Freud sent on to her former patient, Peter Heller, permitting him the use of this material for his book and we see Anna Freud now nearing the end of her life, turning the baton over to others as she must drop out of the relay race.

Anna Freud was originally a teacher, at first an elementary school teacher in the Vienna public school system. Later, with the help of Dorothy Burlingham, her lifelong friend, she founded a private school in which future analysts such as Erik Erikson and Peter Blos worked as teachers. Ernst Freud, Sigmund Freud's grandchild, and Peter Heller were students there, and later other experiments followed. Anna Freud's co-workers included the late Lilli Peller, the late Trude Bettelheim, and many others. I refer to the time after the First World War, a period that was full of experiments and school reform. This was the time when the Viennese Psychoanalytic Institute offered courses for psychoanalytic pedagogues, mainly elementary school and kindergarten teachers, but also some high school teachers.

Anna Freud was not the only one who was active in developing experiments that aimed at a synthesis between education and psycho-analysis. Willi Hoffer, mentioned earlier, and his friend Siegfried Bernfeld, the author of *Sysiphus or the Limits of Education*, founded the Kinderheim Baumgarten, and August Aichhorn was to experiment with delinquent children and adolescents, an experience described in his classic *Wayward Youth*.

There were also other schools of thinking, and I am referring to the work of Alfred Adler and his collaborators. Those were revolutionary days, after a lost war, when poverty, hunger, and unemployment were rife, and small Austria was all that was left of the Austro-Hungarian empire, the monarchy of the Hapsburgs at an end.

It was at that time that I began school, soon starting to sense the strife that went on between the school reformers and those who undermined that reform, wanting to go back to the days of old. I am speaking, of course, about the political struggle of those days, when Austria was to discontinue operating as a two-party political system, an experiment in democratic living which decayed and led to the end of the Republic in 1934.

I think I can best describe the attempts of the left, the social democrats, as they were trying to develop a model educational and welfare system. The Minister of Education at that time, Otto Glöckel, spoke the following words that I will never forget: "The Social Democrats have led the workers from the whiskey bottle to the worker's symphony concert." The anatomy professor Julius Tandler, who was also Welfare Minister, opened a hospital, a welfare center for children, and said in his opening address: "He who builds palaces for children tears down the walls of prisons." In this atmosphere of hope and of deep commitment psychoanalysis flourished, and in this stimulating and challenging day-by-day struggle the theories and techniques of education and therapy developed.

It was during that time that Anna Freud was invited by the Viennese socialists to give lectures to teachers and thus influenced the education of young children. Many of these early child analysts started as educators. I speak of people such as Thesi Bergmann, Siegfried Bernfeld, Bruno Bettelheim, Bertha Bornstein, Edith Buxbaum, Emma Plank, Fritz Redl, Hedy Schwarz, and many others. It was a creative time and most of us hoped that we could contribute to the school system and the new world to come with the knowledge of psychology, of psychoanalysis, modern pedagogy, to a renewal of the school system.

But times changed, the country was surrounded by fascist governments; Mussolini to the south and Hitler to the north, Horthy in Hungary. The Austrian Parliament was dissolved in 1934, elections were forbidden, opposition parties and unions suppressed, the resistance broken, and many of us were soon to fill the concentration camps and the police prisons. Small islands were maintained, and it was during that time that I became a student in the Course for Psychoanalytic Pedagogues, and chose to be analyzed and to follow a career which would slowly lead to work with difficult children, to child psychotherapy and child psychoanalysis, and to emigration. That was true for a good many others, but few of us kept primarily to educational tasks. My good friend, Thesi Bergmann, Peter's governess, was one of those. Fate had it that she and I escaped on the same train and were admitted at Dover, England, on August 10, 1938, free once more. We would not be permitted to stay long in the United Kingdom, later coming to the United States. We kept in touch through all these years and I think I helped Peter to find her again. We occasionally sent each other publications until the time of her death in 1982.

It was during this time of decay and the slow destruction of the positive influence of psychoanalysis in Vienna, indeed, throughout Europe, that I met Peter Heller.

I recall first meeting his father, who interviewed me, and introduced me to his young second wife. I had hardly ever met people who were as well off as the Hellers at that time, living in a beautiful villa in one of the affluent districts, while I lived in a small apartment in the poorer section of the ninth district. Little did I know that the Hellers were very liberal, enlightened people when I began my work with Peter. I dimly recall that sometimes Peter and I would get together by telephone, and I would try to help him with complicated geometric drawings and give instructions by telephone, seeing his work and trying to visualize it all in my mind's eye. Then of course, we lost each other; each one for himself, each trying to get away from the terror system, to begin a new life.

And now there comes a book, the material from Peter's analysis, the things he wrote as a young boy, and the comments he shares with us about his treatment some sixty years later. The book is a remarkable document and I admire the courage that allows Professor Heller to publish this document. I think of this material almost as a kind of archaeological find. It stems from a time when Anna Freud was a comparative beginner. She had published her first book on child analysis in 1927 and it would take almost a decade until she would publish her classic, *The Ego and the Mechanisms of Defense.*

As one reads her notes on the clinical work with Peter, one can study Miss Freud's mind as it changes from earlier ways of thinking, deeply influenced by her father, to the work of 1936. She moves from id psychology to ego psychology without, however, ever abandoning her way of thinking in order to follow the line which had also characterized Sigmund Freud's work, a line of progressive development. While Peter's analysis took place in the years 1929 to 1932, one cannot help but feel that Anna Freud was in the midst of the development of her method, and that in her data on the analytic process in Peter's analysis one can find changes of theory and technique which are of great historic importance. She discusses two basic issues of conflict that came to the surface in 1927, and were discussed in a symposium on child psychoanalysis, a response to her book on child analysis. I refer to the important historical controversy between Melanie Klein and Anna Freud and their respective students. The first question concerns the issue as to whether the transference neurosis develops in work with children, whether the Oedipus complex should be fully analyzed; whether during child analysis, particularly during the beginning phase, both analytic interventions and pedagogic interventions might be necessary. The other issue apparent in the material of the child analysis is one which Anna Freud addressed in her book *The Ego and the Mechanisms of Defense,* published in 1936. One can clearly see how, during Peter's analysis, she developed in part her psychological concepts concerning methods of the mechanisms of defense. In her 1936 volume, she defines and describes an example for the defense mechanism of the restriction of the ego in a boy. This boy became a good soccer player, but then, fearing the aggression of the "big ones," he "unlearns," forgets this accomplishment. Peter Heller recalls this episode as a *key mechanism* in his life.

The style then of Anna Freud's work, the interpretive language she used, her way of listening, changed and deepened. She demonstrates through such clinical examples how, if we only want to, we can learn from our patients and must not remain overcommitted to our theoretical assumptions, but refine them.

While preparing the preface, I discovered remarks by Anna Freud in her interchanges with Joseph Sandler, as they prepared *The Analysis of Defense*: *The Ego and the Mechanisms of Defense Revisited*, a volume published in 1985,[1] three years after Anna Freud's death. There is no doubt that her remarks referred to the analysis of Peter. I learned from Professor Heller that he was then nearly nine years old rather than six years old, as the book states. His parents were separated rather than divorced and he expressed, as he did in the book, the difficulty in correctly assessing the relationship between the analysis of the little boy, his life history, and the man he was to become. He was interned as an "enemy alien" in England. He did not become a pianist, having obtained a diploma in the art. After a marriage that ended in divorce and a very stormy "internal career," he became a professor of literature. Anna Freud, in her discussion with Joseph Sandler, says: "We used to say to child analysts that they should be careful not to disturb budding sublimations in the child, because if you begin to interpret them, to show up their sexual or aggressive sources, you may nip the whole thing in the bud. We used to think that in the therapeutic process elements the child could not deal with otherwise should be given a push toward sublimation. We felt that we had to be careful of these elements, that something might be going on which did not belong to what one has to analyze. But after a while we saw something else during child analysis, that there are many meanings of sublimation which come to nothing, or which are transitory. Now we would say that it is far too optimistic to think that a child of, say, five years or who develops a special attachment to an activity, will keep that attachment in his later life. On the other hand, I remember analyzing a little boy about forty years ago who was then six years old. He was a clever little boy, with divorced parents, and at times his mother would come to visit him. Whenever she left him again he fell into a sort of depression, and in that state he produced poetry. Well, he dictated the poetry in his analytic sessions. It was very nice poetry, and this boy, after a very stormy career, became a professor of literature. I heard from him recently that he was very interested in seeing his early poems, and as I treasured them, I had them copied and sent to him.

[1]Sandler, J., with Freud, A. (1985), *The Analysis of Defense: The Ego and the Mechanisms of Defense Revisited*. New York: International Universities Press, p. 180.

They are quite impressive, and there is no doubt that his present profession and his poetic ability as a child have a very definite link. But at the time we analyzed his poetic tendency, partly in relation to his mother and his feelings of extreme longing and sadness, and partly in relation to his very intense fear of being hurt, which caused him to turn all his attention away from bodily accomplishments to intellectual ones."

The surviving data of Peter Heller's child analysis, my own world at that time, the choosing of a profession, the acquisition of professional knowledge, seem to be phases of the past. Why should one go back to analytical notes, old material, drawings, dreams, and make an attempt to restore the past, the happenings of half a century ago? Should young analysts read this book and trace the development of today's therapeutic techniques? In our pragmatic culture many students are only interested in the immediate task, the instant recipe that is to help them meet a situation, change a symptom, and so on.

Sigmund Freud loved to quote the poet Goethe, who said: "What thou hast inherited from your fathers, acquire it to make it thine and thee." I would like to paraphrase this beautiful quote and not just speak of fathers only, but say that we must acquire what we have inherited from our fathers and mothers and thus have it become truly ours. Professor Heller, the little Peter of yesteryear, has given us a great gift. He permits us to look into his childhood, his life, his analysis with Anna Freud, and we also learn about his present thinking, learn of the success of that analysis. He had an analyst, Anna Freud, who permitted him to learn, who permitted him to doubt, and thus he became an heir to her thinking. He used this heritage well and I feel grateful to him. Peter Heller's father writes about our fate "between two worlds," and I think Peter Heller's contribution teaches those of us in this profession that there is more than one way to bridge those two worlds. The readers of this volume will find it pleasant and useful, as do he and I, to move back and forth on the bridge that is the analytical understanding of the human and societal life cycle.

(Photographs appear after "Prefatory Remarks.")

TO THE READER

Because of the unusual nature of the material presented in this volume, we would like to describe in detail the format of the book. It is hoped that this will help the reader use the parts of the book more effectively and thus enhance the understanding and appreciation of its contents.

INDEX OF PERSONS AND PLACES

This is a glossary containing descriptions of the people and locations referred to throughout the book. People's names are arranged alphabetically according to *first* name because first names are used to a large extent throughout the text.

ANNA FREUD'S COLLECTION OF NOTES AND MATERIALS

Parts 1 and 2

This consists of all material Anna Freud accumulated during her analysis of Peter Heller. Remarks added by the editor or translator within Anna Freud's text are in brackets. The texthead "SUMMARIES" refers to Anna Freud's division of the first part of the analysis into eight phases. Roman numerals I-VIII, inserted by the editor, indicate the *beginning* of each of these phases, while the *end* of each phase is marked by the insertion of Anna Freud's summary of that phase. Summaries by phases exist only for the first part of the analysis. Hence the editor distinguishes Part 1 with its corresponding summaries from Part 2, in which entries are specified only by individual titles (mostly by a heading at the beginning of the entry).

Materials in Anna Freud's collection stemming from the patient, such as letters, poems, stories, essays, are included either in the footnotes at the appropriate date or in the Appendix. Drawings are briefly explained by Peter Heller and are presented within the analysis text pages.

The analysis text will be running on the right-hand pages of the book, in full size type.

Footnotes to Parts 1 and 2

The footnotes to Anna Freud's text are in smaller type and will be running on the left-hand pages of the book, opposite their citations. They are set in smaller type than the analysis text. This will make their function clear and facilitate their use.

Appendix to Anna Freud's Collection of Notes and Materials

This contains various types of patient-generated materials considered too lengthy to appear within the footnotes.

RETROSPECTIVE

This section, set in regular-size text format, contains Peter Heller's recollections and impressions regarding the experiences presented in the analysis by Anna Freud.

INDEX OF PERSONS
AND PLACES

Michael (Mikey) Burlingham: Tinky's younger brother
Mijn Bok: piano teacher
Mumi: Edith Kramer, older friend of P.
P.: P.H., Peter Heller, patient, born 1920
Peter Blos: teacher and principal of the B-R School
Reinhard: schoolmate at the B-R School
Ruth B: schoolmate
Siegfried Bernfeld: analyst
Sigurd: Basti's older brother, pupil at the B-R School
Thesi, Thesu: Therese Bergmann, P.'s governess
Tilly: chambermaid for the Hellers
Tinky: Katrina E. Burlingham, P.'s schoolmate at the B-R School
Victor: son of Eva Rosenfeld; P.'s playmate and schoolmate at the B-R School

INTRODUCTION

All this happened nearly sixty years ago. Am I still what I was then? That hyper, stocky, strong little boy with black curly hair, slovenly and spoilt, pugnacious and anxious; who sometimes acted and thought of himself as a poor, piggish soul, and sometimes as an "immortal," alternating, as a friendly reader put it, between "Klosettmensch und Genie"; that is, the attraction to public toilets and aspirations to genius?

The phrase "disorder and early sorrow" comes to mind, Thomas Mann's formula for a case of premature sexual awakening and confusion brought on by the social tremors and insecurity of the 1920s. What are the links between this bright little Jewish boy, brought up in privileged left-wing liberal, capitalist avant-garde style, and the bald, overweight teacher of language and literature, the diligently literary academic? Between them intervened the obliteration of that privileged milieu which some German contemporaries have called a ghetto of *high culture* (perhaps that term would apply to academia as well). Between them stands Hitler, the genius of the petit bourgeoisie, carrying ad absurdum that cult of genius to which I, the little "great man," adhered with such persistence. Between them came our emigration, the long, strenuous, ever inadequate adjustment to America, an alien continent and alien language. How could I bring all this together? An unmanageable abundance of events seems to rush by, escaping my grasp, as if I were trying to scoop up a river.

So there he stands in a Vienna townhouse, Berggasse 19, in the hallway of a solidly middle-class apartment that has since become a Freud museum and archive. He is waiting for his session with Anna Freud. The great old man passes by: slight (in my memory), bent, seeming to chew or mumble. He was suffering, by then, from cancer of the palate; had his jaw prosthesis, and had had several operations; but he always assumed a diligent, cheerful air. Now and then he patted me hurriedly on the shoulder: "*So groß, so groß,*" he would say. "How you've grown!," which struck me as typical stupidity of a grown-up: as if I could be conned into believing that I had grown visibly in the course of a few weeks. And yet, for *groß* means both tall and great in German, he touched on the nerve of my ambition (did his daughter discuss her patients with him?). It was as if he knew that then, and all my life long, hardly anything would so preoccupy me as the wish to be *groß*, a great man.

Time to go in now, along a dark passage, turning right into Anna Freud's room, past her large, fairly cluttered desk, and Wolfi, a German shepherd, blackish tipped with brown, as I may recall incorrectly (the room smelled of him); and on to the couch, covered with a carpet and brown cloth antimacassars at head and foot. Lying there, I would feel her behind me in her chair, knitting or crocheting, and could squint upward to the left to see bookshelves with volumes of Nietzsche—the Kröner (formerly Naumann) pocket-size edition—in which I sometimes read to shield myself from analysis. Having published a book on Nietzsche in 1970 and being engaged still in publishing English-language studies on Nietzsche, I must ask myself again: Am I still that little boy who made a career out of what began as a defensive maneuver against analysis? It is not easy to gain a sense of freedom and independence in dealing with these memories and the material at hand.

Back to the Berggasse, to Anna Freud, then a young woman, rather pretty and delicate, dark-eyed, with that pure and penetrating gaze which she retained even in old age. I see her before me: the rounded movement of her delicate, skillful hands; the slight stoop even then, the wisp of stray hair across her forehead adding an absent-minded scholarly note. There was the homey, neat, comfortable, yet austere way she dressed: the citified dirndls, the homespun, stylized simplicity she favored, which was unostentatious and in keeping with the emphasis on unerotic, unseductive femininity; a quality of kindly severity.

This was the way she was, or appeared to me, when I fell in love with her; when, in the course of my analysis with her, I came to love and, at times, to hate her, as I continued to do even after analysis and in the decades when Anna Freud lived, as ageing queen of the Freudian movement in its London center, in close companionship with her lifelong friend Dorothy.

Dorothy Tiffany Burlingham, born in 1891 in New York, still a youngish American woman in her mid-thirties, had moved to Vienna in the fall of 1925. She had left her husband, a doctor, in the States. He was said to be mentally ill. His father, a distinguished lawyer, restless, strong-willed, exceedingly bright, educated in the classics, was the influential friend of prominent Democrats, including La-Guardia and Roosevelt. The younger Burlingham a few years later leaped to his death on Park Avenue from the window of his father's spaciously uncomfortable, elegantly puritanical apartment. Dorothy Tiffany herself belonged to a wealthy patrician family. She was the daughter of the American artist Louis C. Tiffany, famous creator of opulently colorful reflections of the fin-de-siècle—stained glass windows, iridescent vases and lampshades—and, so the rumor went, perhaps also an alcoholic. Dorothy had moved with her four children to Vienna to become a patient of Sigmund Freud, and to live, eventually, in the Berggasse, directly above the Freuds, in an apartment which I wanted to be, and which became, a second home for me. For I admired, worshipped, and loved the fair, fine, attractive, sensitive patrician children in their effortless grace, their carelessness, their American sense of humanity, even in their lack of zest or commitment. Their mother, Puritan at heart, an enlightened WASP, magnanimous and decent in intent and deed, became a kind of mother also to me, and one who would not desert her children, as I blamed my own mother for doing. But Dorothy aroused mixed feelings in me. I can still hear her, insisting vehemently: "Absolutely, app-so-lute-ly *not*, Bob!" And this dogmatic vehemence was in accord with an uptight character or demeanor that would erect barriers and enforce a distance between herself and other humans, and stifle spontaneity, quite against her conscious intention. Occasionally though, a teasing, spinsterish sense of humor broke trippingly through the shell of self-righteousness, shyness, and virtuous repression. "Mother," as all of us called her, had dark, fine, sharply chiseled features like those of an old American Indian. She thought of herself, erroneously, as stupid. Her later psychoanalytic publications would also seem to disprove this; but she certainly was austerely limited in perspective. Quite in command of her family (though it shocked me most pleasantly that her American children dared to say such things to her as "don't be silly, mother"), she was utterly submissive in her pious zeal to turn herself into a vassal of Professor and Anna Freud. When she reported: "The Professor thinks" or "Anna says," let alone, "The Professor and Anna think," she was clearly invoking the highest possible authority. Thus, in crass innocence, she came to represent the narrow minded, narrow hearted orthodoxy, the know-it-all-presumption, the petty concern with orders of rank, and the vindictive cliquishness that often made the Freudians so insufferable. Much later, when I married her daughter Tinky, my blonde, slender first love who seemed to me to dissolve in mysterious loveliness, "Mother," of course, became my mother-in-law. Now, decades after our divorce, Tinky, like me, is confronting old age, living in Cambridge, Massachusetts, married to a psychoanalyst, not far from our daughter Anne (named after Anna Freud) who is herself in middle age.

When I first met the Burlingham children, Bob, the oldest, must have been about fourteen, Mabbie, the older girl, about twelve, Tinky ten, and Mikey, then the "little one," a year younger than I, about eight years old. What has become of us all in these sixty years? A fateful embrace stifling the unfolding lives of these children had been created by Mother, the maternal trust fund, the motherly authority, reinforced by Anna Freud (who was the children's permanent analyst, or, at least, one who, again and again, assumed a therapeutic function with them, far beyond their childhood), as well as by the prestige and spell emanating from the center of the Freudian movement. Worldly and spiritual power, fixation on mother, money, transference object (the analyst Anna Freud who was, at the same time, "Mother's" most intimate friend), and spiritual authority (Freud, psychoanalysis, for them the object or a cult, the doctrine of salvation) were, and remained, all one. Who could stand up against that? How did Bob die, and of what? Of alcoholism, of asthma, or was it suicide, by purposefully disregarding urgent medical prescription and care, and doing what was bound to destroy him (e.g., smoking when he shouldn't have)? Did he put an end, in helpless rage, to his life which never matured into the "self-realization" that was preached so intensely by his mother? And Mabbie, our model, the good one who took care of everyone? (Later on, she herself would denigrate, unjustly I thought, her excessively selfless caring for and ordering of the lives of others, as a compulsion, a sickness.) Supposedly prettier, more puritanical, more clearly defined, smoother, more open and friendlier than Tinky, she represented the same freely moving, graceful type.

Characteristically, I thought of her, as a boy, that when she knew the same "dirty" things that I did, they became "pure."

We were all in analysis with Anna Freud at the same time: Tinky, Bob, Michael, Erik Homburger-Erikson, Ernsti Halberstadt-Freud, and I. Instead of observing the separation of the therapeutic and the private spheres which the Freudians postulated, Anna Freud spun, in all innocence, the spiderweb of the older generation in which later so many of us, beneficiaries and victims, got caught. Perhaps, in a menopausal depression (she was not given any medication, because the psychoanalytic faith and authority of the old ladies did not allow it), Mabbie returned in the summer of 1974 to the center of the cult at Maresfield Gardens, to take her life a day later, with pills collected for this purpose over a long period of time.

My relation to analysis remains ambivalent. This is connected also with my relationship to the Burlingham family, and particularly to the Burlingham children. It was a relationship marked for me, among other things, by the opposition between my darkness and their radiance, my brooding and their seemingly unburdened grace and lightness; or indeed—in keeping with clichés of that period—between the Jewish, reflective, intellectual consciousness of guilt and impurity, and the Aryan children of light. For this antithesis—the foundation of Nazi ideology—was characteristic not only of my childish imagination but quite pervasively alive in the infantile spirit of the time. Indefatigably in love with Tinky, I became closely connected with that highly respected and beloved circle. But later, under the pressure of a marriage which was unsatisfying to both of us, I rebelled against all those who were clustering around Anna Freud and Mother, and whose lives were controlled from that center. Or did my ambivalence toward analysis simply stem from the exaggerated hopes which I nourished concerning its powers of salvation? I had been brought up by atheistic parents. Analysis was my substitute for religion, even more so than Marxism. At the same time I believed that these two systems gave us a double key to the fundamental human questions: Marxism to the collective, social world; psychoanalysis to the life of the individual. For the analysts gravitating around Freud and the circle of the Burlingham family in Vienna, in whose shadow I grew up, psychoanalysis was indeed a religion, a church, a cult. Such expectations of salvation deserved, and were bound, to be disappointed. Moreover, psychoanalysis never entirely cured me. After my childhood analysis with Anna Freud, I went back into analysis in my late twenties with Ernst Kris, in particular because I was haunted and driven by confused, bewildering sexual fantasies which compelled me, as it were, to be unfaithful and interfered with sustained concentration so that, quite frequently, days and weeks would go by for me in a haze of vague desires. And of this second analysis too, it seemed and seems to me that it did not free me of my difficulties altogether. Thus, when Anna Freud sent me the material concerning my child analysis with her, I went to the analyst Heinz Lichtenstein for the purpose, I thought, of discussing this material and its possible utilization. But immediately, and now at an advanced age, I began to speak about my troubles, which, among other things, referred me back to the dilemma between greatness and smallness, which had already preoccupied me as a boy, and to the complex of voyeurism and exhibitionism which had also appeared in the childhood analysis. And surely, the present self-analysis is yet another attempt at productive integration of this complex. Finally, to complete my list of reasons for my ambivalence, I also thought I encountered on an intellectual and academic plane a good deal of dogmatic prejudice on the part of some analysts, and this in turn diminished my respect for a discipline which, to be sure, has had a lasting influence upon my life and thought.

My concern here is not to take sides for or against psychoanalysis or to pose an either-or, but rather with an attitude toward analysis determined by a variety of motifs and their fluctuating intensities. Does analysis swallow up one's life, I was asked by an analyst. Again my answer would have to be ambivalent, a yes-and-no, concerning, to be sure, only analysis as I experienced it in my own person and in those around me some decades ago. Analysis, as practiced then, fostered self-observation, but also self-inhibition. It encouraged going back, regression, retreat from presence into the modality of an absence never caught up with, a promise of presence never redeemed. And even if this was and is a condition attendant upon all existence, psychoanalysis frequently intensified it, but without ever eliminating one's hang-ups or their derivatives. Again and again, analysis as I knew it, fostered a surveillance by the analyst and a self-surveillance, which treated every manifestation of life and every new turn as merely provisional, hence to be scrutinized with a view to latent, probably more essential motifs and impulses that might need correction. This resulted in a pervasive mental reservation, a permanent "second look," a worried suspicious glance at one's own life, a reflectiveness raised to a higher power, which did not quite allow one to regard one's existence as definitive or valuable in itself. In a sense, life is always and never provisional; but to live, self-consciously and continuously, in the provisional mode, is surely inhibiting. And for the therapist the exercise of this reflective grip—in keeping with the patient's permission and request for it— often proved a dangerous source of power, and a temptation to exercise illegitimate tutelage.

For analysis certainly could be used and was used to inhibit self-realization in those who entrusted themselves to therapists and in whose lives the therapists intervened. My most bitter reproach to Anna Freud, Dorothy Burlingham, and the circle of orthodox, presumptuously authoritative psychoanalysts has always been that they had an infantilizing and often debilitating influence on their patients, instead of promoting the liberation of man which seemed to be inherent in the potential of psychoanalysis. I cannot forget the expression and tone of voice of some analysts who, not only in therapy but in daily intercourse or discussion, would look you deeply in the eye with a gaze gleaming with indifferent participation, or say in a voice almost vibrant with neutrality: "How interesting that you should say this; it certainly would express your perspective . . ." or something of that sort. And you could always be sure that they were addressing not the expressed opinion, but the suspected latent motives presumably unknown to the speaker himself, and that they were interested in these motives only and not at all in what you said.

And yet behind the pseudo-empathy which never concerned itself with the manifest conduct or content but only with what had yet to be deciphered; behind the false, depersonalized friendliness; the bedside-manner-mask of sympathy; behind the tendentiously penetrating gaze which scrutinized your own, I see the radiant and illuminating eyes and hear the purifying voice and interpretations of Anna Freud whom I loved and revered as a child beyond all other humans. My ambivalence toward analysis has a still more primitive root as well: In analysis I wanted to be loved, and even loved precisely as a patient; and like so many patients, I did not think I was loved enough.

This brings me back to the little boy of whom I sometimes think that his heart was alive and that he had quite a bit of that radiant intelligence which Freud ascribes to children. I have also asked myself occasionally whether this alertness and capacity for strong emotions were not obscured or submerged during some later periods. Were those early years not my best after all? Anna Freud's ability to enter into the world of this boy as she did in the analysis, to understand him, to enlighten him, to draw him out of himself, and to raise him above himself, seems to show her to me in the very best light, in *her* unique, lucid (at times all too lucid) intelligence, her humor, her capacity for a purifying, cathartic, empathic response which did not allow any collusion or complicity with weaknesses, yet did them justice. A moralistic element, a slight admixture of what Nietzsche called *Moralin* may occasionally be detectable but it seems justified by her position as adult and educator. I now recall seeing Anna Freud when I was about to separate from Tinky, who was once again in analysis with her, and her saying to me that I was like a chambermaid who came for a pro forma visit with her notice to leave already in her pocket. Perhaps, as her friend, the analyst Eva Rosenfeld, observed to me in conversation, Anna Freud was freer at that earlier time because "her father's mantle had not yet fallen upon her shoulders." She had not as yet claimed her place as heir and as contender for leadership in a world movement.

The wider circle of my existence at the time was also dominated by Anna Freud. It consisted of the very private Burlingham–Rosenfeld School, which bore the stamp of Anna Freud's personality and of her conception of psychoanalytic pedagogy. In fact, the school was, among other things, although this was denied later on, a progressive and elitist experiment in the education of children undergoing analysis. At first, Dorothy Burlingham had been looking merely for a private tutor for her eldest child, Bob. She found Peter Blos, later well known as an analyst, who, in turn, brought his friend Erik Homburger-Erikson along. The small school of ours then formed around the four Burlingham children whose preeminence, attenuated by American democratic manners, was recognized by their fellow pupils, as well as by the teachers, the more so, as Dorothy Burlingham financed the entire enterprise. Cofounder of the school and participating substantially in its management and guidance was another intimate friend of Anna Freud, Eva Rosenfeld, wife of a Viennese lawyer, who also became a prominent analyst later on. In her backyard, in front of our playground, the little wooden schoolhouse was built.

The administrative director was Peter Blos, a German with a

systematic and scientific bent of mind, and a very young and strikingly handsome man of whom I was somewhat afraid because he was strict, exact, pedantic, and without sympathy for Austrian *Schlamperei* or my personal mixture of slovenliness, tardiness, and apologetic irresponsibility, and my habit of talking during class. His collaborator and somewhat Bohemian painter friend, the Scandinavian Erik Homburger-Erikson (later renowned as a psychologist), taught the humanities interestingly, in a lively and subtle manner, inspiring students to do work which they felt to be their own. I was very fond of Erik, who was quite gentle in characterizing and restraining my aggressively disintegrative, contrary, dialectical debativeness and incessant questioning. We liked him, but also liked to make fun of the blond, tall, rather delicate young man who blushed ever so easily and, as Mabbie would observe, could not pass a mirror without looking at himself.

Peter Blos and Erik were the main teachers, especially for the "big ones," *die Großen,* the adolescents: elegant, talented Bob Burlingham; diligent Mabbie Burlingham, lively, sensitive, and aware; Sigurd (Basti's older brother), somber, angry, menacing, and inclined to be violent, who committed suicide while he was still in school; well-behaved, good Gerda; and the siblings and model pupils who were not in analysis and opposed to it as a suspect and alien thing: Mario Iona, who later became a physicist, and Elisabeth who had a saintly look about her and was to marry an English clergyman. These were, I think, some of the permanent and leading figures; but there were also some transients: such as two all-American Americans, Bobby, lanky, lips pursed, looking as if he was chewing gum, and Judy, dressed self-consciously in a soberly casual fashion, in sweaters and sneakers. There was the beautifully racy, slightly mustached and dark Kira Nijinsky, daughter of the dancer, who was entirely out of line, and contrary to the Burlingham code and style even wore makeup of the kind the Burlinghams condemned severely as "smart lady." Yet Bob Burlingham flirted and fell in love with her. And there was blond, sweeter than sugar, beautiful and lithe Ann Nederhoud, who sang "The raggle taggle gypsies oh!" at Christmas in a fine, thin, high voice. There was, temporarily, the nervous young Aichhorn, who was irritable and fidgety (he did not impress me as one of the "big ones"). He was the son of an arch-Viennese, the dignified, rotund City Councillor with a trimmed pointed beard, a Social Democrat, most proficient in psychoanalysis, author of the pioneering book on *Wayward Youth* (or should it be "neglected" and hence, "delinquent" youth?), who would offer an occasional course for the big ones. The most approachable, however, was the almost too innocuous and gently reasonable Ernsti Halberstadt-Freud (the later analyst W. Ernest Freud), who appeared to me, so to speak, as a small "big one," which he actually was, considering his stature and height.

Erik Erikson and Peter Blos were also there for us, the little ones, supported by Mrs. Briehl (English) or Joan Erikson, a tall handsome Canadian woman with nobly quivering nostrils, who demonstrated and promoted a serious rhythmic kind of gymnastics, perhaps akin to the "Eurythmie" of Rudolf Steiner, and at any rate of deeper and more soulful import than what a tough physical instructor such as Buresch would drill into us. Buresch surely had hardly a notion of something as cerebral and un-German or un-Austrian as psychoanalysis even then, and would deny, of course, whatever notion he might have had of this Jewish science in the near future when the Nazis were in power. As for the "little ones," *die Kleinen*, there was, above all, Katrina Ely Burlingham, called Tinky, whom I worshipped, desired, pursued. Then there was, as the little one even among the little ones, Mikey Burlingham (who later on suddenly grew very tall); and there was my rival–friend Vicki Rosenfeld, son of the family on whose property the school was built. And there was Basti, who was not a very good boy at all but had something of the wiry, intellectually lazy, though cunning and witty street urchin, with a wealth of idiomatic expressions, among them *Dulderitzn-tzn-tzn-tzn*, an endless nonsense word, or *Eierdidi-Wasserkopf* which meant something like egghead-idiot and was perhaps applied contemptuously by him to me, though we got on well in a fighting sort of way. There was gentle Ruthi Bernstein, slightly hard of hearing with a demurely ironic and intelligently sheeplike expression on her kind face; and another somewhat brash Ruth from Berlin; and Sylvia, disoriented, excitable, nymph-and-childlike, not quite awake as yet; and the marble-white, all-too-beautiful Ighino, son of the architect Wimmer; the fresh and coldly sharp-tongued Reinhard Simmel, a clever, witty, rapidly babbling Berliner, though actually sentimental, fragile, and shivering, much in need of warmth, the son of an analyst, who, like Gerda, lived au pair with the Rosenfelds in the main building.

This was our school: a paradise compared to the coarsely compulsory Evangelical Elementary School on the Karlsplatz which I had been obliged to attend up to age eight; or to the bleak, rough, and tedious RG XIV, a *Realgymnasium* preparing pupils for entrance into university, where I served time later on, from twelve to eighteen. I should concede though that I learned a good deal there, mostly against my own will. I was compelled to acquire some discipline and enjoyed a lot of extracurricular experiences including a fair share of unrefined and forbidden fun. The Burlingham-Rosenfeld School was a marvellously promising, privileged experiment, animated and inspired by a purer, more humane, and more sincere ideal of humanity than any school I ever went to. It was suffused with a genuine sense of community and housed in a light, sunny, warm place which even smelled pleasantly of fresh wood and clean linoleum. The people who directed and guided the school were of superior character; educated, cultured, fully formed human beings, not mere specialists in a field, nor mere professional pedagogues. They were conscious of a dominant human concern beyond the concern with subject matter or careers. Young and enthusiastic, as they were at a time when analysis itself was in the vanguard, they were inspired by a sense of mission. Eva Rosenfeld once said to me: "What we did was not nearly as important as who we were." They put together, for a few years, a school where students could learn to love their work. This was so because everything was geared to learning through intensive "free" work on "creative projects," chosen by the pupil of his own accord or assigned to him with his consent.

At the same time there was something fashionably faddish and mysteriously arbitrary about the school, evidenced, for example, by the dilettantic, lopsided, or single-minded concentration on relatively remote topics. I grant that the Eskimos were closer to the consciousness of Americans than to a Central European Viennese. Still, there was an excessive, if utopian concern with their tribes, mores, kayaks, implements, igloos, their tales, their hunting of whales, and the like; all of which was, preferably, to be richly illustrated with self-made linoleum-cuts, a medium favored above all others by the style of our school. And so it came to pass that there was little systematic learning, especially in what the world around us considered to be the major subjects and disciplines. We ultimately failed to meet, or met only barely and skimpily, the scholastic standards and requirements imposed by the state and its school system. It was a chore later on to prepare for the entrance examination into a public school. Nor did our school accustom us to the need to learn and to master techniques and subjects which might not happen to interest us at a given moment. And yet there can be no true accomplishment, even in a field of one's own choice, without the acceptance and the training of this kind of discipline. There was no pampering or self-indulgence, no pomp, no display of extravagance or riches. The school, like the Burlinghams themselves, cultivated the opposite of what an ordinary person might think of as luxury. On the contrary, everything was to be simple, understated, stylized to appear restrained, and expensively unpretentious in the manner of homespun fabrics. Even so, the whole endeavor was a kind of luxury, and especially so in the ratio of distinguished teachers to a very small number of pupils. Moreover, in this privileged environment we were also isolated and estranged from crass, harsh "normalcy" or a commonplace reality, not to speak of the economic misery pervasive in Austria which, shrunken and enfeebled by the First World War, was now reduced still further by staggering unemployment.

Perhaps our school was too good or too sheltered and pleasant to prepare us soundly either didactically or existentially for requirements imposed by the harsher social realities of the world we lived in and were to encounter later on. However, this bleaker, meaner, poorer, and rougher environment represented the true state of the country and indeed of every nation on earth. A similar dilemma has generally been characteristic of educational ventures of this kind, including the "free schools" which flourished at the time. To a lesser degree it even applies to more orthodox establishments. For our schools, and even or especially the best of them, generally prepare us poorly for what awaits us "out there." And yet I cherish the memory of the Burlingham-Rosenfeld School, and of all schools I went to, it remains the one I would regret most having missed.

How did my father come to send me into analysis with Anna Freud? My great-grandfather, I like to imagine, still stood bare legged in the Szasawa River bundling and driving logs downstream from his Bohemian shtetl. Actually, it appears, he was a dealer in, and shipper of, lumber. In 1891 my grandfather Gustav left Bohemia for Vienna, where he was joined by his younger brother, during a period of economic expansion, to start a candy business. In the beginning the brothers could still be seen in their shop window kneading or twisting hot, heavy cords of sugar candy. Hardworking, they succeeded during years of prosperity and rapidly developing capitalism in founding a candy and chocolate factory, the spectacularly successful firm of Gustav and Wilhelm Heller, soon to become "purveyors to the imperial court" of Francis Joseph.

My father belonged to the second generation of money and social status. At parties in their palatial townhouse in the Schwindgasse, his mother Mathilde, who sang lieder by Schubert, Mendelssohn, Schumann, Franz, up to Brahms, Wolf, Loewe, and Mahler, would receive the members of the Vienna Philharmonic of which she was a patron. On festive social occasions, the concertmaster and other leading instrumentalists would come to play chamber music. It was rumored that she had a "Platonic" liaison with a minister of state. I still remember her, in keeping with the style of the nineteenth century "Makart" period, descending a stairway with great majesty, a generous bustle emphasizing her rear from which a mauve train draped. A weighty promontory suggested the vault of a voluptuous bosom, while a diamond-studded choker, sparkling in rainbow colors, encircled a very white, slightly wrinkled neck, and her very pale face was surmounted by auburn hair in which a diadem or ornamental comb would glitter. Her imposing, matronly bearing notwithstanding she was rather witty. However, according to my father, she was a cold woman. He hated her, he felt, because she neglected him as well as his two sisters, the older, bright, rather homely Grete and the younger, pretty, fairly simple minded and affectionate Janne.

My grandfather impressed me as a good-natured, reasonable, dependable man who loved a good meal and good wine. To this day the family remembers the tender-cooked tongue (with horseradish), a specialty of his cook, Fanny, served by a liveried servant who also poured the wine. Grandfather's conversation was direct, plain, sensible, and down to earth. He loved to go hunting, and while the hunt meant of course far less to him than his business, it was a good deal closer to his heart than the fine arts. I remember him as a chubby, dignified man of somewhat less than medium size, in his hunting lodge at Klausen, in a Styrian loden suit. He had a stylish gray mustache, and was a real *Kommerzialrat* (an honorific title created especially for distinguished businessmen), with slightly watery, rather cheery blue eyes, and a bulbous, jovial nose.

My father, rebellious, intellectual, at first disinclined to go into business, advanced in the First World War from a volunteer recruit to the rank of lieutenant. Although he soon began to fear and hate the war, he thought in retrospect that the war experience had turned him from a spoiled boy into a man. During his *Gymnasium* (high school) years in Vienna he had made friends with Otto Fenichel, who was active in the leftist youth movement and was preparing even then for his later distinguished career as an analyst. At the front line, at a solitary observation post for the heavy artillery, high up in the snowy mountains above Rovereto in the Southern Tyrol, my father read Marx and Freud. He thus gained his own access to psychoanalysis and later on, before and during the years of my analysis with Anna Freud, underwent analysis with Ludwig Jekels. He had married right after the war, entered the Heller firm, his father having made this a condition for financing his studies at the university. He attended lectures in economics, obtained his doctorate with a dissertation opposing the Marxist theory of surplus value, and read philosophy (Kant, Husserl) on the side in a circle of colleagues and with Ernst von Garger, the art historian, his closest friend.

Above all, he wrote. He did so in particular under the guidance of another, older friend, the miniaturist and literary critic Alfred Polgar, who cultivated a pure, finely chiseled style in his mordant vignettes. I remember my father's articles in the *Weltbühne*, published during the journal's brief Viennese phase after its retreat from Berlin when Hitler came to power. At that time, the *Wiener Weltbühne* was edited by the stridently clever journalist Willy Schlamm, a close companion of my father. The latter acted as clandestine, financial supporter of the radical left-wing review. Mainly, though, he worked on his short stories, novellas, comedies, dramas, and, most consistently, on three or four novels, among them one of the earliest fictional treatments of refugees, entitled *Ein Mann sucht seine Heimat* (A Man Seeks His Homeland) which was published even prior to our emigration by Oprecht's Europa-Verlag in Zurich in 1936 under the pen name of Martin Haller. Although his attachment to the family business ran deep, he seemed to take his responsibilities nonchalantly, almost as a sideline. Throughout the period following World War I, which ended abruptly with the *Anschluss*, he led the life of an elegant young gentleman, with all the contradictions, characteristic also of the time, that came from being on the one hand a sympathizer with a rather exclusive intellectual avant-garde of the left, and, on the other hand, the affluent codirector and co-owner of a firm that was, in the Austrian context, large, important, and widely known. After emigration, when he had to work his way up in New York, he decided in favor of a business career. In a country favorable to capitalism, he became a successful manager and then owner of a firm which, by American standards, was less than medium size, but under his exclusive control. He no longer felt that he was merely an heir, and shed his mental reservations and sense of guilt about being a capitalist. He always had his own independence at heart, cultivated his existence as his own master and as a boss, symbolized by the little Heller crown on the firm's stationery; as well as his literary, intellectual, cultural interests which included politics, economics, music, art, and psychologica. There were also his hobbies: hunting, playing the violin, and later on, painting, first as replacement for the virtual loss of his native tongue as a viable public medium of expression, and increasingly, as the favorite pursuit of his old age.

He always refused to become dependent on a large corporation as a consistently business-oriented career would have required. He wanted to live well and knew how to secure his own material comfort. I was always somewhat in awe of him, perhaps because I was too close to him to be able to see him in perspective. Even as a true businessman he remained, I suppose, an "intellectual," suprisingly open minded and versatile, with a quick sense for essentials. He was sensitive, bossy, and shy, with many talents, somewhat hesitant and exceedingly cautious, a wealthy dilettante in contrast to the "specialist" consumed by a single interest and career, as I myself was to become later on for many a decade.

In the years when he brought me up, he dedicated himself to me, in spite of his rather nervous and remote manner, to a degree which, given the norm for Central European fathers of his class at the time, was quite unusual. He read aloud to me, took me on his outdoor excursions, talked at length with me, and also talked about his own writings, worried about me, and was most solicitous. He was young then, tall, impressive, at times a bit overweight, a sportsman, well dressed (suits tailored by Kniže, countless tailored shirts, etc.), a host and patron to artists and intellectuals in the Karolinengasse, a large household with chauffeur, cook, two maids and governess. He had, in addition, a separate pied-à-terre in the inner city. Moreover, to protect his privacy, to spare me, and because he could easily afford it, he also maintained a second household, a spacious apartment for his permanently established mistress, Inge, in the Jacquingasse, about ten minutes walk away from us by way of the upper Belvedere Gardens. Weekends he would often spend in the hunting lodge in Klausen near Vienna, but rarely and reluctantly visited my paternal grandfather's ornate summer villa in Baden. He had a house in Grundlsee, a lake in the Salzkammergut, where we spent summers and the longer holidays; and he would rent cabins on the Tonion mountain, where he went hunting (I sometimes went along) and fishing, in which I participated passionately. Later on, around 1933, the Karolinengasse household with governess Thesi Bergmann, and Inge whom my father married at that time, all moved together into a house in suburban Hietzing in the Gloriettegasse, adjacent to the villa of old Schratt, who had been the mistress of the late Emperor. But that was already in the last period of our life in Vienna, after my analysis. In addition to hunting and fishing, we did a lot of skiing, I learned to box, later to dance, and to fence. With all his entertaining as well as his erotic involvements, my father, who rarely mentioned his factory at home, seemed to be interested above all in literature, politics, theoretical thought, and the arts. His friends were art historians, writers, journalists, actors, architects. Thus, I also moved in a direction that did not correspond altogether to the material realities of our existence, nor actually to my father's mentality. For, in truth, he was always deeply interested in matters of money, whereas in my own case a sense of material realities and of money asserted itself only late in life. For at first and for years to come, I appeared to be and frequently acted like an idiot in practical, notably financial, matters.

My opposition to business and obsession with art and culture were strongly encouraged by my mother, a woman with marked literary and intellectual interests increasingly involved in her activity in the world of cinema. Her promising career in this newly developed art and industry began in the late twenties when she worked as script writer for the German film company UFA in Berlin under directors Murnau, Joe May, Kortner, and, most frequently, Curtis Bernhard (then Kurt Bernhardt), with whom she continued to work in the thirties in Paris and London on a variety of movies, including some based on original stories of hers (as *L'Or dans la rue*), or on adaptations and shooting scripts, such as "The Beloved Vagabond" (with Maurice Chevalier and Margaret Lockwood). The most satisfying professional experience of her life was the collaboration in Italy, prior to and during the war years, on treatments and shooting scripts of five films directed by De Sica (and two more directed respectively by Rosselini and Cottafavi) for which she signed under the assumed name of Marguerite Maglione.

In the period ending in Austria's defeat in 1918, her father, Leopold Steiner, had been eminent in the Skoda works (heavy industry, armaments, etc.), one of the most powerful corporations of Central Europe. I remember him standing in front of the heavy wrought-iron portal of the tall yellow Steiner building, which he owned, in the Wattmanngasse, saying: "By the third generation everything goes to the dogs." It occurred to me that if Grandfather Gustav and Great-Uncle Wilhelm were the founders of the Heller "dynasty"—whose members never considered themselves nouveaux riches, but clearly of the elite—the "third generation" referred to me. Leopold, at any rate, was like Gustav, a self-made man, severe in posture, and first generation, according to the bourgeois code of success. He had worked his way up in spite of illness (tuberculosis) and relative poverty in the Balkans. My mother was born in 1899 in Belisce, a small town in Slavonia, near the Hungarian border. By virtue of his efficiency, energy, diligence, ambition, his considerable intelligence, and presence of mind, Leopold rose to a leading position in a mighty enterprise. He was an extremely dignified, very small man, cheerfully pompous and regal in his bearing, as even my mother would admit, though she mostly resented him and found unbearable that he spoke in measured, quotable phrases like those of the "feuilletons" in the *Neue Freie Presse*, Vienna's leading and most respectably bourgeois liberal journal.

My grandparents had rather unsatisfactory marriages. To return to my father's side: When Gustav married Mathilde, her family, the Kreidls, were inclined, I think, to claim a higher social rank than his. This may have contributed to the cooling down of a marriage in which proud Mathilde would occasionally look down upon her husband Gustav with a little disdain and a demanding dissatisfaction. It is not surprising that he eventually established an enduring affair with a comfortable and homey, socially less ambitious petit bourgeois woman, for whom he set up a candy store across from the Opera. I do not know when this liaison began; it was kept secret from Gustav's children and all the world, even after Mathilde's early death, and was discovered only after Gustav suffered a terminal stroke.

Prompted by his upward striving, grandfather Leopold, it now seems to me, fared similarly in his marriage. I am not certain that Jenny or Jenninka, my maternal grandmother, belonged to a Sephardic and consequently more elevated Jewish sphere than Leopold. Given her extreme emotional sensibility and her mental awareness, however, the claim to a higher spiritual plane, rather than to higher social status, was implicit in her very being. She seemed to be made of a finer, indeed of an all too fragile fabric. Unfortunately, I know too little about her. For a short while before her marriage, she was an actress in the Burgtheater. At that time, a man in Leopold's position would not, I think, have tolerated a wife with a still quite uncertain career, least of all in the theater, and at the expense of her maternal and domestic duties. Jenny appears in my memory as a small, delicate, vivaciously ethereal being with a long face and broad Slavic cheekbones, looking at me out of large and melancholy eyes. Her salon was of a more intellectual and spiritual tenor than Mathilde's. It was attended by the eminent Social Democrat Austerlitz; the highly original thinker and author Popper-Lynkeus; the young critic Lukacs; the young minister of state and brilliant economist Schumpeter, and others. I know of that period only by hearsay. Later on, when she was already somewhat isolated, she translated novels from the Russian for her own pleasure, among them, to my astonishment, things that had been translated long before. She developed vegetarian fads and idiosyncracies, refusing foods fertilized with manure, and preached a dietary gospel concerning the supreme importance of a healthy digestion. For years she seemed almost excessively dedicated to her three children and to hate her husband as a cold, implacable, unfeeling, and scheming tyrant. When that aversion began, I do not know. By the time he left her for another woman easier to live with and with more sensual appeal, her children were grown-up, involved in their own confused struggles and affairs, with little time to spare for her. She now felt driven out of her stately yellow Hietzing house, and moved out, only to perish slowly from loneliness and depression. Finally, she committed suicide with sleeping pills which she had been saving up for years, an act that, long after the event, turned out to have the profoundest, most haunting impact on my mother.

Margarethe (Gretl), née Steiner, then Heller, later Daxelhofer, whom I called Mem or Menga, was the middle child between an older and a younger brother. Her loyalty was to her mother whom she loved—mostly. Mostly, she hated her father who, she claimed, never really recognized her and despised her because she was a girl. She was extremely vivacious, at times hyperanimated. She enjoyed striking popularity; worried and grieved in silence. She was well built, small, had broad shoulders, narrow hips, a talent for sports. She was a dashing, elegant young woman (*fesch*, as one would say in Vienna) with dark hair, large, beautifully expressive, dark eyes, and a slightly oversized nose about which she was unhappy. She had intense intellectual and artistic interests; was the center of attention at most social occasions; had a brilliant, dramatic way of telling, and inventing, stories and tended to be radically open and, occasionally, embarrassingly exhibitionistic in her reporting of intimate details. She was my father's boyhood love. They had "waited" for one another during the war. My mother married even before she received her secondary school diploma. Their sexual relations must have been unsatisfactory from the beginning if I may trust my mother's frank accounts.

During the late twenties and thirties, my mother, though never politically active, was at times more rabidly anticapitalistic than my father. At the same time, she always remained in some respects the daughter of a wealthy family, and was quite ladylike, even and especially in the manner in which she adopted the antiladylike, quasi "proletarian" avant-garde style of the literary left. She had brought into her marriage a considerable dowry which, as was customary, was left to her husband to administrate. However, her father Leopold lost his position and his fortune when, after the defeat of Austria in 1918, he first made the patriotic mistake of opting for Austrian citizenship instead of becoming a citizen of the newly created Czechoslovakia (so as to stay with the Bohemian Skoda works). Second he cast his lot in the postwar period with the speculator-financier Castiglione, whose brilliant career was eclipsed by bankruptcy. During the twenties and early thirties, Leopold Steiner was reduced to the status of a merely respectable, upper middle-class property owner, still living comfortably, in early retirement, on rents and capital interest. However, after 1938 he became impoverished. Having sold and lost his collection of paintings and books, he hid his last jewels in the bottom of his trunk, leaving for Italy, where he waited out the Nazi years in precarious circumstances. After the Second World War he lived most modestly and neatly in the cheapest single rooms, among other places in a public old people's home in Bad Aussee, where he reflected solemnly on esoteric religious matters. At the time of his death he owned no more than would fit into his wardrobe trunk.

The young marriage of my parents suffered additional damage when a second son was stillborn (I never knew about this in my childhood) and my mother came down with a lingering lung infection (pulmonary apicitis). There was an obscure, complicated episode: My father had a brief affair with a very young, athletic friend of my mother. Anni, presumably out of love for my father, made a suicide attempt from which my mother rescued her, and/or nursed her back to health. When I was about four years old, my mother left my father, because she had fallen in love with another man, Max Fellerer, who later became a well-known architect. My father was deeply hurt in his love of Gretl, as well as in his self-love and pride. He was profoundly attached to her; he would not accept being left for another man. Yet they did begin to live apart (though remaining friends), and later on, my father also got on well with Fellerer, maintaining, with considerable effort, a "cameraderie" in the avant-garde manner of the twenties. Hans, as I now called him un- or anticonventionally, would have the benefit of Gretl's, my mother's, advice in the choice of his "mistresses," among them beautiful women like the actress Sybille Binder who, I was recently told, had a simultaneous affair with Max Pallenberg, a distinguished comedian, famous for his performance of the Good Soldier Schweyk. In the years of my analysis, Inge Schön, a petite and daintily "luscious" blonde who later dyed her hair red, and looked in profile like a voluptuous, somewhat fleshy Greta Garbo, was the woman to whom my father grew more and more attached. In the thirties he finally married her out of opposition, he claimed later on, to his intellectual friends, including my mother, who was Inge's polar opposite. For they warned and tried to dissuade him from taking this step.

Inge, my father, and I lived together from about 1932 to 1938. I was then in my adolescence, between 12 and 18 years of age. In this period, Inge came to lead an aimless and increasingly depressive life of luxury, drinking heavily, though it was only in a subsequent period that she was considered an alcoholic and underwent treatment. My father's friends thought the marriage a kind of mésalliance with a "barmaid," especially as Inge's slight pretensions to intellectual, artistic, or educational interests and pursuits and the halfhearted efforts she made in various directions, presumably (it was suspected) to please my father, were quite unimpressive. She was beautiful to look at and attractive, and considered highly gifted on the sexual side, but while she certainly did not lack admirers or suitors, she did not earn the respect of those who desired her or slept with her. At the time I knew her, she seemed to me both good natured and malicious, not scheming or money-minded, but rather mindless, childlike, indolent, affected, unfortunate, but also inwardly tough and independent, though without self-respect or pride. Or was she proud of the fact that she was "alive," that is, sexually alive, and later on proud that she had "lived" and knew about "life," namely, sex? And perhaps that was more important to her than all the intellectual, cerebral rubbish, or even money, or her abortive career as a singer in the Rice Bar, where she first met my father, or as a volunteer in the Montessori Kindergarten. Years later, in London, where she had emigrated in 1938 with my father, the Aryan wife of a Jew, she had a daughter. She had long but vainly hoped for a child. Her daughter was to give, for some time, a focus and center to her life. Her husband, however, was not with her then. He had gone on a long business trip to the United States to establish a new life there for himself and her. The child's father was a British policeman, a circumstance which led to my father's second divorce.

In the period under discussion, it seems, I could not help but see my mother in comparison to and in competition with my father. He was about six feet tall, strong, of fair complexion in spite of his sparse black hair. His eyes were blue, his nose aquiline. He was commanding yet shy, even taciturn; nervous in masculine ways, irascible, spoilt, abrupt; often tense; but also sensitive, charming, witty, self-assured, the more dependable of the two. Often his thinking was more rational than hers, more logical and realistic, but then again more vague, evasive, aloof, and without empathy. My mother was extremely mobile, animated, and animating, intense, imaginative, an untiring virtuoso in the Viennese art of conversation, so that, motivated surely also by jealousy, I came to observe with suspicion and annoyance how she would turn on the unfailing mechanism of her sparkling charm. She was considered or considered herself more artistic, more brilliant, more inspired, and imaginative than my father. She was indeed egocentric, yet much less able to look out for her own advantage than my father who, incidentally, did support her for years after their separation. Actually, she remained in some ways incapable of taking care of herself. Later on her "Greek god," the architect from Linz, did not stick to her; he did not, after all, want to marry a Jewish woman.

She was even worse off with her radical lover from Berlin, the charming pseudorevolutionary womanizer Karl Frank (later Paul Hagen), who eventually became a psychoanalyst in New York. Nor did she find peace with other men; nor in her work as a script writer and assistant director at the UFA studios in Berlin for Kurt Bernhardt, for Papst and others in Paris or London.

In keeping with the status of upper-middle-class women of that time, she vaccillated between her professional artistic interests, a career she never took quite seriously enough, and her private life "as a woman," trusting more in her intellectual and erotic charm than in mere professional competence. In the thirties, after her marriage to my father was, at long last, legally dissolved, Hitler's rising power had become a threat, and she feared for her livelihood. She married a young French-Swiss engineer whom she had met in Paris. A future professor at the University of Lausanne, he came from a small town nearby, in the canton of Vaud. He was politically reactionary, in sympathy with the Action Française, a cultivated, good-looking, somewhat snobbish and gruff, yet dandified and delicate, "Aryan of Old Bernese stock" whose name, Daxelhofer, was only to be pronounced in the French way (Daxelle-au-fèr). During the Second World War they first lived in Italy, where my mother continued to collaborate on various movies (notably with De Sica). When the situation worsened, they settled in Switzerland, which gave her husband the upper hand over a woman he otherwise admired for her brilliance.

Again, years later, after she had sued my father with obsessive rage in a futile attempt to retrieve the long-lost dowry which he allegedly had "stolen" from her, she found herself betrayed by her Swiss husband so explicitly that she discovered the inevitable bundle of letters verifying what she had predicted and perhaps promoted long before; namely, that this man who was eight years younger than she would desert her as her father had deserted her mother. In her pride, she thought she had to leave her husband, and he calmly let her go. They had had no children. She had suffered from insomnia for years, taking innumerable sleeping pills. She now had a nervous breakdown, and spent months in a Swiss home for mental patients. Then she tried to join us, my second wife and family, in America, an attempt that proved a failure for all of us. After nine months in the United States, she returned to Switzerland, where she had become an unenthusiastic citizen during her marriage, to end her life in a modest boardinghouse in Lausanne. Finding her reduced circumstances and her age degrading, she took an overdose of sleeping pills which had probably been provided by Anni, the "rescued" friend of long ago, in keeping with a pact they had made in their youth. She died as her mother had done. Indeed, in the course of her later life she had come more and more to think of herself as the daughter of a suicidal mother and therefore fated or condemned to take her own life.

Her last years were darkened by severe insomnia, excessive use of sleeping pills, and intermittent periods of profound depression. I remember her stomping in circles round our circular driveway in Hadley, Massachusetts, in the snow, bundled up in her shabby raccoon coat, with an unvaried, morose expression. I recall also her telling me what an unspeakable burden it was for her to get out of bed in the morning and brush her teeth. "Je n'ai plus rien à dire à personne" (I have nothing to say anymore to anyone) she wrote on one of the notes she would stick in her books. In her last phase she was a furious feminist, a state of mind that had found expression in a Swiss movie on a day in the life of a housewife, and in her best theatrical play, the drama *Xantippe*. She submitted the latter without success in all the languages she had learned to master excepting Spanish; that is, in French, German, Italian, and English versions. In her last work, begun in America, a film treatment of the life of the Amherst poet, Emily Dickinson, as well as in a fragment of a novel about her friend Anni with whom she had been connected originally through their mutual relation to my father and Anni's suicide attempt, my mother's hatred of men—including incisive insights fuelled by deep resentment—was perhaps the last interest to bring an occasional spark of enthusiasm into her life.

At the time of my child analysis, however, she was "brilliant Gretl," adored, so it seemed, by Thesi Bergmann, the good-natured, plump confidante who used to be her impecunious classmate and friend in Genia Schwarzwald's educational establishment, a renowned secondary school. Thesi, who joined our household in the latter part of 1928 and stayed with us for about five years, became a kind of superior governess for me, to take on the role of my absent mother. Her subsequent career was quite remarkable. After obtaining a diploma from a teachers' college, she taught from 1933 to 1938 in schools for exceptional children and at the Montessori School, completed a psychoanalytic training course at the Vienna Psychoanalytic Society, and worked at Aichhorn's child guidance clinic. During the war she worked with Anna Freud at the Hampstead Nursery and taught at a hospital school in England; she then emigrated to the United States, to become a child therapist at a Cleveland hospital and an instructor in child therapy at Western Reserve University. At the time when she came to us, she looked kind, cozy, cuddly with a cheery, amusing little snubnose. But her eyelids, drawn sleepily over hazy eyes, made for a slightly bleary-eyed expression and suggested, despite her kindheartedness, a touch of bitterness that was confirmed by her cherry lips being pulled downward at the corners of her mouth. Her back was rounded as the result of an injury that had left nothing more than a bluish bump. She was convinced that this blemish disfigured her and made her unattractive to men, although, as I found out later, this ran counter to her vivid fantasy life and tormented her. It was taken for granted that this person who blushed so easily, and was excessively shy or modest and naive, was ineligible for the sexual scene, "out of question," and utterly without sex appeal. She was accorded a "touching" character and a kind heart, as well as docility and the ability to assimilate learning. Yet it seems to me that her role as my mother's ally, spokeswoman, and representative tended to be compromised at times by fits of infatuation for my father, which faded away with Inge's increasing assumption of power. The family consistently underestimated both Thesi in general and her intellect. This was partly because of her financial dependency, her somewhat lower social status, her petit bourgeois character, her somewhat petty worries over trivial matters, and her plain humor. She loved rather trite and homely puns. During her years with us, encouraged by my mother, and supported by my father, she took advantage of the opportunity to catch up with and complete her secondary education, taking her matriculation examination (Matura). She was then accepted and went into analysis with Willi Hoffer, probably upon the recommendation of Anna Freud with whom she was in contact (as Anna Freud's notes indicate concerning the boy, P.H., in her care). In those years when she transferred her idolatry to Anna Freud, Hoffer, and psychoanalysis, she laid the groundwork for later collaborations out of which grew, after the emigration, her book on *Children in the Hospital*, first published in New York in 1965 with an introduction by Anna Freud. This miniclassic in its field made Thesi known and "famous" as I wanted everybody around me to be or to become, though perhaps not "immortal."

Her belated training as a teacher-therapist helped Thesi to restrain her propensity for anxious self-renunciation or self-abnegation, and made her lose, if not her baby fat, some of her dreamy naiveté, some of the charm of her credulity, her all too touching and touchy, tender and vulnerable shyness and insecurity. As was frequently the case with analysands, she became less ingratiating, more prosaic and self-righteous, but also more approving of herself and better equipped with claws or elbows for getting and making her own way. This observation may seem to contradict my previous claim that analytic self-surveillance tended to diminish spontaneity. However, the "second nature" inoculated by analysis rarely, if ever, became spontaneous but always retained an element of deliberate and self-conscious posture. Thesi, for all her therapeutic enlightenment and growing professional success, never lost entirely her directness, her childlike charm, her shrewd candor, nor her modesty, or even her timidity. In the sixties, when my mother was gravely ill, scarcely to be rescued from her depression, and came to this country alone, and wrote to her, Thesi did not respond, which I resented. Yet had not my mother's attitude to Thesi been rather condescending? The friend to whom she had offered the position of surrogate always had to be ready to relinquish her place. In a way my mother always had taken Thesi for granted. She had allowed herself to be admired, parading reports of her sexual, erotic, and social exploits and experiences before the less attractive and less enterprising woman, who, to be sure, responded as vicarious participant with live and excited interest. She never treated Thesi as an employee, but always as a kind of satellite. And yet I have often heard Thesi say how she wanted to enjoy, to relish, *die Kleda*, as she called my mother, and how much she did enjoy being with her. Unmarried, she lived for many years with her widowed brother, and after his death, in a lonely life, with his son in Cleveland, not far from where we live now.

I remember the small, rotund, hunched-over octogenarian on her last visit with us in Buffalo in our "wilderness," a piece of land behind our garden, leaning on me, the sexagenarian, to make walking easier. We also talked about this book and, in general terms, of the difficulties I had as a boy. I remarked that in the end, in spite of analysis, people do not overcome all their problems. She said: "What was the saying in Grundlsee?—Once a pig always a pig, and there's no pill you can take for it."

I have now introduced the major figures, though in too cold and literary a fashion, for I feel far closer to them and they continue to live on within me in a warmer, more open, vague, and indeterminate manner than on these pages. This distortion is due not merely to my inability to do better, or to the need for a simplified, quasi-objective perspective, but also to the fact that the present project focuses on the negative, pathological aspects and that I am forced in that direction. It remains an attempt to unearth and, occasionally, even to wallow in the pathological, the injury, the wound, and the wounding.

A last word about my parents, and thus about the main topic of my analysis: My father, a hypochondriac, always complaining of illness and conscious of his neurotic inhibitions, placed great value on the psychoanalytic illumination of self and others, though only with regard to aspects which were adverse or disagreeable to him. Yet he proved in all respects to be tougher and more vital than my mother, the strongest in body and spirit of all octogenarians I have known. My mother, now long gone, was in all respects less fit, more fragile. Why did she leave me? My father, to be sure, made it a condition of his consent to the separation that I remain with him. Intent as she was on adventure, preoccupied with artistic ambitions and without means of her own, she might not have been suited at all as a mother nor attuned to motherhood. She claimed later on that she left me to my father's care because she thought my material future would be secure in his hands. Neither as a child nor thereafter, it seems, could I forgive her, or myself, for her having left; much as she, apparently, could not quite forgive herself for it, even later in life. It haunted her, and her very last, desperate talks about the failures and failed plans of her life referred, among other things, to this episode. And that she left me not only once but many times, returning only to leave again, became the crux of the child analysis and its two dominant themes: the loss of my mother which I could not overcome and the problematic relationship to my father.

My mother, it seems to me, comes off badly in the following account of my analysis. For the sake of justice and love, I therefore insert in her memory some (translated) "verses in prose" entitled *Aquarius*, which touch not on the exhibitionistic, faithless side of her which tended to generate confusion, but on her capacity for insight, her openness and empathy, her gift of critical divination, her sensitive intelligence similar in some ways to that of her mother and younger brother. It was perhaps too delicately textured ever to find adequate expression and adequate understanding, to meet receptive antennae sensitive enough to respond to her own.

> *Always too soon and too late,*
>   *—why did the literati refuse to hear of silent film?—*
> *scintillating in gestures, vital in torrents of words,*
>   *—why did the Jewish woman hung with jewels refuse to hear about*
>   *Hitler?—*
> *unpacking her handbag filled with ideas*
>   *—and the ladies of Lausanne about the sufferings of*
>   *Xantippe?—*
> *for humanity's sake:*
>   *—or the Yankees about the blacks!?—*
>
> *Why, being right,*
> *did my mother get into the wrong, so often,*
> *and babble?*
> *Why don't they use, she'd say for example,*
> *the membranes inside the shells of hardboiled eggs?*
>
> *I think of this airy membrane between*
> *broken eggshells, when I think of my mother,*
> *who visits me still sometimes at night as a moth,*
> *though rarely,*
> *since she took off to the other side:*
> *Daughter of air*
> *on wings of luminal.*

Finally, I should also mention the little girl about to appear as my cousin and playmate. She was the daughter of my mother's older brother who enjoyed the reputation of a Don Juan, much as his young wife proved notoriously successful in the erotic domain and market. The latter became in the thirties the mistress of a wealthy uncle of mine, a domineering, fat, irreverent, witty man who collected decorations and encounters with celebrities, including Empress Zita of Habsburg, Mussolini, et al. He even became aide-de-camp to De Gaulle. I still recall with irritation how, at a festive luncheon when I was a grown man, he presented me condescendingly with a tie. For I felt as humiliated then as I had felt formerly when I suspected him, who got on well with her, of being after my mother. He would pinch my cheek in a patronizing manner that was generally accepted and to be expected from an uncle in those days. Such reminiscences at sixty and over tend to confirm how childish men remain, or at any rate, how childish I have remained; which brings me back to my initial question: Was I that boy? Am I still that boy? What else is an old man but a small boy modified into something less promising? Still I lie when I say this. For however justified such self-disparagement may be, it suggests only a part of an uncontainably complex truth. As for my little cousin with whom I played when she was a pretty, saucy, pugnosed girl with blue-gray eyes, black curls, and porcelain complexion, I was to meet her again in later years, as a somewhat wild young woman, freely and thoughtlessly drifting through life. At times she even turned religious and wanted to teach me to pray; and I remember her again, in another decade, as a shriveled, confused alcoholic and mother of a good many children in and out of wedlock. She was at times a bohemian, and radically left wing for a while. I wonder what her later years may have brought her.

Death, playing a large though scarcely acknowledged part in this child analysis in which all concerns are by preference translated into the language of sexuality, now begins to make peremptory demands. Meanwhile, however, this endeavor is meant to serve the living.

PREFATORY REMARKS

The following materials consist of notes and interpretations by Anna Freud, and of materials, reports, ideas, dreams, observations, scribblings, drawings, letters, short stories, and verse by the nine- to twelve-year-old patient Peter Heller in the years from 1929 to 1932, plus complementary notes, explanatory remarks, and interpretive descriptions of drawings added by me (P.H.) for this book.

Anna Freud turned her notes and materials over to me. This came about as follows: In November 1972 she sent me a collection of poems I wrote as a child, asking me whether she should leave the documents concerning my early analysis to me after her death, or destroy them: Would I find the file which referred to my analysis "upsetting—or merely very interesting?" I answered, requesting gratefully that she should not merely bequeath the material to me but send it to me while she was still alive, which she did, after some hesitation, so that I received the package early in 1974.

I then planned a work in three concentric circles. The first part (which corresponds to this book) was to consist of my own child analysis and a retrospective on the case of a neurotic, privileged only child in Vienna of the late twenties and early thirties. The second part, enlarging the circle of a contemporary problematic, was to describe the Burlingham-Rosenfeld School, an enterprise characteristic of Freudians gathered around Sigmund and Anna Freud, and of the problems and difficulties of an insular educational endeavor and community and its spirit, within a society of an entirely different character and mentality, developing rapidly in quite another, reactionary and fascist, direction. Analogous discrepancies were characteristic also of other experiments of the twenties and thirties, which were, frequently, left-wing, avant-garde, and elitist, such as the Frankfurt school, the Bauhaus, the Weltbühne, et al. The third, most comprehensive circle was to reach beyond both the analysis of an individual case and the perspective on a small community, by way of a discussion of Freud's contemporary essay on the problematic state of Western civilization, entitled "Civilization and its Discontents" (1930),[1] and the critical and utopian reaction of the left, particularly Wilhelm Reich, condemning the author's "cultural pessimism." "The first of these studies," I wrote to Anna Freud in 1974, that is "the case history of the child" would contain, "as in a distorting mirror, the major motifs and figures destined to recur throughout the composition." For I thought and continue to believe that a concentrically expanding perspective would reveal continuities between micro- and macrostructures, the individual and collective difficulties, and the problematics inherent in the cultural matrix of a civilization of which individuals and distinct groups form a part.

My first effort to integrate the materials of the child's case history with the retrospective of a man in his late fifties and early sixties did not succeed. The confrontation with my difficulties as a child made me so intensely aware of analogous current problems that I came to a halt, as if caught in a labyrinth, even before I had worked my way through half of Anna Freud's collection. The second attempt succeeded but was not well received by readers, apparently because of the confusing intermingling of the child analysis with my retrospective, or of the analyst's collection with current reflections, a see-saw movement back and forth between the analyst and the ex-analysand. It seemed appropriate therefore to separate the original collection of materials by Anna Freud from my retrospective. However, a further revision became necessary to produce an intelligible English version.

When I first informed Anna Freud of my overall plan involving the case history as well as the description of the school and Freud's critique of civilization, in order to ask her permission to use the material she had sent me, she thought I should use the case history only for an autobiography, but not in order to describe the analysis which only the analyst could do. I disagreed: The analysand, I thought, was part of the case history. Was it only the patient who should not make a graven image? Besides, my relationship to Anna Freud was an essential part of my childhood. Apart from my mother, and opposite to

---

[1]Freud, S. (1930), *Das Unbehagen in der Kultur*. Vienna: Internationaler Psychoanalytischer Verlag. [English: *Standard Edition*, 21:59–145. London: Hogarth Press, 1961.]

her, she was my great love. When I wrote her to this effect, I got no reply. A later report about the progress of my work was also left unanswered. With some defiance, as if still entangled in the kind of love-fight relation which developed in the course of my childhood analysis, I now thought: Let her speak up if she takes offense! But when I sent her my manuscript in its original form, with a view to publication, raising the question of the availability of the original material and her notes, she did give me permission to use them for my purposes as I saw fit.

However, let the reader be warned: Everything in this book, including the most neutral comment of which I have been capable in my later years, remains somehow within the magic circle of the child's analysis. There is hardly a mention of the major contents of my adult life: my five children, decades of happy marriage, academic teaching, study, research, thinking, and writing. The judgments, the shades of recorded sentiment, even the logical arguments advanced here, are still bound up in the web woven almost sixty years ago; and even this commentary about my own comments is, among other things, still a symptom. Even a man who would have liked to jump over his shadow will eventually have to recognize that he did not succeed.

Anna Freud at the time of Peter Heller's analysis.

Peter Heller, toward the end of analysis.

Peter's mother, Grete Heller
(née Steiner), in the 1930s.

Peter's father, Hans, and Inge,
Hans's second wife, about 1932.

ANNA FREUD'S
COLLECTION OF
NOTES AND
MATERIALS

Footnotes to Part 1

PART 1

I

About the Pavor Nocturnus

Peter Heller enters analysis at the beginning of February 1929. His attacks are described as follows: He wakes up at night from his sleep, stands in his bed with eyes wide open as if he saw something, and usually cries out, "Please, please, please don't." During the day too he is afraid when he goes through the dark hallway; and of death; and that he might be reborn into this world as a weak child. Otherwise he is very cheerful and trusting.

At the beginning of the second week he tells me two dreams:

First dream: There is a large open space, like a field. Many people are sitting and standing around, young girls, women, his governess, and he himself. They are watching a battle. There is a man who looks like Mr. Goldscheider, or like a field marshall. After a while he doesn't like it, he says to his governess: "Thesi, let's go away. I don't want to see it." Then he wakes up and feels uneasy, afraid.

Second dream: There are large boxes in the room with candy, as before Christmas. Thesi points to one and says: Look, it's empty. Burglars were here. They look out of the room and see his father run across the hallway, and holding the door to Peter's room shut. The governess wants to pull the door open; thinks, it's the burglar, doesn't know it's the father. He wakes up and is afraid.

Association: Before Christmas he looked around in the room because one is curious after all; and found two gifts which were meant for him; to his regret.

1. Note by P. on separate piece of paper: "You can't get rich in Tesu's profession. She said: she was impressed by that He said I think: made a great impression. Quite preoccupied with this. But not impressed. In a way Mem loves me as much as Hans." Accompanied by scribbling of the name PH and fragments of the name. On reverse: Musical notes, above: 3 16ths, below: 4 8ths, a group of 16ths; 8 16ths; at bottom only 2 notes or perhaps one whole note.

SUMMARY I

First Phase, Introduction

1) Resistance, dissimulation, annoyance (Example: How does one recognize boys: by their eyes—play with Mädi)

2) Play as transition and fill-in.

Material in the resistance: writers and poets, book titles, comparisons, comparing opinions, plans for the future

3) Gradual, still reluctant admission of fear of death, sudden disparagement of the parents as writers, wish to become greater than they. Prohibition of the wish.

Hence *result* of phase I (after introduction and resistance): Most superficial relationship to parents as an outcome of normal oedipal relations, *curiosity* displaced on books, *jealousy* on plans for the future, *fear of father* on fear of death (he will have to die before he becomes famous).

II

Worry about Thesi's profession[1]

Worry about my laughing

Resistance

Saying *du* or *Sie* [familiar vs. formal address]—Peter—disgusting

Grandp*apa*: *Lacken*bach [Lacke = puddle of urine], Zipfi [penis]

Words from the Evangelical School:
  sh(it)
  peeing
  ass
  Lulu/Wedekind
  Poo poo
  piss (conflagration) [piss = German *brunzen,* conflagration = *Feuersbrunst*]

5

shitter
rentschiet (shouted at him by street boy)

Thursday

1st Dream:
He goes with his school group through a gate, like Schönbrunn, a big lake, islands, the trees are pink.

2nd Dream:
He walks with Thesi on a street with 𝒫𝒫 trees. They speak about Christ. Suddenly the street goes down steeply and he is very frightened. Then Thesi complains to his mother that he is always quarreling.

About 1:
Summer in Weyregg. Franzl, village boys, hunting lodge, shot a squirrel, Bella almost run over. School excursion. Quarrel? Christ, Greeks, model.

Friday

Dream:
He is in the garden with Riki. Riki says: Let's sh . . . , Adelaide is with them or Mädi. There is a wooden fence or house. As he looks at it, it turns into a transparent wire fence. If somebody passed, something terrible would happen. Mädi is on the lookout. He thinks: one can see from the windows, but he doesn't care.

Riki: ⚹
Wooden fence: games with Franzl. Like in school. The things the boys did: playing firemen. ∧ Teacher, I have to go to the bathroom!, a[ss], p[ee], p[iss], etc. The model student *Weiss,* at the top of the class; bad boy Pollak.

Unemployment compensation.

Made a fire, watched out, mustn't tell.

Wire fence: when you drive by [take it away] easily, like nothing.

7

2. Collection of Chinese Poetry (1907) rendered into German by Hans Bethge.

Another compulsion while driving: [imagine one has to] cut through snow piles and stems of street lamps ⌒ , sometimes gets stuck.

Always says: I may do it yet.

Tuesday, May 21

1st Dream:
He sees a giant spitz sitting and is very frightened.

2nd Dream:
He sees railway tracks, a wall, he falls across the tracks and sees a train coming. Mädi is somewhere. He thinks: it doesn't matter, I'll live anyway.

About 1:
Saw a movie, "Rin-tin-tin under false suspicion," looked just as big next to a small monkey. Saw a small spitz and said he didn't like it.

Wednesday

Tells me how he likes going to public toilets!

Wants to kiss me

"gifted boy"

read outside

would like to know about other children.

May 30–June 3

reads poems to me from *The Chinese Flute*,[2] doesn't want to know anything.

Monday, June 3

begins to tell things again, about being embarrassed at the Burlinghams, undressing, going to the toilet very difficult, didn't want to go at all, wants to get rid of it. Mother has left for Berlin.

Tuesday, June 4

is a quarter of an hour late, was in the Volkscafé on the toilet, alone; as he went out a man went in, he went back in. Man only said he should stand in a corner.—Promises hesitantly not to go again, unless very urgent. Speaks of being ashamed.

Wed., June 5

wants to say anal words, cannot really do it, little stories about Basti and Ighino; constantly asking about books, compares greatness, fame.

Thurs., June 6

Dream:
There is a war. He and Basti are in the Belvedere park or the Schwarzenberg gardens. They wage war against the Germans. The Germans are 150 men with a bath attendant in charge as their leader. Then they run downhill. Tinky and Basti's father are standing there. He recites lines from a poem by Claudius: There is a war, etc., I do not want to bear the guilt for its outbreak. He falls down in time with the rhythm of the last verse.

Associations and interpretation:
Remembers seeing his father naked, taking a bath, quickly looked at the penis. Germany big.

Wages war with the father about the big penis, has to check all the time whether all men have such a big one. Therefore *fear of the father*, therefore *going to toilets*, therefore incessant *comparisons*. Guilt, death.

He says: When I wake up in time from the dream, I don't scream, when the dream goes too far, I do.

Dream:
He is at the railroad station, his mother is leaving. Suddenly he says: Gabi still owes me 5 Moncalms. He knows those are cigarettes.

Result: *Railway station* one of the comparisons between Austria and Germany, Germany bigger. The rest contains allusions to all his sins: the day before he lit a *fire* in the garden with Riki, they bought

3. In A.F.'s original a footnote refers to the entry of June 4, 1929.

cigarettes at the tobacconist's and smoked them, figured out excuses that they are for his father, etc. Peter got *matches* from his apartment by lying. Gabi is an allusion to his transgressions with *Mädi*. In this way he confirms that he feels *guilty* about all these things.

Friday, June 7

Wants to touch me, have a best girl friend.

Monday, June 9 [June 10]

Dream:
A famous woman doctor tells him that his grandmother will hang herself in 7 weeks.

Associations:
Park keeper (guard), Socrates not read.

SUMMARY II

Second Phase. Breakthrough to Spontaneous Communication

1) Worry about Thesi's future

2) Worry about my laughing

3) Grandpapa . . . Popo [behind], smutty words
   3a) Resistance: *Du—Sie*, Peter;
                 everything is disgusting

4) Confessions:
   a) about the toilet in the Evangelical School (dream of shitting)
   b) public toilets (form: writing)

5) Reaction to confessions: reads *Chinese Flute* for 4 days.

6) Inhibition: gratification. Cannot go to the toilet at the Burlinghams; instead in *Café* Berggasse[3]

7) Dream of war with Claudius verse. Interpretation of the *compari-*

13

4. Refers to entry of June 6 (2nd dream).

5. Refers to entry of June 7.

6. With letter from Peter during summer vacation: 6.9.'29.: "Dear Miss Freud, very often I would really want very much to find out if you like me. According to the rule, you would have to like all (your) patients. But I don't believe a genuine human being can do that. Devotedly, Peter Heller. [Below: a drawing of a mountain landscape with a menacingly desolate, sadly glaring building.]

sons and fear of death as a compulsion to compare his penis with his father's. Germany—Austria.

8) Dream of Gabi[4] with explanations of the guilt feelings denied during the day: *fire, cigarettes*, sexual games with *Mädi*.

Transference: wants to touch me,[5] have for best girl friend (I shall let him do everything: dream of park keeper).

Summer vacation,[6] promises only half-heartedly and reluctantly not to go to public toilets, but keeps his promise. Screams very rarely.

Result of the 2nd phase: Insight into his *sexual conflicts*:
        a) anal temptations
        b) gratification of his voyeurism with girls
        c) sexual competition with his father followed by anxiety

Mechanism: Repression of guilt feelings.

Form of communication of conscious material: shame, incapable of saying it in words, [hence in] writing; followed by "literary" periods of resistance.

Form of communication of unconscious material: throughout in dreams.

III

Peter resumes analysis on October 28 after the summer vacation. Little happens during the first week, he misses a day because of illness. As to his symptoms, he says that he screamed the last time two months ago in Baden. He can fall asleep in the evenings without anyone staying nearby. On several evenings neither his father nor Thesi were at home. He says he no longer "plays" with little girls or boys. Sometimes he has a strong desire to go to public toilets and that torments him. There is very little shame. He is already finding himself much less interesting. The fear of death is still there. He says a new feeling has been added, thoughts about homelessness. If his father died, he would be homeless . . . During the summer he read "in a Nietzsche," is very enthusiastic about him, reads a great deal to me, especially Nietzsche poems, talks about them. Says he wanted to look

7. Reference to Mark Twain's *The Prince and the Pauper* (1881).

for things he doesn't understand, that he is quite glad when he feels his limits, in school he is doing brilliantly.

On the first day of the second week he tells the following *dream*: My father has given me away to someone else. Lydia is there. I play and flirt a little with her. This other man suddenly says he wants to shoot his children. For there is a war, and so it is better if he shoots them right away. He shoots all his own children. Then my turn comes. He gives me the choice whether I want to go begging or be shot. I run away and think it over, then I come back and say, be shot. He asks with what. I say with a pistol. He takes a pistol, aims at me, there is a bang—and suddenly all of us are sitting peacefully around the breakfast table. Then my father comes and picks me up to take me back again.

Associations:
The other man: an officer he traces back to Lagerlöf's Marbacka, the father of the author. So again the father. The disguise: my father gives me away, takes me back again, serves only to move the entire dream narrative away from the father. That is why the dream is so clear.

Lydia: He has ruined his friendship with two little girls, Lydia and Mädi, by sexual forwardness. Recently Mädi has made peace with him, he wants Lydia back too.

War: is always a representation of punishment for him, one gets shot, he wants to live. Fear of death.

Choice between begging and dying: prince and pauper.[7] London's East End, dirt, misery. Is like in a public toilet.

Pistol: remembers a gift his father just got, a kind of pistol, one aims it at a person, pulls the trigger, and out pops a box of cigarettes to be offered.

Sudden transformation, breakfast table: cigarettes instead of shot.

Interpretation: Yearning to play with little girls heightened by his new love for Tinky. Also to play with his mother, with whom he always wants to do the same things. Feels threatened with death by his father for these wishes. Must either die or go begging, that is: to public toilets, to compare his own strength and potency with his father's. Fear

17

of being overpowered by his father, consoles himself with the idea that it is only make-believe, a joke, not real. Diverts the whole anxiety situation away from the father.

Screaming dream about the castle moat.
After the interpretation of the pistol dream, Peter rests again for a few days, reads a lot of poems aloud to me, but without real pleasure, sometimes scolds the poets, is dissatisfied, then is again captivated by the poetry itself. Does not want to tell very much, but confesses hesitantly to a fear no longer expressed by the thought that he might die before becoming anything, but that he might be grown-up but not amount to much, nothing really great. In answer to my question, he says that his parents are still in the process of development. Thesi thinks that his father might still become something great. Considers my father somebody really great. But doesn't want to say much.

Three days later he arrives and says: today I screamed and also dreamt. At night, during the first dream (of the moat) he got out of bed and ran to Thesi, talked continuously about something terrible, and screamed. Tells three dreams.

1st dream:
He looks down into the dry castle-moat at Greifenstein and says: down there nothing but emperors lie (buried).

2nd dream:
In front of a house with a fence there is a lawn; he runs on it; a girl comes out and scolds terribly. She looks like Tinky.

3rd dream:
He sees two yellow sandstone statues representing David and Goliath. He becomes terribly angry at the David figure, rushes at it and smashes it with his fist.

Associations:
On the day before, he had gone on a school excursion to Greifenstein, but the castle did not excite him at all. He walked the whole time with Tinky and told her about socialism, but was unsure whether I would approve because people always say one shouldn't talk about such

8. On a slip of paper: "Father believed that [I] had been dirty on the toilet. Messed."
"Nose" [with a picture of someone picking his nose].

9. See Appendix, pp. 243–247.

grown-up matters with other children. He likes Tinky very much, realizes that he wants to be with her all the time but has resolved not to run after her as he did with Lydia, because if one does that, things always go wrong with girls and they ditch you.

A very unpleasant thought still comes to mind which he will not tell, but only write down (see note [8]). He complains a lot about his father being so supersmart and scathing, and pretending to have found out some things that are not even true. That happens when one is supersmart. Then he annoys Peter with them. (Father found the toilet dirty and insisted angrily that it could only have been Peter. Also teases him about picking his nose, "mistreats" him.)

Interpretation:
He now loves Tinky and is tempted to get too close to her, to walk on her lawn. That is very dangerous because then she could get very angry. Besides, his father notices everything, as with the toilet. That is why one has to put away the father, and put him where already many emperors lie. That is difficult, because he is big and Peter is little. But it would not be the first time a little one has slain a big one. David and Goliath. But he gets angry at himself for this death wish and annihilates himself, David, for it. The conflict has erupted between the masculine love for Tinky (mother), the fear of the father, the death wish toward him, and the self-punishment for the death wish out of love for him.

The following days:

1) Suddenly great yearning for the mother

2) He brings me his novella, "Revolution."[9] Contents: a man gets divorced from his wife who is at first charming, but only a few weeks after the wedding turns out to be nasty, and he helps himself to overcome his despair by helping the poor and wretched to acquire their rights through a revolution. Connections: The wife's name is Grete like his mother's. After the first advances she gets angry at him like all his girl friends. His idea of himself as the world reformer is thus to help him over the separation from his mother. Sublimation.

3) Conversation with his father, then the father's conversation with Peter about the separation of the marriage. Followed by

4) enlightenment about sexual intercourse. He had always considered this a medical matter, is very astonished, asks if his mother knows this, whether only a few people know it. Is a little afraid, says he does not want to marry. But very satisfied about the new knowledge, very grateful, says it was worthwhile.

5) Increase of resistance alternating with free discussions about his parents, change from day to day, reads a lot.

6) Angry at his mother, starts up from a dream with the thought: mother is arriving. Remembers nothing but scenes from the past where she hurt him, preferred others, about rowing, about Heinerle, is suddenly angry.

7) Increase of anxiety and shame, particularly in front of Margot. Complains that Margot is so cold. When she visited the school he put on a "big man" act by being fresh to the teacher. Thus Margot as mother-figure in front of whom he plays the man, displays himself (embarrassed) and complains about her rejection.

8) Special tenderness for the father, looks forward to his mother's arrival which is expected in two weeks.

Then

Nov. 29, 1929

Dream of the chestnut tree.
He rides with Victor in a horse-drawn cab. They see a poster with writing underneath   ♩ . It shows the boxer Jim Tomy [= Gene Tunney]. He has an unpleasant feeling, believes Jim T. [= Gene T.] is in second place; so he is not the winner, but perhaps he is. They are on a long dark avenue lined with chestnut trees. A man and a woman pass. They are young. He picks up a chestnut and throws it after them. Then Victor and he throw chestnuts up into the tree. Victor's stays up there, does not fall down, and Victor says braggingly in dialect—the way Basti speaks—that his stays up. Peter brags also, in the same dialect, but his does not stay up. Up there, shadowy, there is a girl.

Associations:
Cab: "symbolic" of the rolling on of time as in the poem, means being

grown-up. [Reference to Goethe's poem "An Schwager Kronos" (To Coachman Time)].

Boxer: who is stronger, he or the father; David, Goliath, toilets. Father wins.

Man and woman: I will think they are his parents.

Throwing chestnuts after couple: he chases them away

Throwing upward: ejaculation into the woman

Victor-Peter: competition for Tinky

Basti's dialect: Peter passed wind, Basti laughed

Interpretation: He fights with Victor for Tinky, as he does with the father for the mother. The father is probably the winner in this boxing match, because he is bigger and stronger. When P. will be big and grown-up and will have chased away the parents who begrudge him this, he will try intercourse with a shadowy girl in competition with Victor. Even if he is defeated genitally, he can be stronger in the anal sphere with wind. (Set a record.) The father is rich in money, he in feces.

December 3, 1929

Peter's dream about fleeing

He arrives and says that he had an obscure dream, quite fantastic, but does not know exactly what everything was in the dream; and that is an unpleasant feeling.

"He is pursued from a palace which belongs to the Emperor. He jumps down. There are tailors with him, a tailor. They run across a big field. At the end there is a stationery, no, a tobacconist, and the gate to a courtyard. He goes in, while they run by outside. Then it is like the end of "Circus" with Charlie Chaplin: How he sits there, very sad, then walks away farther and farther, and disappears."

Associations:
Emperor—father

palace—rich man

tailor—his tailor; what does the tailor cut [in German: tailor = *Schneider, schneiden* = to cut]

tobacconist: the game of beaver which Thesi taught him. A Beaver = man with a long beard reaching over his necktie. They go to the tobacconist's to get change for school. There is a beaver in the shop.

Circus: the girl Chaplin loves takes another man.

gate to courtyard: symbol for vagina

Concerning the beaver game: I remind him of how he always had to behead the snow-heaps while driving by. He says, yes. Sometimes he could only cut through them at a slant. ☛ With the telegraph poles, too, he usually could not chop off their heads, but only smash them down (David–Goliath).

Interpretation:
To be read backwards. He is sad because the woman he loves takes another man. The mother allows the father to drive into her gate with his car. For this he wants to cut off his father's penis. But his father finds out and chases him—with all his cutting plans—away from home; wants to kill him.

At the beginning of the hour he (confirms [crossed out]) says that he is especially fond of his father right now and that the thoughts of going to public toilets have come back a little.

12.5.29

Peter's dream of the little bag.
Throughout the hour on the 4th, he reads poems to me which deal with "death." Doesn't want to talk. On the 5th he says that he had the following dream on the night of the 4th.

He is on an outing. Like in the book about Kasperle, the clown. How stupid Floritzl is with his song to the children. They go with Mr. Buresch. Little Frieda stays behind. Mr. B. keeps his hands behind his back holding a little paperbag. Frieda throws stones at the bag until the

27

10. Kasperle, Floritzl: figures from Josephine Siebe's Kasperle books for children.

11. By Frances Hodgson Burnett (1886).

12. Gym teacher.

13. Figure 1.1 shows on its lower half quadruplets, triplets, quintuplets, and nonuplets: The upper half of the drawing shows couples: two positive (with plus signs); one poor and proletarian, the other bourgeois; and an additional problematic one consisting of a somewhat effeminate looking man (father?) with an elongated tail-like thing, who turns away from a woman with a dark wicked look (mother?), to reach out to a smart, bejewelled, doll-like person (lover?). This drawing and the corresponding paragraph (see above) are elsewhere listed by Anna Freud in the context of phase IV (see summary of the latter, p. 41).

contents run out. He (Peter) gets angry and hits her on the head. She runs, howling, back into the house. It has a gate with roses around it.

Associations:
Kasperle[10]: flees on a mail coach, flight.

Floritzl: something suitable for children; my suggestion to put the Little Lord Fauntleroy on his Christmas list.[11] Only wants books which show that he is big and grown-up. Just discussed this yesterday.

Buresch[12]: unapproachable, virile, probably how he [Peter] would want to be.

Little paperbag—back: testicles, seed bag from (my) explanations about sex.

Frieda: runs after him instead of him always having to run after (girls). Connection to dream of the chestnut tree, only this time the girl does the throwing.

Blow on the head: has recently hit Tinky on the head.

Gate with roses: gate of love, (she) runs to another boy.

Probable interpretation:
He is very excited by the return of his mother. Has all kinds of ideas that she should now run after him, worry about him. He is no longer a silly little boy, she should woo him, then he will be rough, chase her away, and she can go to someone else.

On the same day, half jokingly, he makes the attached drawing [Figure 1.1]. Siamese twins who cannot separate.[13] That must be dreadful. A man who already has a woman reaches for a second one. I say to him he is afraid his father will reach out for another woman, because his mother is gone so much of the time, and for this reason he always questions his father who he was with. He finds this natural and acts as if he has always known such things. During the whole hour very critical of me, doesn't want me to say Peter, finds a picture of me ugly, etc.

FIGURE 1.1

14. See dream told after October 28, pp. 17ff.

15. Refers to the dreams reported under this heading, p. 19.

16. See entry of November 29, 1929, pp. 23ff.

17. See entry of Dec. 3, 1929, pp. 25ff.

18. See entry of Dec. 5, 1929, pp. 27ff.

19. A children's song: "Little Hans went alone out into the great big world; hat and stick suit him well, he feels mighty fine; but his mother cries and cries: has her little Hans no more. So the child changed his mind; quick!, ran home again."

SUMMARY III

Third phase. Fear and competition. Rivalry mixed with homosexual stirrings.

1) Dream of officer.[14] Choice between dying or begging. Dying = being killed by father, begging = scoundrel, public toilets, rivalry, homosexuality.

2) Screaming dream about the castle moat. David and Goliath,[15] he no longer slays Goliath but David.

3) As actual experience: father finally enlightens him about the parental *separation*. Defense. Sexual enlightenment on my part, greatest *intellectual* interest: "That was worthwhile."

4) Novella "Revolution" (1 1/2 years ago). After disappointment with woman activity in social domain (homosexual?), intellectual.

5) Dream of the chestnut tree[16]: competition, anal.

6) Dream of fleeing[17]: fear of father, genital.

7) Dream of the little bag.[18]

Result of the third phase. The genital enlightenment arouses only intellectual interest, no excitement. A shift from castration anxiety to wish for castration becomes apparent alongside rivalry.

IV

Mood of Little Hans . . .

December 6, 1929

Feels uncomfortable, doesn't look well, has the feeling he is getting sick. No fever. Annoyed with several people. Pretends to translate Chinese writing for me, improvises a little folk song about loathsome Memka. "There was a horrible Memka, she went far away to Berlin," the son's feelings hurt. Then reads from *Chinese Flute* "The Friend's Farewell," and sings *"Hänschen klein . . ."* [Song of Little Hans].[19]

20. The series of "Hänschen klein" (Little Hans, Figure 1.2) shows on the first picture the crying little boy, while the ladylike mother walks toward a big man with an artist's beret and a big penis; in the corner again the little boy observing and looking backward. In the second picture he goes into the mountains. The mother, who does not look ladylike anymore, call after him: "Dear son, come back!" He: "No." In the third picture he returns, bald and with spectacles, to the now fat matron, who says to him in a mannered way: "Dear son, I have longed for you *so* much." Now the clumsy other man has lost out and *he* must cry. The interpretation that here the father, too, has "reached out for another woman" (see p. 35) might apply to a preceding picture of couples (see Figure 1.1) or to another drawing (see Figure 1.3) of a woman with an oversized head and a similar man whose head is connected as if by a wire to the hand of a young girl; while on the reverse side, treating the theme of "marriage," the "dark point" in a snail shell rhymes with "boasts and swaggers" (in German: *Punkt* and *prunkt*).

Mood: When his mother comes, he wants to leave, then she should yearn for him. Or get sick. The enclosed drawing shows that he knows exactly that his mother is leaving a male friend behind in B(erlin), just as his father has reached out for another woman here.

When I offer the interpretation that he takes his anger against his mother out on me, he picks up a knife to sharpen a pencil, and says suddenly: I'll stab you! As a joke, but unexpected in its surprising speed.

The drawing renders the mood in a semihumorous way.[20] It confuses him that I am not sitting in my usual place but stand by the stove.

December 8–14

Mother here; empty, resistance, reads aloud book titles from Christmas catalogues for hours. Finally, on Friday, he admits to an *anxiety about his eyes*: has to draw figures with protruding eyes [Figure 1.3]. Is afraid somebody could pierce his pupils with a needle. I ask if he wanted to see something forbidden. Thinks once, his mother, when he found her door locked when he came to her. Thought that it was all right for a child to see his own mother.

Inwardly very excited all week, as if trembling inside. Does not want to tell me anything but always expects me to get angry when he conceals something. Then, as a conclusion to the week, Saturday evening.

big outburst like a *wide awake screaming*. Tells me about it on the following Monday (Dec. 16) before interruption of sessions. Beginning: Thesi laughed in a funny way, said: when the *young pig* comes home from school. Thereupon big outburst against Thesi and mother with crying and screaming, all his complaints about punishments during the summer, wrong treatment, unfair, I say so too. Does not let his mother leave for a party, gets terribly afraid. She stays. Finally change of mood. Remorse, they are right.

Explanation: the cook mentioned that Thesi might *get married*. Connected it with mother. So he is the young pig, the little one, slighted, demeaned, mother and Thesi marry others, treat him badly. Dammed up, outburst.

FIGURE 1.2

FIGURE 1.3

21. See entries of 12.5.29, pp. 29ff, and 12.8, p. 35.

22. See entry of Dec. 6, 1929, p. 33.

23. See entries Dec. 8–14, p. 35.

SUMMARY IV

Fourth phase. Return of the mother.

1) Poems about death, drawings which fantasize that mother and father have to leave someone in order to get together, Siamese twins. Protruding eyes in picture.[21]

2) Hänschen klein [Song of Little Hans]. Chinese Flute,[22] illness—substitute for death—as punishment for mother. Transference of anger to me.

3) Anxiety about his eyes after return, nervousness, inner trembling, resistance until

4) big outburst like "wide awake screaming"[23] ending in anxiety about his mother. Occasioned by cook saying Thesi will get married.

5) Conflict between mother and me.

Result of 4th phase: Repetition of the original hurt by his mother: if she doesn't want him, he will leave her, become ill, die.

V

Dec. 20–Jan. 12 [1930]

Over the Christmas Holidays: LTT

After the *outburst* he still comes to me once or twice, not much can be done. Then he leaves with Tinky, Reinhard, Victor, and Margot for Breitenstein. When I ask if his mother would visit there for more than a day, he says: No, I would throw her out.

Stages

LTT

theatrical unhappy love for Tinky. Quite superfluous. Takes R. and V. into his confidence, interprets everything about Tinky, everybody speaks about it. Screams once at night. In the evening he cries in front of Margot because of Tinky. After his

24. A.F.'s notes, in themselves continuous and numbered, are here interrupted to insert the summary of Phase V which concludes with a reference to the first entries of Jan. 18–25.

he gets sick after one day of analysis. Angry when mother dictates to Thesi, says he wants to go to school to Tinky.

[LTT probably = "Liebes-Theater-Tinky," Peter's staging of a theater of love or "Love-Theater-(with)-Tinky." See also p. 309.]

Interpretation:
drowns out the secret love for his mother with the noisy love for (Margot [crossed out]) Tinky which he wants everybody to see. Therefore the hurt. After the interpretation he admits that he has perhaps done something once, and since then his mother does not like him any more. We talk about *masturbation*. He says: in the past; now only without feeling and then it doesn't matter, like picking one's nose. Relates a dream (with screaming) from the days of his illness.

Dream about the daisy

"The little guard of the Belvedere park walks around, picks very large daisies. Does something wrong. His father is there and says: You see?! A blackboard from the new desk . . ."

Interpretation:
Guilt feelings about masturbation, father threatens. Because of masturbation mother (Tinky, etc.) cannot like him any more.

Jan. 11–18

Nothing for a long time, only
    1) feeling that everything is being set up for him,
    2) that mother was in analysis,
    3) fritters away time with his love for Tinky.

Jan.18– 25

1) Dream of the pig wallowing in mire, thief, Margot, toilet. Toilet wishes.

2) many questions (what does the female look like?)[24]

25. See entries of Dec. 20 to Jan. 12, 1930; pp. 41–43.

26. See the novella "Revolution," Appendix, pp. 243–247.

27. These entries are repeated here in order to maintain coherence, see above, footnote 24.

SUMMARY V

Fifth phase. Transference to Tinky.[25]

LTT on the Christmas holiday. Relationship to mother played out with Tinky:

    a) rivals

    b) being unloved

    c) do something to his detriment in her eyes

    d) despair

Talk about *masturbation:* Warning (by Euli) of catching an illness; "harmless" form, smelling.

Dream of the wallowing pig: anal love.

Result of phase 5: conviction that m(other) has left him because of his sexual transgressions, that is why wife leaves husband (novella).[26]

VI

1. 18–25

1) Dream of the wallowing pig, thief, Margot, toilet, toilet wishes

2) many questions (what does the female look like?)[27]

3) fear of peasant boys, wants to get rid of cowardice,

4) afraid to invite children, punishment.

5) wants to send Thesi and mother to me, give them a modern outlook

6) Thesi's visit, tells about the disappearance of anxiety.

7) Interpretation of fear of inviting children: could get too intimate, play. Immediate liberation and invitation.

    Surface: Thesi might scold (him)
    deeper level: temptation

28. See 2nd dream under "Pavor Nocturnus," above, p. 3.

29. Figures 1.4A to 1.4I show: Figure 1.4A a "pilgrim" with a miserably twisted figure in the background; on the reverse side (Figure 1.4B) the procreation in "Vienna"—coffinlike cupboard, a reptilian creature, signs for vagina, penis, sperm, "Hel"—to which a spiritlike child-creature, P. "Heller," owes his birth; Figure 1.4C "woman in twilight" (mother?) persecuted by a little child-creature; on the reverse side (Figure 1.4D) a "seraph." Figure 1.4E a host of angels, foolishly rehearsing choruses, standing around in the presence of God; on the reverse side (Figure 1.4F): with "He," Hell, Helle," the face of a wretch with a penislike tongue. Figure 1.4G a man with misshapen nose and beard between angry twilight-woman and a little devil glancing upward maliciously; Figure 1.4H a huge, broad-shouldered villain with a feather in his hat (as in *Freischütz* = "Schreifritz": familiar twisting around of the name of the protagonist of Weber's opera, to mean, in German "screamer, *lit.* "screaming Fred"): finally Figure 1.4I "The Judgment": the woman in the twilight pronouncing accusations before a high male (divine?) authority—above her: angel in front of heaven's gate.

1) He asks religion teacher about Freud, thus resistance,

2) Tries to offend Tinky by talking about Ernsti. Strong urging on my part to be discreet, admits to conflict between me and mother, believes I dislike his parents.

Dream of Herod's hall

We all sit in a hall like Herod's. The teachers say one mustn't go into the antechamber; we boys say we will do just that. There two women are seated, one in a blue gown with a train ∿ They say something to one another, perhaps about socialism, but not that—

Dream with added drawings

Dream of candy

He is with Mem. She offers him candy ◉ yellow rim and stick. He takes one, leaves the rest for her. Then a man comes with a loathsome face, a barber or a housepainter, and helps himself too. Then it is the Karolinengasse, he sees the man skulking around, suspicious that he's a thief! The man slinks over to the candy, grabs some. He screams loudly: Thesi, a thief, a thief! (Not a screaming dream.)

Interprets himself:
Candy and stick—penis. Father's penis so big, because he took mother's. (Brings to mind initial dream of burglar.[28])

Comes to me directly from his mother, feels very strong, reads [Goethe's poem] Prometheus.

Makes the enclosed drawings [Figures 1.4A–1.4I]:
    angel
    God
    spirit
    pilgrim, etc.[29]

FIGURE 1.4A

FIGURE 1.4B

FIGURE 1.4c

FIGURE 1.4D

FIGURE 1.4E

FIGURE 1.4F

FIGURE 1.4G

FIGURE 1.4H

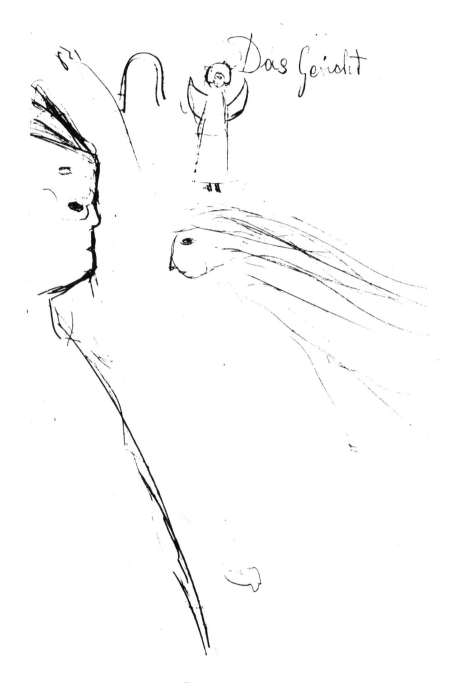

FIGURE 1.4I

30. Figure 1.4J shows a shapeless girl with flower in her hand, with a dark splash and the remark "a blotch on the ass"; on reverse: fiercely marching girl or woman (Tinky's mother?), below: a small, intimidated creature; see Figure 1.4K.

31. On a piece of paper: "because of *smelling*, smelling" (with clown face and penis).

Fear of peasant boys. Remark about Tinky (see Figures 1.4J,K)[30]

Connection of the three facts
 a) fear of inviting
 b) fear of boys
 c) conflict between mother and me, Thesi and Margot, parents and Dorothy.

Fear of temptation in all the above, divorce due to mysterious sexual transgressions.

2.4.

Resistance, blinking, reading catalogs.

2.5.

After much urging: masturbation ("harmless" form) *because of smelling*.

Shame over smelly feet ([See] enclosed.)[31]

Dream [crossed out] (among the dogs who protect him, one is against him).

2.7.

Dream of Wolf
He passes my garden fence, Wolf barks at him, squeezes through the fence, further and further, Peter knows his head must be through by now and Wolf will jump on him from behind, grab the nape of his neck. Gets terribly frightened and runs away.— . . . Then the Number 58 Streetcar is waiting.

Associations:
first dream of dog who rears up.

Interpretation:
Wolf = penis, will jump out (fall off), then he is a woman.

Fear when masturbating.—

FIGURE 1.4J

FIGURE 1.4K

32. On the reverse side of the sheet with the entries of 2.7 and 8, Anna Freud's schedule:

	Mon.	Tues.	Wed.	Thur.	Fri.	Sat.
8–9	Judy	Judy	Judy	Judy	Judy	Judy
9–10	Ribble	Peter	Peter	Ribble	Minna	Ribble
–						
11–12	Liszi	L	L	L	L	Bok
12–1	–	A + B	Levy	Hitsch	Friedr	
–						
2–3	Tinky	Ribble	Ribble	Tinky	Ribble	
3–4	–	Bob	Bob	Ernst	Bob	
4–5	Erik	Erik	Erik	Erik	Erik	
–						
5–6	Peter	Ernst	–	Peter	Peter	
6–7	Bob	Tinky	Tinky	–	Tinky	

Thus there were in analysis: classmates Tinky and Bob Burlingham, Ernst Halberstadt (Ernest W. Freud), and Judy; as well as their teacher Erik Homburger-Erikson. (Mijn) Bok gave piano lessons; Hitsch = E. Hitschmann?

33. Death of Anna Freud's friend and relative, Mrs. Tom Seidmann-Freud, who wrote and illustrated children's books.

34. The drawing with A.F.'s note "Tom's death" (Figure 1.5A) shows the dead woman next to a man (death?) and a boy who waves goodbye in several poses; and contains the question: "whether one may tell everything even though it might hurt you?" you = A.F.—On reverse side: "dead somebody. Peter How come you give analytic hours? Do you not find it so disagreeable?"

35. In Figure 1.5B God appears as (ill-humored?) Catholic priest with a broad-rimmed hat; behind him, the angels like children. On reverse side: God with penislike beard; the woman similar to the one in the evening twilight, or Tinky? A man watches as she speaks with God.

Is afraid he might love Mabbie instead of Tinky—when near Tinky he reached down with his hand, did she notice? Attempt to spoil things.

2.8.[32]

Resistance.

2.9.–15.

2.10.

Tom's death.[33] Is full of thoughts about my grief, ashamed to talk about it, takes her picturebook down from the shelf, very kind and tender.

Drawing I [Figure 1.5A][34]

2.11.

Discussion of *religion*, what his father has told him about "The Future of an Illusion," looks for the same opinion from me. [Attached on a piece of paper: "Your father does not consider religion necessary. Not for everyone."] Wish to quarrel with the woman who teaches religion.

Drawing II [Figure 1.5B] the heavenly hosts
Woman who speaks with God[35]

2.12.

Much resistance, tender quarreling.

2.13.

Is afraid that Tinky likes Reinhard as much as him, does not favor him. After much probing, it turns out that he had been angry with Mem because she "imitates the Burlinghams." Thus displaces, expects his punishment from Tinky.

FIGURE 1.5A

FIGURE 1.5B

36. Scrap paper with musical notes (sounds); and the words: "Tinky passed a sound [= wind]." "You can tickle me in the ass."

37. See above, p. 45.

38. On the sheet: "Excuse me, I must make a ——. Close the exhaust pipe." On reverse side the giant sum of: "568.920,000.000,682.000,035.000,000.000,000.000."

39. Drawing: Many men looking in *one* direction and an angered woman on whose chest a second face is drawn (breasts–eyes, navel–mouth); below, the words: "play with your . . . ," "pushed away"; on reverse side: musical notes, among them four that form the word *popo* = ass.

Comes in saying: Be quiet, I have to think! Whole hour of restlessness and resistance. Finally during the last few minutes, written communication.

Sheet III,[36]

that Tinky "made a certain sound." Asks if I may be called "monster": produces nothing but swear words: bitch, beast, sh—head, lick my ass. The boys in the Evangelical School said this, pointing rearward.—I ask whom he wants to scold with these words. He says: Tinky; does it sometimes for fun.

Thus: anal love, see dream of wallowing pig.[37]—On the same day fear that he would have to love Mabbie.

About this week

Fear of boys has almost disappeared. Observes that it comes only when he is safe in bed in the evening, not where boys are.

Thus unrealistic. Somewhat fearful of skiing, but works it through by himself and transforms the fear (Look at him! (he skis well)).

At the beginning of the week a little excitement in the evening after call from Mem and complaint that she never sees him.

Frequently angry at Thesi.

February 17

Great agitation, forbids me to speak, "Say nothing at all!" With much anger and passing of wind he tells me in writing that *Mem passed wind in his presence* (sheet a).[38] After that he had a row with Thesi who accused him of *masturbating* instead of getting washed (b).[39] Eula once said this makes you sick; took it back later.—Greatest resistance in speaking.

Interpretation:
Apparently his fantasy of intercourse, Mem's (Tinky's) wind an invitation. He reacts with masturbation.

He says: so the "harmless" playing and touching (without feeling) is not so harmless after all.

Dream with great anxiety. In reply to my question whether he screamed, he says: a well-behaved boy does not scream.

Dream of the lame uncle

He is at the Rosenfelds, then goes up to his grandmother's house. On the doorplate, which should read, for example, Dr. Heller, it says: The lame uncle. He gets terribly afraid, runs away.—Then he is in the garden with Thesi, and says: The lame aunt. She says: Why do you always say the lame aunt; it does say: The lame uncle.

Dream of the masseur

He goes toward the masseur, quite stiffly, as if he were showing him his penis—

Associations:
Uncle Wilhelm has a *stiff foot*. Thesi has had something wrong with her *foot*. The *masseur* always speaks of *hygienic*. When you cross your eyes (squint), they get stuck that way (eye anxiety).

Interpretation:
Masturbation the day before, excited, afraid of erection, afraid it might stay, squeezes it all the time to make the stiffness stop. Is afraid of harming himself, of losing his "foot" like uncle and Thesi, because he did something unhygienic.

Interpretation of eye anxiety: when he fantasizes intercourse between f(ather) and m(other), squints at them (to look), has an erection while doing it, his penis could remain stiff, fall off.

About destruction

On the same day he breaks the leg of a table, touches a Chinese dog. Perhaps he has to ruin other people's things like his own member.

40. Refers to entry 2.3.

41. Refers to entry 2.14.

42. Refers to entry 2.17.

43. Refers to entry 2.18.

44. Explanation: The founding of an absurd "movement"—purely for the sake of its name—which was to manifest itself everywhere through propaganda, lists, proclamations (*Heil Zobeltitz!*). The name—Fedor von Zobeltitz, also Hanns von Zobeltitz—suggested to P.H. authors of "conservative" kitsch novels.

SUMMARY VI

Sixth Phase. Masturbation as discharge of oedipal excitement.

1) Fear of peasant boys (homosex.)[40]

2) Fear of inviting children   <u>Thesi scolds</u>
                                     temptation

3) Resistance. Wants to hear people speak badly of psychoanalysis. Relig(ion).

4) Utmost resistance, excitement: "Be quiet, I have to think."

Finally: Tinky passes wind.[41]

Swears (anal language), whether one may call me pig, wants to call Tinky these names, anal love. Admiration by boys instead of fear of boys.

5) Like 4): "Say nothing at all." Mem passed wind.[42]

Temptation by Mem. Intense masturbation.

6) Dream of the lame uncle. Masturbation anxiety, connection to eyes: when you squint, it stays that way.[43]

Erection, hygienic. Interpretation of the eye anxiety at the return of the mother.

VII

February 19

Conceives the Zobeltitz plan.[44] I have to talk him out of it; but he cannot be prevented from stopping strangers in the street asking for addresses on behalf of the Zobeltitz project. Thesi notices it, becomes uneasy, rightly suspects a repetition of the toilet stories. He wants to hear from me too that he should not approach strangers because they might seduce him; claims he would like very much to experience this once so that he could say no. Thus: *Accosting strangers on the street*, [literally: *on language [Sprache]*, misprint for *Strasse*] *attempt to be seduced by men.*

Promises this time quite easily not to do it.

Summary: His idea of intercourse is that the man and the woman pass winds into each other. When he observes father and mother (greeting one another) and thinks of it, as he squints over to them, his penis gets hard. He fears it could "stay that way" and break off. Then he will be a "lame uncle." But he would like to do the same not only with Mem but also with his father and the boys. Therefore fear of boys and approaching people in the streets. He is especially dirty and forgetful these days.

February 20 to March 3

After discussion and interpretation of this phase, extreme resistance. For more than a week he is insufferable, boastful. Talks about his analysis at home, brags about it. Everything he says is phoney, and repetition of interpretations. He does not play or read during the sessions, but is *unpleasant* in every way; also dissatisfied with me. I tell him all this, especially about the playacting, the phoniness. Once he betrays himself and tells me that his father has left for the Semmering several days ago, but not with Mem; alone, in order to finish a literary work.

Surmise about resistance: Angry at father's journey for two reasons, jealousy for Mem, jealousy for himself, father leaves them both. Surely suspects that father is traveling with another woman. I don't tell him that, but put pressure on him through my dissatisfaction with him.

March 4

Finally—as a result of this—a dream

Dream of the coal
Mem has bought coal, many tons of miles [*kilogrammeter*— combination of weight (kilogram) and distance (kilometer)]. He says: when Mem buys coal, then it's every man for himself!

Associations:
Coalmen: sinister people—seducers

45. See p. 19.

46. An enclosed sheet concerning this and the following dream includes the drawn itinerary Vienna–Milano–Cannes, railway, figures, and snakes that can bite. On reverse side: "It bothers me so when I have a hole in my stocking. Like now."

Kilogrammeter (Kilometer): Km—car—father as driver and speeder. Mother easily anxious.

Every man for himself! In the last week he frequently felt anxious and worried about his father.

Interpretation:
This is really about his father's automobile trip. He would like his father to seduce him, not the woman he probably took along. Dream of David.[45] Fear of automobile accident, something should happen to father as a punishment for deceiving him.

He adds as an experience of the day: His father was displeased with him because he left his little friends in the street after having been together with them in the theater, and drove back in his car [driven by the chauffeur], instead of taking them to their homes. Apparently, he imitates his father. He leaves the others behind and drives off in the car, as father does to Mem and him.

March 5

He tells another dream, supposedly also from the previous day.

Dream of the train
He takes a train with Margot and others. She is still outside and he is terribly afraid that she will not get on in time. However, she manages to hang on at the last moment.

Association:
On a trip to Cannes, which he wrote about,[46] father and he were outside to eat, while Mem and the governess were on the train. He was terribly afraid that they would leave without him, then he would have been left behind *alone with his father.*

Dream of the pond with the frogs
He is on an outing with Mr. Blos and the other children. They sit at a pond where it is very muddy, squooshy.

Associations:
On the outing with Mr. Blos he had stayed back repeatedly, he would

47. Reference to entry of Feb. 19.

48. Reference to entry February 20 to March 3.

49. Reference to entry of March 4.

50. Reference to entry of March 5.

51. In the complete series of summaries quoted here, there is no entry after the words "Result of Phase VII:"; while a variant (see p. 123) connects the three dreams (of coals, railway, and pond) with the closing remark: "fear of homosex."

52. The enclosed sheet with these words also shows the drawing of a boy constructed of letters (AB are eyes, CL nose and mouth, R penis, etc.), and musical notes forming a figure whose forehead and eyes are represented by a bass clef, with two notes placed one above the other in the way of a third as nose and mouth, and an E standing on its three arms as body.

have liked once to urinate publicly. There are frogs in such a pond. In Carinthia there were adders and sand vipers. Whether they are dangerous; whether you can die from a bite; whether it matters where they bite.

Interpretation:
Is afraid of seduction by father, of being alone with him and of ensuing punishment. Attack by the snake, castration as consequence (as prerequisite).

SUMMARY VII

Phase Seven. Relation to father.

1) Zobeltitzes. Homosexuality[47]

2) Prolonged resistance, behind it: father's trip to the Semmering, surmises, homosexual jealousy.[48]

    a) Dream of coals—death wish[49]
    b) Dream of train—fear of being alone with f(ather)
    c) Dream of pond—temptation through snakes[50]

Result of phase VII: "Fear of homosexuality."[51]

VIII.1

March 6

Peter is very excited, throws himself onto the couch on his stomach. Admits that his penis is hard. Tells that he would so often like to *show* it. Describes this at length, until I say that he apparently would like to show it to *me*. Hence: attempt at seduction.

Stops suddenly. Produces associations, draws nothing but fat people, suddenly throws himself again on the couch, writes on a piece of paper for me: I made some air behind just now; evidently passed *wind*.[52] I think he made a twofold attempt to seduce me, at first *genitally*, then *anally*. Consciously, nothing worthwhile takes place between us.

53. Sheet: "The storm roars. I look on. There flies a black shadow. A cloud is racing about, it has lost its way, finds its place. The storm roars. The waves roll onto the shore. Their lives are over; devoured by others. No use it was to them to have advanced so far. The storm roars. A leaf is swept up high by the storm. See who I am, it seems to say, a big tree is dead, and I, a little leaf, am alive. The storm is roaring."

March 7

Is nice and cheerful. Has again discussed the whole LTT episode with Tinky, told her that he behaved stupidly. For the first time again he reads poetry to me ("The feet in the fire" [by C. F. Meyer]). I show him the whole scale, genital–anal–spiritual. For anal he spontaneously uses "dirty competition." Makes a resolution to be less dirty and forgetful, but his face is all blackened and yesterday he forgot to give me and Mijn Bok the money from his father.

March 10

Writes the poem *"The Storm roars"* down for me (see insert[53]). Says he wanted to do it differently at first: that the children of the sea would have to go down into the depths because on the surface a storm is roaring that is too strong for them. But then it came out like this. To my question what his mood was, he says: "Whether *wind* has anything to do with my winds?—Yes."

New game with Reinhard. Mrs. Meier and Mrs. X, concierge and laundress. They speak in Viennese dialect about old times, modern youth. "If we had behaved that way!" Drunken men, child thrown out the window, all the fault of the Jews.

Tells me about a comic magazine that interested him. There was a very fat *naked* man and that thing was very big. Did not understand the joke, but had to look at the picture. As he says this he suddenly lets a *loud wind* pass, turns dark red, throws himself on the couch, is terribly *ashamed*. How terrible it would be if it happened somewhere else, terrible here too. I interpret: He thought his penis is not as big, *but* instead he can make a loud wind. He wants to get rid of that, is astonished at the way the body joins in.

March 10–19

almost nothing new. Is bored in analysis. One day of play. Several rows with Thesi, some anxiety in the evening. Has to think of *A Christmas Carol*, how the ghost appears and *warns* against bad deeds.

54. Country place of the Burlinghams near Vienna where P.H. spent several days with the Burlingham children, their mother, and Anna Freud.

secretly offended because of Neuhaus,[54] hidden *jealousy* of the other children. Fantasies, half in jest, of *killing* me. What would Wolf do? What would I do? What would happen to him? When I say: reformatory, he is very alarmed. Says it's strange he takes it so seriously since the killing was only meant in fun. Keeps dangerously close to my desk, surely wants to knock something over. I warn him that one easily *kills things* instead of people.

Relates two dreams:

Dream of Sigurd
Playing ball in school. Sigurd throws so hard, he jumps just high enough over the ball so it won't hit him.

Interpretation: is sometimes afraid of the strong big boys in school who beat him when he is very fresh to them; but he continues to be fresh; he doesn't want to show that it hurts him.

Dream of Tinky
Unclear dream. Something about the Matador building set. They are building, everything is scattered around—

Associations: Tinky reproached Reinhard for not cleaning up the other day after playing. Reinhard became quite small in front of her.

Interpretation: Afraid of Tinky, as of Sigurd before. Does this signify his feeling small in front of men and women, father and mother?

Next day he scolds me a lot, does not want me to speak. Finally confesses several things: that he is often surprised that grown-ups (for instance on stage) *have a body*, go to the *toilet*, etc. Apparently, he has to imagine *me* in such situations.

Tells about a fantasy leading to masturbation which he began in Cannes. That children *pee at each other in different positions*, etc. There he once heard a boy say: I'll shit on your head, and at that he had to smile a certain way. I explain to him the connection with being dirty, that is: with "dirt-love."

93

55. Enclosed: Drawings of women who look as if they were wearing a pair of pants on their heads instead of a hair-do.

Very restless, again he can hardly stand me, tosses back and forth, says: "Be quiet, whenever I speak." That it makes him so uncomfortable when he thinks beforehand: Now it's time for analysis. I interpret the resistance: that he again has dirty thoughts about me. Admits to it, says: Yes, if I said all! Forces himself eventually, brings up several categories:

1) Drawing: first a pair of pants, then makes a head of it.[55]
So: instead of thinking of people's faces he has to imagine what they have in their pants.

2) What did Nils Holgerson do when he had to go to the toilet? [i.e., in Selma Lagerlöf's story of the boy who travels on the back of the migrating wild geese.]

3) What does one do in a zeppelin?

At some point he interjects that he wants to marry me. I say: because you think: If I were grown-up—etc. He says: Perhaps [crossed out] I think it without the *if*.

As punishment for these thoughts he has fallen out with three people: a) made Tinky angry, b) Thesi, c) tried to read his father's manuscripts.

Tells about literary projects: the story of a boy whose parents are divorced, and what he suffers.

Thus new attempt at competition:
he is:
    a) more gifted
    b) more to be pitied
than the preferred children.

March 21

High point of transference

Again very excited and angry, scolds me, tells me not to speak, calls me disgusting, I should not smile. Suddenly shouts at me: *Where did you get this necklace?* I do not want you to get such presents. Like a jealous husband. You should not have a *private life*. Then jealousy of the Burlinghams whom I like privately, him only professionally. How

56. A sheet with the words: *Sessr, Pessr, Ressr, Hessr,* followed by correct spelling of "Sessel" (chair), and proper names: Pessl, Ressl, Hessl. For L.T.T. see above, p. 45.

it would be if I were suddenly to *kiss* him. That his Mem spoke well of me, wants to come and see me. I say: Tell her I shall look forward to it. He: I will not tell her this, because it is a lie: That he would like to be the most loved person in all the world or be loved as much as the person one loves most (summit-love). Shouts, kicks, but asks cautiously in between, whether he is making too much noise. Takes leave very tenderly with both hands. I promise that I will some day knit a sweater for him too.

At the beginning he writes down words and says: I am writing only words with an r:

> Pessr

> Sessr etc.

The omitted letter is always an l (L.T.T.) (love).[56]

At the beginning of the hour a dream which remained uninterpreted.

Dream of the music

Hears music by Grieg in the street car. He says, he doesn't like it. Mem says: I used to like that very much, better than Beethoven. Where is Thesi? He says: she just went to get her board, in order to get up the stairs (from the subway, as if she had a lame foot). Then she leaps up, he says: she doesn't need the board at all.

Associations:

Grieg: at the Christmas celebration with the Burlinghams.

Board: as in the gym class with Edi Polz

Mem's judgment—his collecting of judgments

lame: lame uncle

Interpretation:

Different judgments about something important.

57. Reference to entry of March 6.

58. Reference to entry of March 10.

59. Reference to entry of March 10–19.

60. Reference to entry of March 20. Concerning "fear of ball" see also "dream of Sigurd" (March 10–19), and below, pp. 103, 328ff.

61. Reference to entry of March 21.

62. Drawing of a boy, P.H., and a woman watching him. He says: "Temperature doesn't get taken under the arm." Below: "Heller Peter's chocolate" (and a vague picture of a doctor).

63. See Appendix, pp. 243–247. The "copy" for which he is grateful was made by A.F. for him.

SUMMARY VIII.1

Eighth phase: Attempt to seduce me.

1) Wanting to *show* erect penis[57]

2) Wind (dirty competition) storm roars[58]

3) literary

4) Joke about the fat man while passing wind (my penis not as big, but—)

5) Has to imagine me anally. Old fantasies about children who pee on one another. Dirt-love[59]

6) Agitation, cannot stand me, dirty toilet thoughts about me. Marry without if. *Fear of ball.*[60]

7) High point of transference,[61] wild, rebellious, affectionate, necklace, private life, kiss.

VIII.2

March 24 (Monday)

Again very restless, headache, tosses around. *Jealousy* of Ernst with whom I had gone shopping. How dreadful it would be to have a private social relationship with me. Excitement, tosses around, says: semi-hard. I reassure him: this would be quite natural.

As he complains of headache, I ask whether I should take his temperature. No, too private. Writes: Would be terrible if he were still little: "One's temperature does not get taken in the armpit")[62]

I *interpret* his excitement: When he likes someone, me or Mem, he wants it only nicely from *above,* in the upper sphere, but the *lower* mixes in and wants to join in too. That is natural, but cannot happen yet, later, with a woman, yes. Therefore protesting, screaming, anxiety. I repeat the explanation.

Great *relief.* Finds the copy of "Revolution,"[63] very grateful. Relates that he is writing the story of a boy, how he goes to a childrens' party, cannot step on cracks, etc.

64. Enclosed: Drawing of a labyrinth. Next to it the figure of a boy as if boxed in by a frame.

On leaving he says gratefully: So I should not take it so seriously!

March 25

Arrives in friendly mood, *cannot remember* what we spoke about yesterday. I slowly recall it for him.

Speaks about Goethe's verse ". . . durch das Labyrinth der Brust" [through the labyrinth of the soul], what does it mean, whether the inner world? I say, as it is with you. During the rest of the hour draws labyrinths, out of which I have to find my way.[64]

2 days vacation for Budapest, very friendly goodbye.

March 25–31

Rivalry
Arrives complaining as if he were ill: his knees and hands are chapped and they hurt. Then he remembers a dream.

Dream of one's chances
Somebody says about him, Peter doesn't have a chance, not a chance. He is very sad about it.

At first nothing comes to mind, then he says, but that isn't part of it: that Tinky has taken her napkin away from his side and sat down next to Reinhard. So he has *no chance with Tinky.*

Suddenly asks for anatomic details, what is it about his penis that will still change. I promise still more exact information with pictures.

Tells that he has been standing at the streetcar stop next to a public toilet, people went in, the wind kept blowing the door open, people could have seen inside. Did not go in, but thought: this way all the women could see inside.

March 31

Very friendly and in good spirits, quite natural with me this week. Mostly lying on the couch. Inquires about my explanations which are

65. See above, p. 93.

not ready yet. Tells me that in gym class he finds Mabbie's *feet disgusting*.

Reads the beginning of the *story* of 5-year-old Peter to me. Very well written, description of a childrens' party, quite superior, knows that it is himself.

Reminds me of his ideas about *eternal life,* has me again explain *fear of death* out of the *wish to kill*. Says that what came out about destruction was really true, he had been in a bad mood. Thesi lectured him, a *glass* literally leaped out of his hand. Why is it that he is such a sissy, always thinks that dying hurts? Fear of boys.

Feels hurt because of ball game, regresses, is no longer such an admired player. I remind him of *fear* of the *big boys*. He takes up the thread eagerly: the *feet* reappear, fear that they might knock his feet off with the ball. I remind him of the dream of Sigurd.[65] He says not a dream, but rather before falling asleep, demonstrates how he jerks up with his legs. Establishes connection: feet—penis through smelling—sweaty feet, castration anxiety, stops playing well out of fear.

"You don't have to knock off my feet, I am really not a good player at all!"

Very enthusiastic about interpretation, congratulates me.

April 1

Beginning of termination?
Very cheerful and friendly, I produce the requested drawing of the scrotum, he asks something about female details. I repeat the process of reproduction, he listens very quietly and with interest.

We speak about his parents very openly, he is very pleased that I praise their way of being protective of him. We speak of his analysis as of something past; that we will arrange with his father that he will come later on only once a week. He is very happy about it, embarrassed.

We speak about cow, bull, ox, etc.

66. Reference to entry of Monday, March 24.

67. Reference to entry of March 25.

68. Reference to entry of March 25–31.

SUMMARY VIII.2

Eighth phase. Continuation.

7) Jealousy, excited, *semihard, measuring*.

Interpretation: love from above and below[66]

Great relief

Plan for his story about children.

8) *Cannot remember* on the following day. Labyrinth of the soul[67]

9) Interpretation(s). Accepted:
    wish to kill—fear of death
    wish to kill—destruction
    Fear concerning feet/ball (sweaty feet—smell—lame). Interpretation and resolution of inhibition about playing ball.

    Solutions, supplements to sexual enlightenment[68]

VIII.3

April 2

Secondary gain from illness!
Cheerful, friendly, brings magnifying glass along and tries to burn holes in blotting paper and wool. Very happy when it succeeds.

a) what does it mean: *jump out of your skin* [*aus der Haut fahren* = idiom, to get frantic]? it makes him think of beef tongue, so soft that you can pull, scrape out the meat. Funny feeling. (Has torn out, then lost pages of his music notebook). Whether there could be a connection between first tearing out and then losing.

b) very cheerful, says he thinks: if one can no longer be sorry for him, because he is always sad and frightened, one should at least say: *he is always cheerful*. Thus change, instead of pride in illness, now pride in health. I encourage him strongly, say instead of being sorry for him, one can then admire him.

c) asks whether it makes sense to chase fear around from one thing to another: eyes—feet—tongue.

d) tells about *competition with the shower*. That he must always urinate when he stands under the shower.

April 3

Precursors of termination
Very cheerful, humorous. Mem should die, then people could feel sorry for him. I suggest other calamities: broken arm, broken leg, impoverishment, going blind. Rejects everything indignantly, nothing should happen to him. (I understand on the following day: if Mem dies, I will be his mother).

We discuss that he *misses* his illness, how healthy he is, how much has disappeared. He gets frightened, it could soon be over, digs up all the symptoms, is difficult to calm down. Wants to be a severe case, have a long analysis like the Burlinghams.

I tell him *not* to scream at night in order to show how he still needs analysis. He promises that.

Can play ball again. Very proud.

April 4

Fear of termination. Screaming.
As I have prophesied, he screamed at night in a dream, leaped up and quickly slipped into Thesi's bed. In the morning he himself knew nothing of the screaming.

Dream of the birds.
I. He sits behind a kind of curtain. He is very sad and Margot tries to encourage him. She says: so the story with Tinky is now over, and you would have preferred anyway to stay with Mem. As if Mem were leaving.

II. Birds fall to the ground, each bird is wrapped in flowers. He too shakes a tree and one also falls down in front of him. He plucks a few feathers from it. He asks Margot: why are they wrapped this way? She says: so that they are protected.

107

69. Paper with the words: "I thought right away: it is a sweater for me" (and drawing of scrotum).

III. There is a strong wind. Margot holds him in her arms like a package (baby). She says: we want to light a fire. He says: impossible with this wind. She: but we are doing it in a tube.

Associations:
Why Margot?—because she smells, her body odor.

Protected?—I have said about semen that it lies protected in the scrotum.

Interpretation:
I want to abandon him, like Tinky and Mem have done. But I must not, I should hold him like a baby, otherwise he has to light a fire again, pass wind, masturbate. Exposed to all dangers. If I leave him, he will be *bad* again. Therefore looks for Thesi's protection.

He discovers that I am crocheting a vest for him, is terribly embarrassed,[69] scolds me the rest of the hour. It is "too private" for him, is afraid of everything that the private could entail.

Interpretation of yesterday's material:
Mem should die, so that *I* can adopt him, *I* should feel sorry for him.

Monday, April 7

Has a cold; affectionate scolding culminating in "I'll throw (pillows) at you." Apparently an anal phantasy applied to me.

I shouldn't *touch* him, since he is not allowed to touch me.

Why do I not get angry when he is rude. I say: because I know that it means the opposite.

Tuesday, April 9

Sick with an earache.

Wednesday, April 9

Excited, angry, is afraid of getting nasty again.

a) Now, instead of losing, he has *taken* something, by mistake, a

70. Paper: "It seemed to me as though there had been a spot on Tinky's underpants." Alongside snails and snail-shells (as symbols of crawling into a hole for shame?). On reverse side: "Perhaps I think I want to marry her."

71. See April 3.

72. See April 4.

music notebook from Tinky. Reversal. If no woman, then doubly a man.

b) Tinky spot on her *underpants*. *Excitement* in telling about it.[70]

c) Wants to marry me.

Thus: repetition of *anal transference*.

SUMMARY VIII.3

Phase VIII. Beginning of termination.

1) Difficulty giving up secondary gain from illness[71]

2) and me. Screaming during the dream of the birds, i.e. if I leave him, he will be bad again.[72] Mem dies, I mother. New height of transference.

IX

March 10 [April 10]

Peter ill again. Visit from father; very pleased with improvement, asks me to break it to Peter (when there is chance) that he has a lover. (Cf. trip to Semmering, Peter's ucs[=unconscious] surmise was correct.)

March 11 [April 11]

Back again, arrives very ill-mannered, sticks his tongue out at me to show that it is full of pastry. Once screamed a little, "because he was angry that Thesi was away," knows nothing about it, chambermaid said so (night before last). No dream, but dream last night. (Account somewhat vague.)

Dream of the couple on the balcony

He is in his room and suddenly has the idea that burglars may come. The door to the balcony opens and he sees a man and a gaunt woman. He is very frightened, then Mem comes and he calms down again.

73. P.'s woolly toy dogs, successors to his imaginary sons, which he kept until age sixteen, included an orange-reddish giraffelike dog, a spotted, black-and-white dog with floppy ears, like the great dane Bella, and the much-beloved "Bonzo" dogs with sad Jewish faces.

Associations:
Door to the balcony—the cat always goes out at night to *marry*
Gaunt woman—witch—I

Interpretation:
The dangerous thing happening there is the marrying (breaking in). *I*
apparently marry his father, who already appeared as a *burglar* in the
very first dream. He calls Mem for help.

———

Does *not* ask what his father and I talked about, reports only that fa.
said so many times that he would come and see me, that he, P., ended
up by finishing the sentence for him. Great restlessness, reads, touches
everything. I interpret to him the fantasy that there is something
between fa. and me. Accepts the fantasy.

[up to] April 30

Father's lover.

Speaks about relief, dull dreamy despair is gone. Long conversation
about father's girl friend. Seems to accept the fact, though very
unwillingly. He asks whether it is a very bad thing, whether he is to be
pitied, or does that happen to other children as well. That he always
thinks: the friendship between Hans and Mem is still worth more than
the other relationship. About good and bad marriages. Is very moved,
touched.

But suddenly takes everything back: it is true that fa. has a girl friend,
but he doesn't do anything with her, not even kiss.

———

2 days later perfectly cheerful, normal, friendly. We play. Telephone
conversation with Mem, great praise for analysis. He has a literary
project: what his woolly dogs tell him.[73]

74. Figure 1.6 shows the familiar villain, bad father, wild hunter, man in feathered hat with wide mouth, glaring teeth, wide shoulders, also Freischütz-Schreifritz, plus grotesquely pitiful figures, two of them mirroring one another; and perhaps a second, *sad* wild huntsman.—On reverse side: "It seems to me as though you [i.e., A. Freud] were crying. I thought perhaps your father [is sick: crossed out] is not well."

indecent in identification with father

1) Tells dream, supposedly of some time ago.

Dream of the Jantzen bathing suit.
He pulls his shirt way down with his hands so that one cannot see him.

Associations:
to the bathing suits of Mem and Thesi, where you believe it is just a skirt; but underneath there are pants, and one doesn't see anything.

Thus: to show—to get to see.

2) Long, confused dream:

Dream of the journey to Breitenstein
He is in the train with the other children as he was at Christmas time, a lot of vague "indecent" things are happening. He is wearing a turtleneck collar around his neck (he himself interprets: foreskin wrapped around penis).

Interpretation:
very unfriendly, excited during the hour, hard to get him to talk. Says he was unfriendly with Mem, rude with Thesi. When I ask him about events: nothing; to question about Easter trip: everybody there. When he leaves I go to look for the car, he says: oh yes, fa. on Easter trip with car. Suddenly understands dream and bad mood.

Thus: he goes on a trip like his father and does things as indecent as those he assumes his father does.

Great relief. [Figure 1.6.][74]

SUMMARY IX.

Phase IX.

Father very pleased (wants Peter to know about lover).

1) Suspects me and father (dream of balcony).

FIGURE 1.6

75. Reference to p. 113 ("Father's lover").

76. The following *variants* were enclosed (on folded sheets) with the continous, presumably definitive series of the summaries as they are given in our text at the end of each respective phase.

77. Corresponds to sections 1 to 7 in Phase II of the definitive series.

78. Corresponds to Phase III and the first four sections of Phase IV in the definitive series, see above, pp. 33–35.

2) Accepts lover, but he [= father] doesn't do anything with her.[75]

3) Easter trip. He is as indecent as father.

SUMMARIES: VARIANTS TO THE DIVISION INTO PHASES OF PART 1 OF THE ANALYSIS[76]

Phases of the analysis[77]:

I. Play, poets, plans for the future, book titles

II. Fear of death, disparagement of parents, wish to become greater. Prohibition.

III. Worry about Thesi's future

IV. Worry about my laughing

V. Grandpapa etc.

VI. Dream about sh— Reports about school; about public toilets

VII. Reads to me poems for four days: Chinese Flute.

VIII. Toilet in Café. Dream of war.

Phase III[78] Mother

Love for Tinky.

1) Dream of officer.

2) Screaming dream of castle moat. Talk with father about divorce, sexual enlightenment by me, great interest, novella "Revolution."

3) Mem's return, he angry at her, complaints about Margot, tenderness Hans

4) Dream of chestnut tree, competition on anal, not genital, level.

5) Dream of fleeing, fear of father—genital, notion of vagina

6) Poems about death, dream of little bag, return of the mother, drawing of Siamese twins, marriage, triangles, Hänschen klein! [song]

Transfers: anger at mother onto me.

79. Reference to entry of December 8 to 14, 1929.

80. Corresponds to the end of Phase IV (above, p. 41) and the major part of Phase V (above, p. 45) in the definitive series.

81. With the exception of (1), which in the definitive series belongs to Phase V (see above, p. 45), this entry corresponds to sections 1 to 5 of Phase VI of this series (see p. 83).

Return of Mem
1) *Resistance,* transference conflict.

Eye anxiety, excitement, inner trembling, doesn't want to express anything until *great outburst* screaming while awake.[79]

Explanation: cook: Thesi marriage.

Phase IV[80]

Turning away [from] Mem   L.T.T.

Transference from Mem to Tinky. Clarity, then dark period.

Talk about masturbation.

Phase V[81]

1) Dream about the *wallowing pig,* anal love (stain on ass)

2) Fear of *peasant boys* [change] into active behavior [toward] boys, homosex.

3) Fear of *inviting* children: <u>Thesi</u>
                                            temptation
   disappears after interpretation

4) *Resistance,* must hear bad things said about Freud, religion. Must hurt Tinky by talking about Ernst. Finally admits conflict between Mem and me, that I do not like Mem and Hans.

5) Dream of thief [crossed out] candy, that Hans has *stolen* Mem's penis, therefore his so big.

6) Thoughts and drawing about God, religion, pilgrims, spirit.

7) "Be quiet I have to think." Finally after resistance: Tinky *made a sound.* Whether one may call me pig, anal scolding. Would like to swear at Tinky that way: anal love. Transformation of fear of boys into *admiration.*

8) like 7 "Don't say anything!" Mem passed wind. Masturbation "harmless playing." Thus temptation by Mem; masturbation in the past.

82. Corresponds to Phase VI, section 6 (see above, p. 83) of the definitive series.

83. Corresponds to the first part of Phase VIII (sections 1–7) of the definitive series (see p. 99).

Phase VI. Masturbation[82]

1) Dream of lame uncle. When one squints it stays that way, erection, hygienic. Interpretation of eye anxiety. Attempted interpretation of [tendency to] ruin things.

2) Zobeltitzes, homosex.

3) Long resistance, clarified by father's trip [to] Semmering
   a) dream of coals. Homosex. jealousy
   b) dream of railway
   c) dream of pond
Fear of homosex.

Phase VII. Seduction in the transference[83]

1) wanting to *show* hard penis

2) Wind (dirty competition) (Poem of storm)

3) literary
Interpretation of dirtiness [crossed out]

4) Joke accompanied by wind (my penis not as big, but instead—)

5) Has to fantasize me anally. Telling of old fantasies, where children urinate on one another in various positions.

   Dirt love. *Fear of ball.*

   5a) Agitation. can[not] stand me, dirty toilet thoughts about me, marry without if

6) High point of transference. Necklace, private life, kissing. "Summit love." Wildly rebellious, tender.

Footnotes to Part 2

1. Letter, with date inserted by A.F., "May 1930, Berlin":

Dear Anna Freud!

Hans told me who is his lover, so to speak, and it was, as I thought, Miss Schön. You know, when Hans told me, I said sort of quickly "she is very nice" and that has become another sentence that hounds me. I am sleepy now although it is morning, and I think (though Thesi is also sleepy) that it also has something to do with your and Mem's leaving. Don't you think so?

The fear of the dark is really not quite gone yet. When I stand in our nursery and there is a strong wind blowing outside, I am always frightened. So often now I am afraid that other people (namely Tesu) could die. Do you think it means I also want to murder Tesu?

Well, and now it seems to me suddenly as if everything I have told you is really phony. Generally, I am furious at you now. I think I can't do analytic sessions in writing. Have you seen Mem, most likely her filmscript will not be accepted after all. Hans's children's story will be marvelous. I like to be with him so much now, and I think only now am I not afraid of him any more. Sometimes, that is, in the Diana Bath [*Dianabad*, public swimming pool], the wish to show my body comes again. Could you tell me once more what the rule about that was?

But now I know nothing more to say and must go and practice the piano. I already play Schumann and Min says I will catch up with Tinky. That makes me proud. I hope you will be able to decipher or read my handwriting.

In addition, many greetings to you
      Peter Heller

Added: drawing of a short fat figure: below: "I"; on reverse side, the remark: "Confidential matter of the recipient."

2. Allusion to the "communist doctrine" of mother's friend (Karl Frank) condemning fishing as a capitalist pastime.

PART 2

Five months' interruption, my fault, from May 1 to October 1 [1930].

During this time two letters (enclosure,[1] second letter unfortunately missing).

a) contains reaction to talk with father about his lover

b) written from Dalmatia (July). Content: finds himself disgusting, was in public toilet, is unfriendly, dissatisfied with himself.

Additionally, two talks in Grundlsee. Begins to speak without difficulty, tells about Dalmatia. Nothing real occurred, only temptations to do dirty things, is often angry with Thesi and feels insincere.

Interpretation:
if they knew how I really am. Naughtiness out of a sense of guilt.

Other communications:
Frequent occasions for excitement and jealousy, very active love life of both parents, nudity, etc. (Kreuz im Grundlsee [settlement on Lake Grundlsee]).

October 1.–12.

Jealousy

Resumption.

Unfavorably changed by atmosphere [at Grundlsee] im Kreuz, attempt to acquire the modernity prevailing there by skipping over the neurosis. Evening anxiety without screaming.

Comes in saying: I am against *fishing*, but I fish all day long (Frank, communist doctrine).[2]

Had been thinking that he would *prefer to be in analysis* with one of

3. Regarding enclosure a) forbidden talking about analysis or reporting of Anna Freud's opinions at home, there is a note: "That you have also told me one can read The Count of Monte Cristo without being afraid." b): Political drawings (Figure 2.1): the hard-edged, sharply profiled, spiky head of the leftist revolutionary Karl Frank and another revolutionary figure with beard, glasses, and proletarian cap (representing a former leader in the Youth Movement, leftist analyst Siegfried Bernfeld); a hanged man with a red flag, next to him the Star of David, to the right the swastika, below: the revolutionary with the cap; German escutcheon with swastika; people with intellectual, somber, revolutionary looks; a man with the communist star as a nose and slanted eyes; an Austrian red-white-red coat of arms plus red flag, swastika, Star of David. Regarding c): drawing of the bearded man (quasi Chinese), a small roundish person (Thesi) in the background.

4. A sheet showing how people are replaced by dogs; on one side among many human faces, the remark: "I wanted to kiss them too"; on reverse side: only animals scurrying by.

the others there *rather than with me* (they would find nothing wrong, he would learn that it is all right to have affairs, and he would not be sad about his parents any more).

How *they made fun of God* in a play (God is drunk).

How the *married people there* [i.e., at Grundlsee] do not act in love with one another, but are friendly with other men and women "they do not really care for."

His mother returns but he is angry, jealous, suspects her with a number of different men and women. Seemingly he is angry with me all the time, affectionate *scolding* (charlatan, worse than Zeileiss [a faith healer]; letter to my father as formerly: [my being famous is] "on account of father only"; reappearance of old symptoms, asks many *questions, compares,* tries to draw out my opinion, reports it at home which he should not do. (Enclosure a.) Makes *political* drawings (b) [Figure 2.1] (Frank?), the same *head* over and over again (Bernfeld?), (c) thinks Thesi fell in love with Bernfeld.[3]

Dogs. We speak about mother, he lies down, talks about his woolly toy dogs. He sleeps with them, claims that he masturbates sometimes with them, kisses them instead of kissing people, but not mother, Tinky, or me (d).[4]

Is afraid of becoming famous only after his death.

Works very well at school. ("That would be tactless—").

Attempt at interpretation for me: Transference of his jealousy of his mother onto me. To save himself from jealousy, attempt to justify Mem by modern theories. Renewed fear of the father because of renewed aggression toward men.

(As the mother wants to greet him, he rejects her caresses because *"Hans doesn't like it when she is like that with him."*)

October 13–20

Transition of identification from writer to communist

After a conversation with his mother Peter's state becomes clearer. She has in fact fallen in love this summer with the communist Frank, who

FIGURE 2.1

is now the object of Peter's jealousy. (Frank is against fishing, Hans fishes all day long.) Peter's initial remark about fishing therefore means: I want to be Frank but am still Hans. Mother will move to F. in Berlin, which she has not told Peter as yet. Peter's thoughts revolve around the fact that he no longer wants to become a poet, but a great politician.

Relates the following dream:

Dream of America and Paris

He travels to America with other boys, like Bob. There are many exciting things there, he is put in jail. Then he is in Paris, there is a woman who wants to poison him with strychnine.

Interpretation: His parents are separated like Bob's parents. If he wants to keep his mother he has to become a communist like F., also be put in jail. His father has just been in Paris. Peter wonders with whom. In *The Count of Monte Cristo*, a stepmother poisons her stepson so that her own child may get the inheritance. If Hans marries his lover and has another child, the stepmother will poison him so that the new child gets the factory. (Shortly before, he spoke about the fact that his profession is determined by the factory, he cannot make his own choice like Bob.)

A few days later his mother informs him of her departure. He is quite melancholy, but wants to deny it, reads Rilke poems. In the midst of it he looks up and says: It's not like it used to be with the poems. I think the dear communist disturbs me.

Doesn't speak of his father with admiration any more, but very disparagingly as someone on the same level as he. Finally realizes that his mother is leaving his father the same way as she is leaving him. Evidently he has continued so far to value his father still as the possessor of his mother.

October 22

Confirmation of the new jealousy by way of symptomatic actions.

Peter comes with a headache which we interpret as an attempt to tie the mother to him through illness.

131

5. Note: "The same shape as the thing. And also grows."

For the last two days he has been playing incessantly with a fishing reel tied to a string, throwing the reel away from himself, then pulling it back with the string.

Interpretation:
   a) fishing or not, Hans or Frank
   b) sending mother away, pulling back
   c) fishing is like murdering, letting out rage
   d) Peter's spontaneous interpretation: he rolls the reel like his penis, masturbates very frequently now and in doing so wants to get everything to be "nice" and smooth (keep mother by having a genital like a man).

Says about my weaving: this too is man and woman: the thread goes into the hole.

Relates suddenly a—compulsive—symptomatic action: wherever two things *lie on top of one another*, he has to separate them. Then he thinks: It's still lying there but at least it's now lying on the floor.

We recapitulate his situation. When he is afraid in the evenings he should say: Dear F., I'm not doing anything to harm you, so don't you do anything to me either. He should try not to get sick and remember that Hans is still Hans even if he is not the possessor of his mother.

He is very friendly, looks sad.

November 3

Plays with a finger cot the entire hour, blows it up a hundred times, shows evidently that he is masturbating more.[5]

November 4

Fear of boarding school.
Brings in daily an election poster and reads it aloud with pathos. We speak about Bolshevistic communal education. He suddenly becomes very anxious, turns against communism. (Doctrinal opinions entice, seduce.) It turns out that he is very much afraid of being given away. Hans once said, better for children, but there are no good boarding

schools in Austria. Is surprised about being so afraid since he liked so much staying with the Rosenfelds. Evidently fear of something else.

November 6

Suspicion of Mem. Fare beating

Comes in and says: I am not afraid any more at all. But I wouldn't advise you to break off the analysis at this point. (tiddledywinks).

November 7

Has been afraid again, realizes he is keeping secrets. Tells dream from past few days:

Dream of fare beating

He is with Mumi, she is a communist. A policeman arrests her, they have to take the Nr. 60 streetcar to the police station. Mumi doesn't pay the fare. Then she says, let's get off and they get out.

Associations:

Mumi—Frank—communists—Mem

Fare beating—man without being married

Admits: He is worried. Mem hasn't written for a long time, but had things sent to her (blankets), perhaps moved. Suspicious of Frank, concubinage.

Tells, half humorously, as an inscription for foundation of church, his parents' marriage: Mother unfaithful with many men. Child wastes away, treated with by now antiquated method (link to story of fire in "Revolution," apparently Frank sets fire to the factory), carries mother off, goes to Asia where incest is permitted, marries her. Keeps showing with a thread how loosely the marriage is tied, tightens the knot only at the moment of speaking of the incest-marriage.

I tell him as a rule: Every anxiety can be transformed back into a thought.

6. Copy by Anna Freud [See Appendix, "A Dream," p. 266.]

Jealousy of Miss Schön
Guarded, comes in with the exclamation: "I really don't know any
more what you want of me, I am perfectly healthy." I pretend to go
along with that, make plans to reduce (weekly) sessions to three.

Playing "baby" with Reinhard during overnight visit. That the other
might be a girl friend (lover), very pleasant exciting feeling.

During a distracted game of tiddledywinks he finally admits that *Miss
Schön* had been at his home which excited him very much. Afraid
Hans will marry and have another child. Baby therefore is *substitute*
for father's girl friend. Is sexually aroused the whole time, experiences
it as pleasant.

Continuation after pause of two days

Exclamation: "I have suffered immensely!" Father spent night away
from the house. Will surely get married. What would Peter say if father
asked for permission: It would be a pseudo-question, he would have to
say yes. Says half in jest that he will be kind to his brother, protect
him.

Ruthi and *Tinky*—he'd like to marry both (then he will have two wives,
father only one). Ruth said to him the lesson about Napoleon was very
interesting. She gets personal: she says *little one* and *idiot* to him, thus
affectionate.

That it doesn't make sense to think about his father all the time,
decides to write his list of wishes for Christmas.

November 20

Mother's arrival, slight jealousy displaced to Thesi
Mem arrives unexpectedly, he is again somewhat disturbed, jealous of
Garger, whom she sees more than him. Reads during the hour, then
rows with Thesi.

A poem about the pavor nocturnus "A Dream."[6]

"Collected works," proud.

7. Reference to Sigmund Freud's "Psycho-analytic notes on an autobiographical account of a case of paranoia (dementia paranoides)" (1911), *Standard Edition*, Vol. 12, pp. 3–82, London, Hogarth Press, 1958.

November 21

Fear of Ruth's foot injury
Says he could not love Ruth any more, is sickened by the sight of her foot. Not in swimming or in gym, that wouldn't matter. She *sprained* her foot in school, he saw the foot. Sickening.

Interpretation:
Memory of the lame uncle, castration anxiety.

[My] talk with his father. Promises to keep Inge at a distance in order to spare Peter the excitement.

November 22–December 5

Persecution from behind. Breasts.
New thrust of anxiety, fear that someone could pounce on him from *behind*. At the same time feeling that he is getting fatter, he bumped against something with his chest, believes his *breasts are growing*, the other children would notice when he goes swimming (cf. Schreber[7]). Anxiety is associated with Hans.

Restlessness, excitation, especially in the evening when father is in room next to his. Disturbed about not seeing Inge any more. Dirty, forgetful (piano keys).

Interpretation: Attempt to turn into a woman in order to replace mother and lover for father. Castration wish, wish for anal intercourse, cf. dogs.

Peter replaces the dogs by an observation concerning pigeons which he now makes continuously from his window. She acts coy, the cock approaches her from behind. Calls his anxiety now "cock pigeon." Restlessness diminishes, but he has indeed put on weight recently.

Until Christmas outwardly very good, inwardly very excited, continuous alternation between homosex. love for father, heterosex. love for mother, jealousy regarding both.

8. Attached, a note with a list, drawn up by P.H., of his attacks: "*Steinhaus*: 1. Margot (fever)—*Vienna*: 2. Hans' return. Memka beast. In the margin of 2: a small figure raising his arms between two book covers falling shut and threatening to squash or kill him. 3. Miss Schön. I shall die tonight. Memka! Thesi! I'm dying! Tinky." Below, twice: "Katherine" [= Tinky].

9. "Poems," with A. Freud's notation: "Christ(mas) 1930"; see Appendix, "The Murderer" (p. 265), "Poem" (p. 265), "Yearning" (p. 265).

Great relapse
4 attacks worse than ever. All about 10:30 at night.

1st attack:
New Year's Eve, with a fever (slight flu with earache on ski trip with Burlinghams in Steinhaus. Screams terribly loudly: *Margot!*). Dreams that 2 sleds collide, plunge down into depth. Had expected Mem to visit. When ill, Thesi came. Cries at her arrival.

2nd attack:
At home, Mem and father in the house. Mem ill, vaginal bleeding, psychological breakdown. Father traveling in Grundlsee with Inge. On the evening of his return. Screams: *The books are falling on me and killing me. Memka leave, you are a monster.*

3rd attack:
Before Mem's departure, Miss Schön is in the house: *Memka, Thesi! I'm going to die this night.*

4th attack: 2 days later:
Look, Thesi, help me, free me, I'm going to die this night. Something about *Tinky*, about *telephone*.

Behavior in analysis: very concerned, very agitated, tries extraordinarily hard to find the reason.[8]

Says regarding 3rd attack: I can't stand it that one is leaving and the other is coming.

3 new poems from Steinhaus [a resort], see enclosure.[9]

In the associations: *Hans and Frank are really one person. I have never yet seen them together.* Sounds as if taken over from the mother's ucs [= unconscious].

I see Mem red. Is she bleeding from down there? Hans shoots it off her.

With my mouth I shall be a woman and a man below.

Writes Katherine, over and over, does not know why (show naked?).

10. The blind man, however, is also the revolutionary Frank, surrounded by women, turning his eyes toward the poor and oppressed (see Figure 2.2A).

11. (See Figure 2.2B.) The grim sage, top middle, is flanked by the blood-king and the woman; helper and God on left and right margins; the visionary with glasses and beard, Bernfeld?; his enemies (below), a Red and a follower of the swastika—Nazi—(original drawing in color). On reverse: "I am celebrated" (a famous man; "celebrated" in English in the original).

1st picture:
A blind man who has visions,[10] behind him his exact likeness. Sees nothing but women [Figure 2.2A]. It is he himself, looking inward. Visions—during pavor nocturnus?

2nd picture[11] [Figure 2.2B]:
The blind man with visions (Peter)—a god who helps him (Freud)— the blood-king (Hans)—his wife (Mem)—a helper— below: enemies of the hero.

The blood-king threatens the wise man who knows how one could lure the unfaithful woman back, but doesn't tell him.

January 16

Wild sexual associations regarding seeing red, shoot off penis, mouth as vagina, questions about having children; much more obscene than what he was told.

Searches obviously for an observed missing sexual scene.

Disturbed in his piano playing. Has to do everything like Mem (clearing throat, shivering).

Remarks:
Can I be nice again before all is well? (Picks quarrels with Thesi.)

I used to be proud, not any more now. When I criticize Basti, I can't help thinking: and I scream at night.

1.18

Remarks in associations:
1) If I could go to the Pope—(sin?)

2) I'm going to die this night—if the boy next door makes such noise. (If the parents next door make such noise?)

3) It is the park keeper at the Belvedere. He spreads sand and

FIGURE 2.2A

FIGURE 2.2B

12. See nightmare in "Pavor nocturnus" (footnote 6).

scolds me for walking on the lawn. Then he sticks me into an infernal machine.[12]

January 20

Said on preceding day he will dream.

Screaming dream of the bull.

"He goes hunting with Hans. Father and the forest ranger walk ahead, he and Thesi behind. The trees stand in rows, also bushes. There are bulls or oxen. They keep going in and out between the trees, always in and out. He says: why doesn't one shoot them. Thesi says: but you don't shoot those animals.— Then Hans does shoot a bull and guts it. Slits it open, tears out the guts. Next to it a syringe is stuck in the ground, it wobbles back and forth, they tear it out too." He screams.

Associations:
rows of trees, bushes—(body hair?)

bulls: man, Hans; but why do they keep going back and forth; when you marry, only once (points to something seen, not known).

gutting: that is the way the cook cleaned out the guts of a capercaillie, the cock, no a partridge. The intestines are so entangled, this is perhaps the confusion that enters into every dream

blood: Blood-king, Hans, Mem.

Syringe back and forth: the exhibitionist's penis in the public toilet moved like that.

Capercaillie (cock): prances and clucks to lure the female

Interpretation:
The "vision," intercourse. Double castration, which evidently happens to Mem and him. Knowledge, otherwise not available to him, of the thrusting and the blood.

Talk about sexual matters. Castration of ox, castration of tomcat, courting call of capercaillie.

13. Enclosed: sheets with faces (see Figure 2.3) whose eyes have been pierced; on one of them with A.F.'s remark: "explains himself: earlier, nose always like penis; then like vagina, hole; now again penis." On reverse side: avenue with trees and cars.

Statements:
1) That there would be very much less in this world without love, even if children were produced mechanically. No art. No technology either? Yes, technology for defense. Thus the world is fighting and love.

2) That he will very quickly forget all these rules again (fear of renewed repression).

3) In a way very egoistic that he doesn't want to let anyone get married; whether one knew in earlier times that human beings were so bad.

4) If I don't scream, I dream of Tinky.

January 23

Real situation of mother.
Begins to question me whether Mem went to Berlin not only for professional reasons, does she have a lover. I say, not only. P.: I knew it. Suspects that it is Frank but says: she cannot lie that much (has supposedly seen him only once). I tell him to ask Hans, he says: no, it is her private matter, I don't need to know. Wants to maintain the illusion with all his might that she does not lie,

doesn't want to know anything,

rationalizes with nice tact and discretion.

While drawing, he speaks about Frank, says: perhaps everything in the world is Frank, only in different form.

Punctures all drawings [Figure 2.3], says: out with the eyes.[13] I have the feeling he is stabbing me.

January 26

Everything is dirt

Screaming dream of Tinky
(screaming is reported only the following day.)

"He is with Tinky in a ruin near Steinhaus. There is a golden-brown stone. He has a feeling similar to what he had awhile ago when Reinhard was with him."

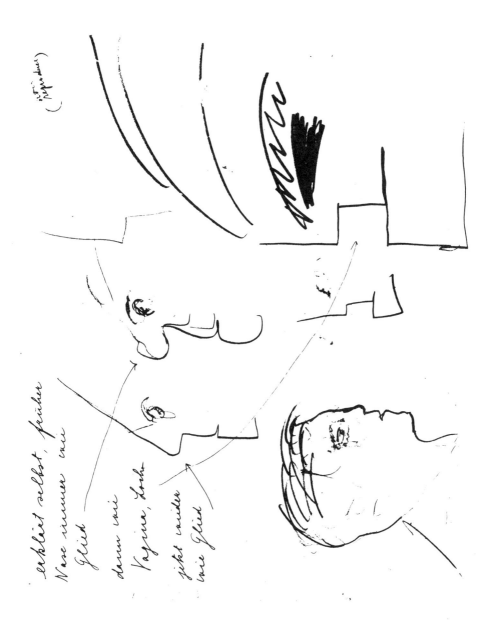

FIGURE 2.3

On the following day at school he has a special feeling vis-à-vis Tinky, has to remind himself that he didn't spend the night with her.

Associations:
Ruin: a special feeling as in Greifenstein, "many emperors (lie) buried (there)"

Golden-brown stone: Alchemist Thousand, brown like dirt.

Believes he screamed when he was in bed with Tinky.

Interpretation:
The father must be dead, he must make as much gold or dirt as father in order to marry Tinky. Scream?

Associations of the day: everything is *dirt* over and over again, all people are dirt. Remark of the previous day: if Hans didn't have money, he too would just be a dog.

Symptoms: Complains that he has to do everything *three times* over. Complains that he is afraid of school as he had been at the Evangelical School, particularly when he forgets a *pencil*.

Interpretation: homosex. danger, when he is without a penis.

Inquires about positive–negative, which stands for *active–passive*. Apparently from the vision: 3 times, active.

January 27

Jealousy of Thesi and Jekels, Menga's "secret chambers." Menga shall die, he will smile coldly. Anger at analysis only apparent.

January 28

Screaming dream of the globe

wakes up at 10:15 p.m., screams: the globe . . . the screw is missing.

Associations:
In school he shifted the globe from which Elisabeth had to copy.

Australia, but it wasn't Australia

14. A humoristic water color (by Lasker?) of St. Anthony's sermon to the fish hung in the "anxiety" hallway of the apartment in the Karolinengasse.

15. The sheet (original in color; see Figure 2.4) belonging to this hour shows two enormous, stern adult faces staring at each other (repeated in background), between them the little boy as if crushed between the two, with feet, arms, hands turned outward as if he were an erect beetle or frog. On reverse: man with diabolically oversized penis like a pointed tail; scribbles; and as a written communication: "Hans: A.F(reud) told me that Prof. F(reud) said: 'In our family there are no neurotics.'" Followed by pierced drawings.

tries very hard, can find nothing

"if Elisabeth . . . didn't have such beautiful legs" Eva has big breasts. Breast—globe?

Ununderstood dream of sledding
"He and Hans are in a canoe, there are terribly many fish there. In Grundlsee (that is like another dream of Grundlsee. Bob sits on the terrace, Menga is not fully dressed. From above one sees a great many fish as in the picture of the sermon to the fish.[14] He runs down to fish.)

Then he is on a sled with Thesi. She says no, not down there, it is too steep. ⤵ He says: what did you make a hole down there for?

He tries very hard but we don't understand anything.

January 30

Dream of the broken window
He and Basti are sitting on a windowpane. Suddenly a piece breaks off ⟩ . He says: Oh yes, Hans will be angry.

Associations:
Basti—he is one of those "bad" guys; what B. said to Ighino a while ago: they wanted to climb out the window at night, urinate against a tree, climb up.

Breaking off—castration

Possible interpretation, also of yesterday's dream: Hans is angry when he wants to castrate himself for him, doesn't want him. Same reproach as for Thesi: what did you make a hole there for? Bob is circumcized, can no longer castrate any woman (?)

Fishing? [Figure 2.4][15]

February 2

Smug smile
Has been on an excursion with Hans to the Rax mountain, was praised.

Complains about a "cozy" self-satisfied feeling, smug smile, talking

157

Figure 2.4

16. Paper with wild scrawls and the words: "alone in a room with a woman I am. *To fall in love!!*"

17. Neighbors of the Hellers in the Karolinengasse.

18. On loose sheets (see Figures 2.5A, B) regarding "Dream of Sesostris and Mary Stuart" (A.F.'s notation) there are 1) ugly, wicked-looking women with evil eyes, 2) picture of the mighty pharaoh: "Sesostris" [in profile]; "Ramses" [crossed out].

19. Savage, broad-shouldered man, massive "hood" or "proletarian" with bowler hat, beard, and powerful, bared teeth (see Figure 2.5C).

Jewish jargon; gossips about the analysis with Thesi, criticizes the other children.

Who is that?

Dream forgotten, empty, "alone with a woman in a room,"[16] Halma board (game), suddenly recalls, to his own greatest astonishment.

Dream of Sesostris

He is in the bathroom, Hans too. Hans leaves, goes over to the Portheims[17] in his shirt-sleeves. A stranger arrives, asks him loudly and wildly: Where is Herr Doctor (Heller)? When was that with Menga? He sees suddenly how Hans drags and crowds Menga, and pushes her toward the toilet. He says as if indifferent: . . . Oh, that's a long time ago.—Hans comes back and he tells him what the man had asked. Hans says with a smile: Oh, Sesostris.

Then there is a very fat person like their laundress, who talks with others about Maria Stuart, what a bad queen, serves her right to be done in.

Associations:
Portheims—so fine and stiff, one could not go there in shirt-sleeves.

Sesostris—Egyptian history, founder of a dynasty, like Napoleon.

Toilet—Eula [= Lilli K.] dragged him into the toilet, locked him in as punishment

Hans's tone of voice—oh well, Garger (Frank?).

Part of what he observed?[18] [Figures 2.5A, 2.5B]

No dreams, small additions, new type in drawing: man with teeth.[19] [Figure 2.5C]

Traum v. Sesostris u.
Maria Stuart

FIGURE 2.5A

163

FIGURE 2.5B

165

FIGURE 2.5c

20. Accompanying paper with list of suitors: "No. 1 renegade; No. 2 *adorer*; No. 3 turns insane; No. ? *hero, adorer, renegade* [composite type?]; No. 4 coward (conceited); No. 5 tyrant." For text of the fairytale see Appendix, pp. 249–254. On reverse side (Figure 2.6A): drawing of Germanic, blond woman: "Miss S." (= Inge Schön).

21. The enclosed drawing (red in the original; see Figure 2.6B) shows, in the shape of an actor and acrobat who displays himself, the soaring, torerolike protagonist (signifying man's progress and elevation—as teacher—, as well as: erection) on a stage decorated with banners.

Maria Stuart and *Elisabeth*, that E. was perhaps a man. (Dream of the globe?) Perhaps theory: all women are men before they are married.

Cannot sleep over at Basti's because of screaming, sad, will "never forgive me for it."

He is writing a fairy tale "without meaning or moral."

Princess who gives each suitor 3 riddles and beheads them. The 100th is a nobleman, very gifted, etc., solves one riddle—Is also beheaded. One would have expected that he gets her.[20] [Figure 2.6A]

Thus: *no one* gets Menga, all die because of her.

Very pessimistic at school; cf. fairy tale.

(A prince whom she loves doesn't care for her, calls her wild sow, in a rage.) Sow = lover; everything is dirt = wish fantasy = everything is love. Drawings: mouth with teeth appear. Vagina dentata?—Woman who kills all men—Princess of the fairy tale?

Second Dream of Sesostris

"Erik calls on him, asking him to tell about Sesostris. He doesn't know anything. Tinky says, but I have the book, and brings it. He opens the book, it starts with the cave men. Then it goes on higher and higher (symbolic), so that he is teaching all the people, he climbs onto the table higher and higher, or is carried, a feeling of tightness. He wears Basti's swimming trunk; his or Sesostris' penis rises, coming out."[21] [Figure 2.6B]

Otherwise, ill-humor, phony, play-acting.

Dream of strong man

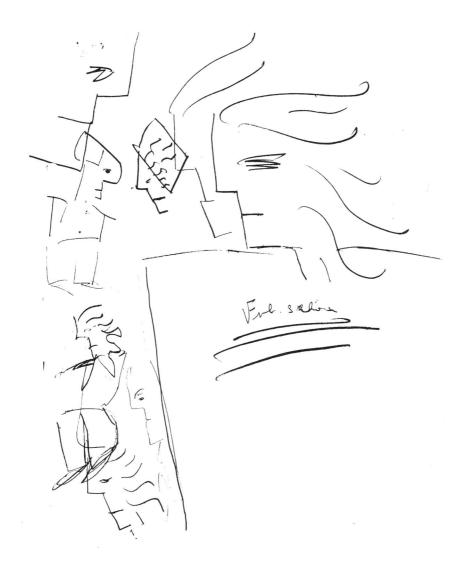

FIGURE 2.6A

FIGURE 2.6B

22. Attached sheet with: "Rosalin(d)," "Jaromir" (from Grillparzer's play *Die Ahnfrau)* "Thesi Bergmann" (indicating visits to the theater).

23. Explanation: "Father should give a half answer": i.e., tell him only half the truth: mother did not go to Berlin because of a man, but in order to undergo analysis with Hanns Sachs, to clarify her thoughts.

He dreams of Rosalind in "As You Like It." The "strong man" fights with Orlando. Blood flows.[22]

He calls out in his sleep.

Mood continues to be agitated, he is late, hardly good for anything. When I admonish him, he promises improvement, takes a taxi on the following day to be in time.

Transference: Will I feel hurt if Erik turns into a better analyst than I? Why I am not more ambitious. Of course, I don't care if 10 years after my death I will be forgotten, he does. 3 kinds of women: wife and mother—genius—governess. I would be g[enius] if analysis would let me.

2.18

Pumsi[*fart*]
Excited interesting hour. Angry at everything, strong resistance, Thesi should not treat him like a child, little fight with Thesi. I clear everything away, declare everything to be fake, finally we touch ground. He writes with great embarrassment: Thesi used the word "Pumsi" from his childhood language as he passed wind. Anal seduction as with mother, he reacts with "fight" = love scene.

Realizes this.

2.19

Question regarding Menga's lover.
After this hour, in the evening in the bathtub, small outburst with Thesi: she should tell him who Mem is with in Berlin. She refers him to me or father.

Father's visit:
a) Menga's situation: father should give him a half-answer, now no man, analysis for clarification.[23]
b) father's situation: to ward off the constant spying, he should question his father once a week.

24. Enclosure: Poems about "Life" (Appendix, pp. 266ff) and about being in love (To Tinky) (Appendix, p. 268).

25. Reference to Figure 2.6A.

5 poems "Life."
Comes in radiant, cheerful, will dictate to me "200 verses standing on one foot." Very approachable.

Discussion of conversation with father: whether I have agreed on anything with fa. As I described to him the effects of his spying, tears in his eyes.

5 poems.[24] Doesn't understand them himself, wonders, especially about "The dreams we live is life that we dream." Repeats this again and again, finds it meaningless.

Attempt at interpretation (for myself): He doesn't know what is real, the bloody vision or the harmless reality. Vision probably made up of two observations: intercourse + menstruation. Bleeding as consequence of intercourse, lies ahead for him too.

Interpreted to him: where the blood comes from, that m(other)'s illness was [menstrual] bleeding.

Drawings of February 1931:
small selection
a) "Kathrin" [Tinky] pursues him, he can't get [the name] out of his mind after his return from Semmering, following a dream which is reminiscent of the birthday dinner at K.s, but remains uninterpreted otherwise.
b) see a)
c) male and female shapes of nose and mouth
d) great "red" excitement
e) same
f) stabs me; eyes out
g) new "Chinese" shape of face
h) to: Elisabeth as half man, first Egyptian
i) mouth with teeth (for the first time)
j) Sesostris
k) women with closed mouths (see drawing of Miss Schön)[25]
l) open, closed mouth, curls

26. See p. 67.

27. See Appendix, p. 252.

28. Drawings: Ugly things: donkey-men with elephantine noses—one with a round semihard hat; others with birdheads; on another sheet: in the background birds, in the foreground an animallike old man with silly ruminant's head consulting a desperate birdlike figure. A dog talks with a pipe-smoking elephant, beside them, lizardlike, a stretched-out little dog. In contrast to these creatures, with the intention to make them beautiful: large flowers on long stems rising out of deep calyxes, drawn with the side of pastel crayons; three tree tops or treetoplike blossoms, framed by rocks or large leaves.

29. Enclosed sheet with animal-men and the confession of having played the analyst: "she has perhaps inner resistances"; "that I told you this about Tinky and that you will some day, when you have time, talk with her about it"; "that I wrote an Oedipus complex poem."

30. Poems appended. See Appendix, pp. 268ff.

a) *Dream of Bella*

He is in his room (nursery). Suddenly the great dane Bella runs in long leaps past the window through the door into Hans's bedroom. As stretched out as the black dog earlier.[26]

Associations:

then—1½ years ago I had interpreted = erection

Peter's interpretation:

Could it be said that he wants to go to Hans like that? homosex. wish.

b) Continuation and new addition to fairy tale[27]

The nobleman overhears the answers to the first 2 questions at the window. (Something scurries past the window, just as the princess answers the 4th prince.)

c) Playacting, phony, talks for an hour with jocular pathos during tiddledywinks. Compares again (himself and Hans as poets), reads Rilke, Tagore.

Loves Tinky, doesn't want to talk about it for fear of interpretation.

Animal pictures.[28]

Beginning of March

Much *playacting*, constant self-mirroring, suffers from it after I make him conscious of it.

Gossip:

 at Grandmother's about analysis
 with father: "Oedipus complex"
 about Tinky with Reinhard: "inner resistance."[29]

Poem about the Oedipus complex which I do *not* copy.

Poems: "Life"
 Fairy-tale of man (top and bottom)
 Music (sexual symbol, tone top, bottom)[30]

Interpretation: of playacting and self-mirroring as continuation of the vision: somebody looks at him instead of his looking. Other continuation of vision: a) top and bottom, position

Dream of the three slaps in the face

Mr. Erik is with them. He is very excited, screams and scolds Eva. Eva says, very fresh: "Do you think we are oxen?" Erik takes a swing and slaps her three times. She sinks down, sadly.

Associations In this way he slaps his penis when it is hard, until it is limp again.

Eva: gets hit by all the boys.

Why Eva = penis?

Dream of the wind

They sit in a circle. One of them says: you just passed a wind. No, he points, that one. Once again. Next to him lies a girl with a red sweater, he is sure that it is Tinky. But to his amazement he sees Tinky over there sitting in the circle. He lies as on a table, on his stomach. A feeling as if he were lying squeezed in between two people.

The evening before there was a *party*; he again on his toilet at his observation post, door not locked, Garger came in. Miss Schön was there, jealousy.

Hans read *Love's Journey* to him; jealousy; whether he will once, must be nice for Hans.

Jealousy, erection (control of penis like a strong Erik), being present as a third party (attempted resolution) being observed instead of observing.

Very angry with Thesi!

March 11

Rests after big events.

31. Two drawings (Figures 2.7A, B): 1. Our society? Adults as men with masks. 2. Many demon-beings enclosed and contained in the head of one perplexed human being.

Wants to be comfortable, relaxed, take it easy, no analysis, talks about *Eula* and past.

March 12

Drawing of *visions of demons*.[31] [Figure 2.7A, 2.7B]

Rows with Thesi. Warning, how it would be without her: "with parents no big deal."

Acts the *big man* vis-à-vis Thesi, scolds: "that's none of her damn business!" Behaves similarly toward Tinky.

March 15–22, 1931

Wish to get away from home
Serious, depressed, matter-of-fact. Doesn't want to stay at home any more. *Calm* jealousy: "Even if I manage the analysis, this I can't deal with." "I know that it goes without saying, but I am alone all the same." "With Menga it would be the same thing, only worse, and I can stand it even less with her." Wants to go where there are children, to Rosenfelds or Burlinghams. But fear of separation from father breaks through occasionally. "Even if there were also a father at the B.s, I would not want him." "I can visit with Hans."———

Interpretation (for myself): In response to dissatisfaction with relationship to father, attempts to give it up. Attempt to get well?

"What is the sense of Hans and Inge taking me along, they only have to restrain themselves in my presence."—

Revolt: Hans complains about disorder. Thesi too. "They can go to hell."

Disorder in school. Then phony, talking Jewish jargon, histrionics with me.

Interpretation: he must turn into a "*disagreeable*," unattractive person because his father does not care enough about him. Under *these* circumstances at home! people shall say.

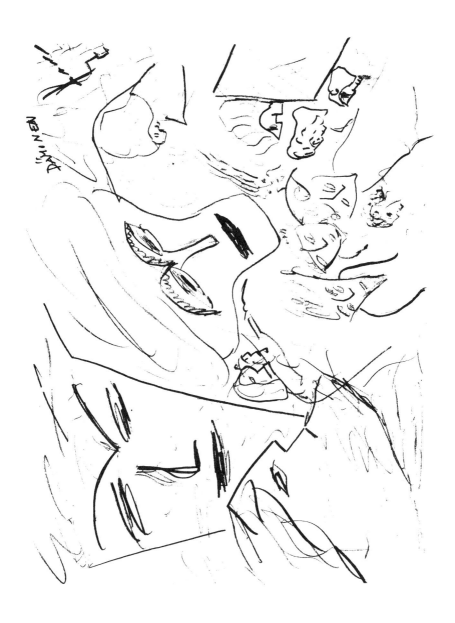

FIGURE 2.7A

FIGURE 2.7B

32. On a piece of paper: "He said when it wiggles, my bottom looks like a pudding, and he gets hungry right away."

33. Drawings: a series of faces one above the other along a median axis which cuts them in half. "Ass-faces"? They have something deadly about them. Also skeletal elements on the margin. On the reverse side: A suckling pig prepared as for New Year's Eve with a spit through its snout. On another sheet: Brutal fellows, one a devil with a wide belt fitted with brass knuckles.

34. Sheet of paper: P.'s summary: 1) "One should pay close attention to [negative] qualities in the people of one's surroundings . . . [in order to] acquire the bad habits of one's fellow-men" [etc. as above]. 2) Revenge on whom? For instance: on father. Note what he dislikes; then do it with greatest perseverance (disorderliness, tardiness, negligence. secretiveness, spying). 3) Conceal your genuine feelings, display artificial ones. 4) Do all of this only in the presence of father, be particularly nice to other people [so they will say:] What does the father expect of the boy! 5) Secretly swap gifts of parents. 6) If possible, read only forbidden trash." The written text on these sheets is run through with lines suggesting pointed mountain peaks: similar to drawing of mountain ridges on the reverse side.

Basti makes the comment about his behind.[32] He has again some school anxiety as at the Evangelical School.

Drawings of faces divided by lines?[33]

March 22–29, 1931

How to become unattractive and disagreeable
Peter got into trouble in the Diana-Bath swimming pool, gets into an argument, is fresh in the streetcar, reads on the toilets, throws book out, turns visibly seedy, "neglected." I interpret this for him as revenge on father. We (write [crossed out]) discuss an article: "How to become unattractive and disagreeable" or "How do I revenge myself on my father?"

1) Imitate disagreeable qualities of others (for example: use Jewish jargon, be fresh, thumbs in armpits, sharp criticisms in wrong place)

2) Acquire characteristics that displease father (disorderly, unpunctual (Peter excludes sitting on toilets), secretive, spying)

3) Conceal sincere feelings, pretend false ones.

4) All of this only in father's presence, otherwise nice: "What does the father want of the boy?" (4) Peter's addition)

5) Trade parents' gifts (steam engine for typewriter).

6) Read only trash (Peter now reads only Tom Mix, Karl May).[34]

3.24

Dream in hexameters.
"There was a woman—half man, half beast . . .—a fury. It is like in the Iliad. She takes a hero of the opposite side for a husband. They fight, and behind them one sees their armies only like a stream of blood. They fight by day, by night they sleep together in a little bed, like Peter's bed. The man is perhaps Diomedes (who always removes the armor from the defeated; Peter has to think: then they lie naked).

189

35. Sheet of paper: "I always feel as if you were my wife and I quarrel with her." Picture of a woman with virile traits, two breasts or eyes, penis? On reverse side: men and women shaped from clay.

36. Enclosure: Poems by P.H. typed for him by A.F. See Appendix, pp. 269–271.

Then something drops like a curtain and there appears a thick page from a (sturdy) children's picture book; such a corny picture of yellow chicks; and with that again a verse like: But the chicks, the innocent ones, pick their little grains in the sand—"

Interpretation:
Again the vision, strife between man and woman, blood, nakedness.

Final image a) that is where children come from
          b) children do not know anything about all this

———

Heralded the day before by anger and attempt to quarrel with me: "I think you are my wife and I quarrel with you."[35]

Anxiety
again in the hallway and evenings: maybe over conflict with the woman? The Fury, he says, = remorse.

[March] 22–29.

Dream of the toilet
"He has his arms around Tinky, they walk in a meadow. It looks like the place on an excursion where he and Basti went to the toilet."

Going to the toilet = marrying.

Visit from father.

Does not want to give Peter away, will take education in hand again, in spite of danger of renewed homosexual bond.[36]

Before Easter vacation

Rapprochement to father

Dream of Reinhard
"They are on a boat. He and Reinhard go down. He slaps Reinhard (as Eva earlier, taking a swing). Then they jump onto a moving streetcar.

37. Pulp magazines of Tom Mix, the master detective, Lord Lister, the gentleman thief, Buffalo Bill, and so on.

Peter runs beside it, tries several times as one does to jump on a train, and finally gets in with a jolt."
Associations:

Boat—that's how it was in Tegel, caught Reinhard's finger in the door.

Slap in the face—dream of Eva—make erect penis soft

jump on—movements of intercourse into the woman.— Vision.

Interpretation?
His member gets hard as he watches coitus.

His state of neglect disappears again as father pays attention to him.

[Easter vacation, 1931]

Yearning for mother
Easter vacation:
With the Burlinghams in Neuhaus, very nice, but a little elegiac and nostalgic. Relationship with Dorothy revives in him yearning for his mother. Speaks about this with Dorothy.

Dream of the train
He makes all the noises of the train in his sleep, then tells me he thinks he took the train to Berlin in his dream.

Makes up a story in which he is a famous detective, there are many divorces, terrible women, unhappy children.

April 5–12

Again slovenly for father's benefit.
Between Neuhaus and father's return.
One day he claims he is getting to be perfectly healthy, all symptoms have ceased, he is so very content. The next day he comes in saying: "I am a pig, really a pig, but inside, not outside."

New edition of "unattractive–disagreeable"
   a) has compulsively bought cheap pulps[37]

38. On an added sheet an accounting in this manner: "2 rides 64 Groschen, 10 streetcar tickets 3 Schilling, Basti 1 Schilling 5, 3 rides 96. . . ." On same sheet: "An 80 year old man, fast eater, has been eating (including dinner parties) for about seven and a half years."

39. A vague sketch about how you could see from the crib in the nursery (via mirror) to the parents' double bed in the next room. On reverse side: Road to Alland, home town of P.'s first governess.—On a further sheet: The Goddess Fate (one of the Parcae) with scissors, opposite a cloud king (God?). Between them two men and a woman stepping forward to come before the scissors.

b) has spent his fare for them, is very astonished that I offer to lend him the money

c) wants to give father a false account of it[38]

Interprets himself: he prepares for father's return.

Little outbreak with Thesi: in the evening he was out of sorts, wanted to write, she forbade it. Then she said: Are you hurt? and he cried. (If Mem were like that?)

Calms down after father's return, more orderly, cleaner.

Regarding the vision.

Out of context he says suddenly that he knows how it was in the vision and draws:

Parents' beds
His crib with a blanket over it, over which he peers [39]

April 13, 1931

Little outburst out of a feeling of abandonment. Father, Mother.

a) Was in Klausen over the weekend with his father, it was very nice. Father left on Sunday night, whereupon he was very depressed, angry with Thesi because she forbids everything. Then Thesi brings him a glass of lemonade all the same, he suddenly has to cry, gets a feeling of being hot like *when he screams*. (How does he know that? Since he never seems to remember? Claims suddenly, he always remembers.)

b) He doesn't like anybody at school, they can all leave, even the Burlinghams, to America, he wouldn't feel hurt, he doesn't feel anything. Tinky is not nice to him any more. He doesn't like the B(urlinghams) so much any more.

c) He can't stand the two girls from Berlin, Eva and Ruthi; they are so nasty and will make everybody nasty.

Interpretation of this mood together with him:
He doesn't want to be reminded of Menga, or he starts to long for her. Thesi reminds him, when she is nice; Dorothy; that's why the B(urlingham)s should leave. Eva and Ruthi remind him of Berlin, when Mem stays away so long she gets to be so nasty (E. and R.

195

40. Enclosed: Sketches of pieces of furniture: table, desk, armchair, indicating colors (red, brown) as the architect Franz Singer had used them, also in the case of P.'s folding bed.

41. Many loose papers. On one drawing: A girl scolding her lover, calling him a Don Juan; a man, master of the house, scolding his wife; the wife, in turn, scolds her son; the son "passes the blame on to his brother"; and a child screams. On the same sheet, however, there is also a person who has written an "Ode to Nature" and another who composes a "Symphony to Nature (C minor)." All this leads to the conclusion: "Only Art can endure." On the reverse side and the following sheets, among scribbles, faces, color spots, disjointed phrases such as "gallant crew" [in English], "Tuscany," etc. There is also a draft for a poem, dated by A.F. "May 26, 31." (See also Appendix, pp. 254f:

> "In the wide spaces I found an evening. And man become aware of limits around him. Trembling foliage pierced by evening rays; black shapes against the huge sky. They stand in front of nothingness, always seeking. Man is small. When he has defeated dangers, he thinks himself elevated, and yet is only elevated enough to sink into his own dust. . . . What is this? The earth. Only thoughts, maintaining themselves like wavering dots, remain, alone on the wide meadows, while men wither away in the rustling foliage. . . . Down there where a few trees stood in smooth rows, was his home, he thought."
>
> "Rivers flow, men perish, sink into the eternal current of life. . . . Where you think you are standing, you are not. Nothing endures. Everything passes by, goes away, forging its own way through the screaming crowd. Everyone lives his own life, everyone thinks he is alone: soon comes the end, death, which will let you drown in darkness. Dark is life, dark is the night; and the day is bright, but can illuminate itself only as semblance and only as semblance can life maintain itself. Yet what is true? Death, nothingness, the gaping abyss.—Silently night came into the village. Drunkenly we spent all of life in a frenzy. The end is coming, the end approaches. Soon death will rule the earth. Let us tune our lyre, let it resound, let us live in frenzy. Come to me. I come to you. Let us hold fast to one another until death redeems us."
>
> Many more sheets follow, among them a red sheet with little holes and the words: "tense, tense, tense"; a paper scrap with accounts; men with penislike beards, one of them penetrated by a projectile; an androgynous person; a God-prophet flying through the air; and so on.

corrupt the other children, Tinky). He doesn't want to feel hurt, it's all the same to him. It's all right when Hans is there. If Hans leaves too, it overcomes him.

Quarrel + being affectionate = vision.[40]

Moods, financial accounts and drafts of poems[41]

Up to vacation

Lives with the Burlinghams, displays mainly 2 symptoms: loses money, misplaces things, looks for them desperately.

Interpretation: He treats things as his parents treat him.

Longing for Menga.

Resumption, October 1 [1931]

Has *not* screamed all summer in spite of all kinds of trials: spent some time with father and lover as well as mother and her male friend. Was sometimes excited and sometimes depressed because of frustration (he doesn't get as much pocket money as others—is not loved as much).

New Information:
a) venereal diseases

b) prostitution

Connected with a) slight anxiety regarding size of penis.

This summer *fishing* means who catches the *bigger* fish.

b) See later with reference to me [p. 199].

Strong *tie to Menga*. After 3 days he asks for half a week's vacation as long as Menga is still here. After [Menga's] departure *transference* to me with much loud anger, reproaches, culminating in the reproach that I am a *nun* (remark by Menga about my private life). This for two sessions, then

interpretation: Menga should not have any man (be a nun) so that she wouldn't leave. Anger about criticism of Menga turned toward me. Very turbulent and unmanageable, with much excitement, wants to

42. These drawings include Figure 2.8A, the sketch of a fair-haired boy—Ferdinand—hero of the projected novella, who runs away from his parents' house, and ends up in a reformatory (see Appendix, pp. 258–261); also broad-shouldered boxer-types, of one of them it is unclear whether he has two fists or two penises; girl with curls (Tinky).

43. Plan of apartment (Figure 2.8B). Anxiety spots are concentrated in the corridor leading from the nursery past father's library and study, and around the hallway leading to the toilets and main entrance.

44. At the same time—see Figure 2.8C—he is also an evil insect with sharp teeth.

45. On attached slip of paper.

stop analysis. As I go along with it, only suggest a trial week, tears in his eyes. In the following night

Dream

"He again takes leave of Menga."

Menga = I.

Decision: he will stay but is now to do grown-up analysis.

Drawings beginning of autumn [1931][42] [Figure 2.8A]

Early October

Frightening places
Plan of apartment.[43] [Figure 2.8B] Marking places in the hallway where there is anxiety, immediately next to them there is none.

Anxiety = small, fat, broad, squashed-up man.[44] [Figure 2.8C]

Around October 20

Beginning of a novella about prostitution
Story of deranged man who comes to realize that he has to pay women to love him.

Transference: Reproach against me that I love him only for payment. ("You are still afraid!" "Me? afraid?—*You* are afraid that you will lose a patient!"). After Menga's departure he turns his love to me, is disturbed by above-mentioned thought.

Around October 22

Scene

Wild hour full of reproaches, insults, quarreling, little wild *screams* ("I have to do it this way!"). Tears in his eyes, doesn't want analysis any more, erection, wants it after all, always opposing me, ends up writing down ("because decency alone forbids saying it: it seems to me:
that I love you"[45]).

199

FIGURE 2.8A

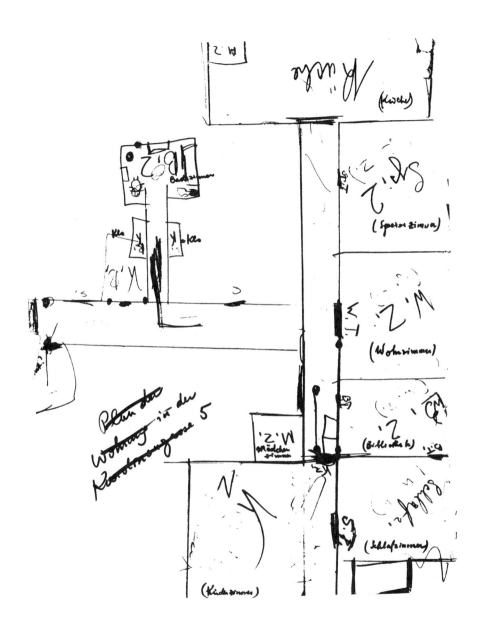

FIGURE 2.8B

FIGURE 2.8c

Interpretation: Enacting of the observed scene, screams—detail of what he overheard.

October 27, 1931.

Peter's wallowing in filth plus hangover
Visits Basti over Sunday, feels exceedingly well and comfortable. Anal jokes, scuffles, and swearing with village boys. Chasing "broads," girls with whom one is allowed to do everything. They walk together through the dark house to the toilet, Basti stands at the door, aperture at the bottom, talking all the while: "Haven't you shat enough yet?" etc. Hears him *pass wind.*

Reaction afterward: he is so alone, nobody is with him, he sets everybody against him with spiteful remarks, etc. Turns all his self-reproaches *outward.*

Menga and I: are old-fashioned and moralistic (his own morals bother him).

Tinky: is conceited, and irritable (has complained about that regarding himself)

Erik: is a pig (his own piggishness with Basti).

Transference: he is as angry and critical with me as I ought to be with him.

He accepts this interpretation and adds: like a man after he has been with a paid woman.

In connection with this interpretation, talk about the fact that it is not easy to have such pleasures, because other needs interfere. He complains that he is not unified: when with Basti like Basti, when with Tinky like Tinky.

October 29

Dream of passageways and stoves
"He dreams that he is walking through long passages like in a ruin. There is a room open to the sky, a stove, he lies down in front of the oven door."

207

46. Copied and typed by A.F. who added the date: "Beginning of Nov. 31." See Appendix, pp. 271–273.

In addition, there follow "Poems about the End" (see Appendix, pp. 254f, a revised version of the draft given above in footnote 41), "A Fairy Tale without Meaning or Moral" (Appendix, pp. 249–254), a poem entitled "The Regicide" (Appendix, pp. 247f) and "Poems about the World," dated by A.F.: "Spring 1931" (Appendix, pp. 255–258).

Interpretation. Associations;
Passageways—like at Basti's, going to the toilet

Oven door—woman's hole. Stove–dirty.

Opposition: with Basti in the toilet or at woman's hole. Because the woman leaves him, he regresses to the anal stage and turns to the man.

Height of transference.
He becomes aroused as soon as he is with me. He says: that has to stop, otherwise he can't do analysis.

October 30–November 7

Isolation, quarrel.
He withdraws entirely from children, divides the transference between Thesi and me. I am his principal wife ("You always appear so conceited to me when you say that!")

Form of love: quarrel, insults ("Your pennies!", etc.).

Repetition: Tries very hard to lose Thesi and me to other men, like Menga. Encourages us.

Why no love for children: too dangerous because of temptation with boys and girls.

I interpret everything to him, and stress in particular how he will spoil and ruin his life with quarrels and repetition. Accepts it seriously.

Poems.[46]

November 16–21

Glandular fever with two fits of screaming
Gets sick after the 4 days of vacation I allowed him. Glandular fever, over 39 [102] degrees. In two subsequent nights dreams in his fever in which he speaks etc., does not really scream.

Calls Thesi, jumps up, takes off his pajama top, runs half naked to her bed, it takes him a while to wake up. Thesi reports exclamations:

"Don't let me drown!" (as if there were water somewhere in his bed). *"How did you get on the ship?"* and as she wanted to waken him: *"Don't speak, don't blur it for me!"*

Explains this himself, after return on Monday:

November 23

The Ship of the Dead

After his return he doesn't want to admit that he has screamed, says it was because of the fever. To explain his exclamation: While sick, he read the novel "The Ship of the Dead" [by B. Traven], that deals with the destiny of stateless people who have no passport and are shipped from one country to another.

Stateless—parentless = Peter.

Anger about Menga's letter

Criticism of Thesi's mother and Burlinghams.
Very annoyed about Thesi's stories about her mother, who, as a young widow, dedicated herself entirely to her children. Thesi says her mother appears faultless to her. However, Thesi criticized Menga on the occasion of a letter to Peter which irritated him (adult letter, dealing with the treatment of birth control in films; divorce or not because of child). Doesn't approve of the fact that Thesi's mother and Mrs. Burlingham do not remarry, unnatural. Criticizes the Burlinghams because they don't use make-up.

Interpretation: Thesi's mother and Mrs. Burlingham are the good mothers, his parents are bad. Menga is getting a divorce, father has a lover who uses make-up. The more he rejects such criticism during the day, the stronger it appears in dreams:

he is homeless, has bad parents, Thesi good ones ("How did you get on the ship?")

Then he asks: but are my parents really bad or good?

I say: They like you, but they also want to live a life of their own.

Provoking separation from me
Now he knows everything, nothing more can come, we should stop.
Repeats this endlessly.

Interpretation: he now has to get me to leave him like Menga did.

Talks about being dirty, all kinds of mischief.

Interpretation: thinks that Menga left him because of dirty things, wants to repell me. (He says: being indecent is not the right thing to deter an analyst.)

Speaks and reads about venereal diseases, reports little inflammation on his penis.

Interpretation: Thinks he has venereal disease himself, then you can't have a wife, then I will certainly leave him.

Obviously he wants to repeat his earlier misfortune.

Comes in the next day and says we shall continue anyway.

Tommy
He is full of his cousin Tommy whom he enlightens about sex and to whom he explains analysis. Talks with him about *prostitution, venereal diseases*. When Tommy gets disgusted with girls, *interprets* that he would like all too well to do this thing with girls.

Interpretation: He uses Tommy for *revenge*, does to Tommy what was done to him. Menga told about *P. and G.*, he believes I think that was not good for him. Revenge for analysis. Simultaneously identification with Menga and me from both of whom he is separating himself (mechanism of homosexuality).

I reproach him for *using* Tommy; the reproaches touch him greatly. Talks compulsively about them, seeking arguments, "so you really think—." Evident defense against self-reproaches. Complains that he has to ramble on about these things. Says suddenly, "Mabbie also

47. Sigurd: older schoolmate; Nurmi: sprinter, Olympic champion.

48. Not a poem but an essay, see Appendix, p. 261.

knows everything I know but with her it is *pure*, as you would say in a novel."

Imagines that he writes a novella about boys in 2 versions: one for children, one for adults. (Boys in a school, one poor, one rich, who want to be leaders, are replaced in the favor of their fellow-pupils by a third boy.)

No pressing to terminate any more; again clearly in love in the transference.

Dream of Sigurd and Nurmi
1. Sigurd fights with Nurmi, many onlookers.[47]
   Nurmi = upright, stiff = penis
   Interpretation: S. masturbates, is already mature, P. not, how long will it take

2. something about girls (Mädi) and being dirty
   Interpretation: perhaps the regression?

December

Menga's return
As usual excited by her coming, feels that he expects her with a *lover's* intensity, is ashamed of it.

What the others think about you, that you have to be something different for everyone.

Interpretation: what the others think about *Menga*.

Increasing criticism of Menga, expressed in the poem: Long live the New Generation,[48] compulsive also in criticism of *others*.

Jealousy after her return. Great disappointment only 2 days after arrival because of F[ellerer]. She has apparently not come back for Peter's, but for F[ellerer]'s sake.

Great excitement akin to screaming, in one hour, hundreds of empty phrases begun and broken off.

Interpretation: "All Menga says is nonsense." He admits that the

49. "Circus Director's Speech" (Appendix, p. 274).

50. See Appendix, "Ferdinand": revised version of the first three pages, p. 258ff.

excitement serves to *veil* his feelings. Serious talk about wrong method, very affectionate and trusting. Warning against screaming!

Peter at school party
High point of performance as circus director: Ideal versus money, in the end as a little child: I listen anyway! Humor, uninhibited, superb performance.[49]

Christmas vacations [1931]

Calls me on the 1st holiday, absolutely must speak to me. I have him come on the next day.

Did not scream, but did dream, very agitated, wants to clarify everything for himself in order to keep from screaming. Dream is about Hans and a second man, Hans threatens Menga and him, second man his ally, shooting, rescue. . . .

Long discussion of the real situation with jealousy in all directions, effort to love Menga unconditionally. Strong transference to me, that he can see me in spite of the holiday, happy about it.

January 1932

Interruption because of his and my flu.

In January only 3 sessions, first he sick, then I.
Content: looking forward to birthday celebration with great excitement, beginning excitement about Menga's departure.

February 2, 1932

Resumption
Departure of Menga, resigned. Started afresh, *wish to go to boarding school*. Reads the novella about Ferdinand to me which he has reworked brilliantly.[50]

Discussion of *competition*. Interpretation: as long as he has doubts about his penis, he will have to drown them in competing.

51. Aunt Janne: father's younger sister; Aunt Gabi: Mädi's mother.

52. Story of teenagers by Willy (Wilhelm) Speyer (1927).

Dream of Janne and Gabi[51]
Comes twenty minutes late, by way of placating me tells the following dream:

"Janne is in her garden, that's what she likes best. Her youngest son Manki is sitting in a little bed, all around are plants with fleshy leaves. She has a dog. Somebody says she only has it until she has a child. Janne is seated on a kind of throne, very fat.

"He runs into a kind of underground passage, he wants to go to the toilet. Nearby, Gabi gives gym lessons. He says I only want to make a telephone call. He urinates in a toilet.

"From Janne's garden he goes back again across the street."

Associations:
Janne: Menga says, a good mother, so solicitous about her children.

fleshy leaves: penis, leaf covering the penis on statues.

garden: from the manure pile in this garden, Tommy observed coitus in the neighboring house

dog: in *Kampf der Tertia* ["Battle in Tenth Grade"][52] the proud girl has a dog that bites the boys' legs = girl's pride.

Gabi: flirts, wears make-up.

gym lessons: exercise the penis.

telephoning: Basti always says it instead of "leave the room" [to urinate]. He always has to call home, report, "give an account of himself."

Interpretation:
(The day before, he was upset that I didn't dispel his fear about his penis more forcefully.) Juxtaposition of good and bad mother. Janne, the good mother, only does the indecent thing in order to have children, is not proud, shows herself naked, gives the child a big penis. The whore-mother, on the contrary, does the indecent thing with strange men, her child has a bad penis, has to go to public toilets and

to make comparisons. The phrase "giving an account of himself" suggests that he is keeping something from me.

Dream of the car ride

He and Thesi go and pick up Menga. Mr. Erik is there too, they are to drop him off somewhere. They arrive there, Thesi excitedly tells something about Peter. There was a boy, very dirty, with an abscess on his hand. "And imagine, the child goes and touches him. How upset madam was! But the child didn't know better!" Mr. Erik then walks away arm in arm with the chauffeur, they fetch Menga—About the beginning: The street was the street to Laxenburg, the place where they stop on a bridge over a dirty river.

Associations:

Ride: as to Basti with Walter, that is, to dirtiness.

River: canal which empties into it, again dirty, toilet.

pick up: they really did pick up Menga from Schönbrunn where her friend lives nearby.

take Erik: to his wife.

chauffeur: Erik came along, thanked the chauffeur, not him. (homosex. jealousy.)

abscess: book about venereal diseases, Franzl in Baden, other children with whom he "played."

Thesi: no, Eula, talked like this.

Interpretation: Erik goes to his wife, Menga to her friend, the only thing left for him is regression to the anal stage; it is unclear whether the punishment for it, the venereal disease, then follows, or whether the abandonment by the objects (of affection) is part of this punishment, because—etc., therefore father and mother leave him. I think rather the other way around.

The exoneration: he doesn't know better, is part of it.

About the scary hallway:
Remembers that he always was afraid that a child with open pants would run after him crying. I think he himself is the child.

Associations:
Eula [= Lilli K.] beat him only once. He knocked over a little child, was happy about it. When they came home she opened his pants (age 4), gave him a thorough thrashing, then locked him into the dark toilet. There he screamed and roared. Then she got him out, he ran into the room and played. He wanted to continue being angry but couldn't.

(I think he was anally aroused. He used to masturbate anally. Connection with the vision.)

[February 1932]

Plans for the future
Talk with the father about next year. He should ask Peter what he would *think about living with the Burlinghams*.

Apparent work
Peter realizes something is bothering him that we do not know yet, appears to be making a great effort during the sessions but is *20 minutes late* without cause. Admits that something oppresses him constantly, as if he were expecting something evil.

Form of resistance:
As soon as we find an interpretation, something in him says immediately: this is all now, nothing more can come. As though he had great fear that something else could come up still.

February 12

Attempt at honest thinking
On the day after my conversation with his father, he ignores it, speaks explicitly about his childhood, something he has never done otherwise. Thus important: something current. It is difficult to get him to touch

53. Menga was critical of the muscle-building gym lessons with Edi Polz at the Diana-Bath, which had been recommended by the Burlinghams. Peter took over her attitude.

the subject of the Burlinghams, says suddenly: "They don't think enough about politics, only about matters concerning the individual." I ask if he would miss that so much. He says: no, that has nothing to do with it, but it is just so important.

I interpret: he is afraid Menga would feel hurt if he went to the Burlinghams, Menga criticizes the Burlinghams, he has to go along, as earlier about the gym lessons.[53] Why can't he think this straight through, rather than via politics. He says he cannot.

We interpret: He creates opposition Menga-Burlinghams as well as Menga-father, Menga-me. Why he cannot simply say that he loves Menga most. He realizes suddenly that consciously he cannot decide between father and mother. At the thought of preferring one to the other, he immediately becomes very anxious, shies away and covers the conflict with the decision:

I like both equally.

We try to remove the protective cover, he realizes that at the thought of *preferring Menga* he becomes frightened of? for? Hans. The opposite is easier because then he knows that it's not true anyway. I compare his protection against anxiety with his *life after death*.

He is impressed with his inability to think about this freely, and to choose.

February 17.

Hans absent, crooked thinking.
Father traveling to Munich for 2 days. Peter as usual upset, in bad mood (after semester break) doesn't like coming to his sessions. Insincere, tortured. At the end of the hour interpretation succeeds.

He would like to ask:
    "Has Hans taken Inge along?"

Instead he thinks and asks:
    a) What is a lesbian marriage?
    b) Does the piano teacher have a venereal disease?

54. See Figure 2.8C.

c) Sybille Binder is sterile

d) Whether I am having an affair with my father

After the interpretation he remembers having asked his father a catch question whether it wasn't unpleasant alone in the sleeping car. Then repressed. I show him the
>*crooked thinking*
that makes him insincere.

Following day. February 18.

Anxiety dream of Eva Johannsen
"It is a narrow street, like the (scary) hallway in the apartment. On the sides are kiosks. He is afraid, as in the hallway, that someone might stand behind the door, forces himself not to turn around. Suddenly a ragged man is there with frayed pants, protruding blue-gray eyes. He shrieks and wakes up. (Nobody actually heard him scream.)

Associations:
Hallway: place of anxiety

Kiosks: in Hietzing where he bought and sold the Tom Shark pulps. Nearby telephone booth where he and Basti played tricks on people.

Frayed pants: from which the naked legs stick out like penis out of the foreskin

Eyes: like Eva J.'s; New Year's party with theater people and Menga. E.J. has a lover who was unable to attend because of a strike of the stage hands.

Shrieking: like Tilly who was frightened by him.

Interpretation:
As always when father is on a trip, he threatens: he will do all the forbidden things, will buy detective stories, Basti, telephone calls, toilets, prostitute.

The anxiety man[54] is a woman (prostitute) with a penis. The eyes suggest looking.

Defense through comparison.
On a ski trip with the Bs Peter has not been as well behaved as usual, but he doesn't know it. His behavior can be interpreted as defense of his parents. Father thought one could go to the Rax mountain. P. was fixed on that idea, compulsively started to talk about it over and over again.

Interpretation:
When he is at the Bs, he has to identify with his father in order to assure himself that he loves him more than the Burlinghams. (See father-mother, mother-Bs, mother-I.)

Two slips of the tongue.

After an interpretation he says on leaving: "I shall certainly *deny* myself this" (instead of keep in mind) [In German: *vorenthalten* instead of *vorhalten*.]

He reports about a ski accident on Sigurd's tour and says to his own astonishment: His fiancée was along and the awful thing was that Sigurd and the friend had to *kill* (instead of comfort) the fiancée. [In German: *töten* instead of *trösten*.]

Artificial in Menga's defense:
We look for instances where we find him "phony," and for the reason. E.g.: Speaking about Tilly, he says: she is very nervous (and then, in an affected manner:) *she needs to be in analysis*.

Associations:
Tilly is nice with Inge but against Menga.

I: This is the way Menga would talk.

After that he has to hear me say: In Menga it would be genuine, his imitation, phony. —Otherwise it would be again a criticism of Menga and that would be mean of me.

We surmise that defending Menga plays an unexpectedly big part.

Considerations whether boarding school or not run through all this.

55. See Appendix: "Ferdinand" pp. 258ff.

56. See below: "Dream of the two directions."

57. Regarding "Ferdinand" see Appendix. The scenes referred to here are missing.

February

Work projects
Brings new installments of the novella[55] and 2 sheets of paper with outlines for new projects.

1) Integration of Marxism and psychoanalysis, the former deals with the external, the latter with the inner conditions of man. In connection with it, a little story: He sits in the hallway, my father goes by, he fantasizes being asked what he is reading. He wants to show: Marx is a greater man than you.

2) About juvenile books. A list of many very intelligent questions (maybe 20): whether didactic; or anxiety provoking; children's attitude toward the anxiety provoking; whether a fairy tale, technology, or realistic; how much about love, whether this only discourages children because it makes them feel their smallness, etc.

He would like to discuss these questions but immediately becomes obsessive in talking about them, as he did in the very beginning when, in talking about poets, he only wanted to argue.

The emotional background that produces this appears in the dream of the following day.

He comes in the next day very angry, finds as a reason that Hans said of a book he had taken out for himself: That is not suitable for you yet.

Then tells dream.[56]

Intellectual and physical exhibitionism

A

On that day he brings in the novella Ferdinand, continues to read it to me: splendid.

Most beautiful scenes
a) Ferdinand in bed after the battle, cannot admit to himself that it was cowardice and not courage to beat up the small boy.
b) Ferdinand is dishonored and beaten in front of the others by his drunken father. The children's reaction
c) Father's soliloquy.[57]

On the following day he wants to continue to enjoy being admired, works himself up into state of excitement through obscene words, sentences from books, etc., which he produces for my benefit.

Interpretation:
wants to show his penis as he had shown the novella.

Dream of the 2 directions
A dream that he can only draw:

"There is something there like a vaulting-horse in the gym and two directions."

Associations: in the gym he once landed on a vaulting horse so flat that he hurt his penis.

Interpretation:
The two directions [German *Richtungen* = directions, movements, tendencies] which he has to bring together are Hans and Menga, analysis and politics (Marx and Freud). One says: children may read everything, the other: that is not suitable for you. His sexuality is the reason Menga left, the parents can *come together* again if he gives up his claims *on both, castrates himself.*

He finds as a reason for his dishonesty: because the parents always put on an act of loving each other.

Allusion to the vision?

He screams when the parents have intercourse, disturbing them.

If he remained quiet, they could continue.

Fantasy from earlier days: that all 3 of them would move to Hietzing, live together.

March 1

Dream of Capitalism
"He stands with Ruth Nathan at the subway station. He has rubber bands for pea shooting. Ruth encourages him and says: Shoot! He

58. Rommel School: public secondary school in the 14th district, directed by Rommel, Social Democrat and Nestroy scholar. Bondy directed a progressive experimental boarding school in Germany.

59. See Appendix, pp. 258ff. End of novella is missing.

shoots (at the conductor), who gets very angry. He says, but don't get excited, I haven't even shot yet. He runs through the barrier to the platform, Thesi is already ahead of him. The two Wolf brothers (the young Hellers) are pursuing him and threatening him. Thesi assumes such an odd position. She is barefoot, she holds her stockings in her drooping arms (hands). Her feet are soft and fat, a very long big toe, spaces between the other toes. The Wolfs take her foot and rub it against the wall which is gritty. It gets caught somehow on the irregular surface. Then the Wolfs lie on the ground, position like a machine (2 machines):

a) cleaver   b)

He says: That is capitalism?!"

Dream of the Lahngang Lakes

"They ride on a train, between rock walls, Menga is so cheerful and chats. Suddenly, in the middle of it, she changes to another car. He asks: Can you do it this way, through the panes of glass? She says, oh yes."

Then an old dream comes to his mind: "He jumps off a moving train, the Burlinghams are shocked."

Interpretation: Capitalism = castrator; whoever has the bigger penis, has the woman.

Transfer = change of trains = change men.

Juxtaposition of [ways of] life

[Before Easter 1932]

a) Dream of the two *schools*.

He has a dream in which he compares the Rommel School in Vienna with Bondy.[58] The *interpretation* shows that he weighs the schools one against the other with respect to their homosexual temptation. In the end Hans and Inge bring him back by car. Thus he returns to his present situation.

b) Continuation and completion of the *novella* about Ferdinand,[59] who in the end (like Peter) runs away from the parental home seeking

opportunity for sexual adventures, is frightened by a child-seducer, runs away again, then stabs a little boy with a knife (first passive, then active) and finally goes to seed in a reformatory.

c) *Work on details* of two main features, his sexual questioning and his affectation. His reaction to a cancelation of mine shows all too clearly that he has to inquire into the remotest and darkest sexual secrets instead of asking: why did you cancel yesterday?

Affectation appears always where the mother comes into question.

Trip to Berlin

He is to travel alone to Berlin over Easter, to visit Menga. He reacts with great agitation, especially on one day, when he is beside himself with joyful excitement, cries on the slightest provocation, etc. During the hour we discover that behind the exaggeration of his joyful anticipation of seeing Menga, there are negative feelings toward her, affection for Inge, reluctance to leave her and father by themselves, distrust of Menga's love for him. After this interpretation the agitation subsides.

He would like to ride in daylight, is supposed to take a sleeping car, cries at home. He wants to travel as an adventurer, not as a capitalist; again the opposites.

Criticism of the mother
We work on his being "natural" as opposed to bragging; whether he can continue to do that in Berlin. He says suddenly: What if Menga likes the other better?—Discussion of whether he could not love Menga but have opinions different from hers. He cannot conceive of it yet.

New literary form: "Impressions"
He writes a number of small poetic mood images in which he sets down everything that he has acquired in analysis, that is: looks down upon himself from a great height. E.g. traveling in the sleeping car, the conductor who calls him "young man."

Departure for Berlin
Special harmony, affectionate with me.

60. Short prose on an attached sheet (Appendix, p. 275).

Peter. After return from Menga.

Longing. Angry with people here, then suddenly turning away from Menga, almost with aversion.

What has she done:
a) Scala
    Cabaret
b) Admitted to jealousy of Tinky.

Here he is ashamed because of cabaret, doesn't dare to love anyone, so as not to hurt Menga, feigns:
unhappiness (faithfulness)
no friends (faithfulness)
secrets from Hans (faithfulness)
poor progress in school (revenge, self-neglect)

Dream of the waiting room

The waiting room. Entrance to the Scala (they are playing Shake-speare). He is admitted to a prostitute, she shows herself, he shows himself. Downstairs Menga waits for him, he knows she doesn't approve.

His own *interpretation*: both are Menga, prostitute and mother. She makes a grown-up of him, entices him, but she doesn't give him anything. The prostitute is Macbeth?, a biblical figure, the sacred she-devil, the "men let down their pants with her."

Waiting: He suddenly recognizes that he is waiting instead of living, doesn't want this any more, wants to be active, a good pupil.

Next day

Continuation of novel and *little stories* in which he utilizes the analytic results.[60]

Bed-wetting?

Thesi thinks that he has nocturnal emissions because there are stains in his bed. He doesn't know about it, but then admits that he wets the bed to console himself that he has no ejaculation.

61. Enclosure: 1) A Life (Appendix, p. 275f); 2) Time (Appendix, p. 276); 3) "We must study" (Appendix, pp. 261–264).

Thus: Acting like a baby from wanting to grow up?

Small relapse into unhappiness, waiting, conflict between Menga and Burlinghams clarified quickly. Interested in history, reads to me a good paper on Otto I., wants to read historical works. Active enjoyment.[61]

APPENDIX TO ANNA FREUD'S COLLECTION OF NOTES AND MATERIALS

1. THE REVOLUTION

[Written prior to analysis at age 8 (1928); see also p. 33.]

PART 1
Chapter 1

I am now thirty years old. At twenty-one I was absolutely convinced that there was nothing that could really drive a person to despair, and only an idiot would commit suicide. A year later I went to visit some relatives. It was a nice visit, contrary to my expectations, for there was a girl there I liked very much. We met often, my love for her grew, and in a very short time (two months) we celebrated our wedding. All my friends had warned me about Grete, which was my bride's name, and now that the marriage was so successful I went to see them in triumph and proudly said, "See what an attractive person she is! It was good that I married her."

They said being married for two weeks was no criterion, but I said that I would love her 'til I died. But then I would have had to die in the following month, because after · that I hated her. I had every good reason to hate her because she was horrible to me. She was a real shrew and tyrannized me all day long. She could do nothing but scold. She showed her true spirit. At first I was sad that my wife, who had been so sweet a while ago, was now so unbearable. But then I became desperate, I didn't know what to do. I couldn't stand it any longer. And then I got angry. I wanted a divorce. A peaceful separation was impossible. What was there to do?

Chapter 2

Now I became serious about the divorce. I took the case to court. We walked to the courthouse separately, but she kept shouting horrible things to me from across the street. I had never seen her so excited. And now we were standing in the courtroom. My wife got more and more excited. Every answer I gave her only made her more angry. But finally we were divorced and I had to support her. I was fairly satisfied because I had achieved the main thing—I was rid of her. After the hearing I saw her with her old friends talking about me and the proceedings, but I went to my friends for our own discussion. Now there was a lot of work at the factory. We had to produce more or we would go bankrupt.

Second part of Chapter 2. The Great Disaster

There must have been something like a hole in the cellar so that I could see some boys smoking in the storage place where gasoline was stored. My God, to smoke in a gasoline storage room was really something! I ran like crazy into the storage room. Of course I wanted to chase them away, but they had already seen me. They threw their lighted cigarettes into a crack in one of the gasoline containers and then ran away. I could see smoke coming out of the container. I ran to the phone, called the office, told the manager to come downstairs with all the workers because the storeroom was in flames. He came at once. Then I ran to the alarm and reported the fire. At last the fire engines came. At first we thought the factory could be saved, but that evening we saw the ruins of what had once been a great factory spread around. Our manager, the owner of the factory, was in despair. He simply couldn't grasp it—his factory which had been so beautiful in the morning, now was in ashes. But the mother of the boys who had been smoking cigarettes in our factory, whom I got to know later, told me that her boys had come home that day terribly upset, and for a long time she couldn't get them to say why, until one day one of them told her that he and his brother were guilty of the factory fire because they had been smoking cigarettes in the gasoline warehouse. She was horrified. Other people would have tried to hide this incident, but she knew she would not be able to live with herself so she went to the court and told the people there with great conviction that she had found out that her sons had caused the fire at the factory. This was followed by a long inquiry, but the whole thing was settled amicably. The children were too young to be punished and the mother was absolutely innocent. The manager came out pretty well too. He couldn't have the factory rebuilt, but he was able to live on the insurance. As a matter of fact, he became a quite congenial retiree. It was all the same to him whether we starved or not.

PART 2

Chapter 1. THE SLUM

Our manager had given me two months' salary but the money just flew because the time flew. I became poorer and poorer. All my savings were gone. I had sold everything. But in comparison to the others I was a Croesus. There were a lot of people there who almost starved. It is terrible to witness how, on one hand, two thousand people pocket their money while on the other hand six thousand starve and freeze. Oh, there is of course the middle class, but of the millions who live in this city, only 2.5 million are middle class. The misery in this city made me so sad that I didn't want anything. And the main thing, life, I didn't want at all. I thought: I can't help these people in their misery. I was very close to committing suicide, but then I felt I must try to help their misery. For that I had to get a job first of all, and there I really had great luck because in a very short time I found a job as a mason. As far as I was concerned I was lucky, but to free a whole city, perhaps even a whole country from its misery, you needed more than luck. For that you needed a lot of intelligence and know-how and many friends besides. Yes, this is a difficult problem.

Chapter 2

I had plenty of friends, but whether they agreed with me was another question. And political questions are often a matter of life and death.

And it was too much to expect my friends to endanger their lives on my behalf. First of all I had to spy around and find out whether I had enough friends for my purpose. If anyone were to betray me, I would be lost. I really had only one friend on whom I could rely absolutely. But even if there was only one, he was worth more than all my other friends, so after I had really taken his measure, I revealed my plan. He was thrilled with it, but said this was no child's play.

People were running around the streets in desperation. Poverty is a dreadful torture.

Now my friend and I were not on firm ground. The two of us couldn't possibly make a revolution. At first we considered everyone very carefully, but then we thought the worst rowdies and delinquents would be happy too if for once they didn't have to steal or sink into poverty.

Now we already had a lot of people. Not as choice as in the beginning but they were people, and if we were nice to them they didn't behave too badly toward us. Late one evening, my friend said to me: We should really still give it a try to come to positive terms with parliament. Let's go there and ask those people. Perhaps it'll work.—And actually we told our people about it the next day. Naturally they were very much in agreement, but they said they had to get this and that ready first. When we got up the next day, our people led us at once to our workshop. Proudly they showed us the flags and other things they had prepared. Then we really did go to parliament in a terribly pompous parade. When we got there, my friend and I walked into the house of parliament. There was a long conference during which it was my intention to get parliament to do more for the poor. I said that after all the state was not poor at all, and that it was only unjust. Two hours later they rejected our plea, so we left. Outside, our people were waiting impatiently for us. They were terribly eager to know how things had turned out. Now we will have to resort to force. Sad but true.

Chapter 3. THE ATTACK

Then, one day, my friend came running to me all excited. He said he simply had to talk to me. We sat down and my friend told me that he had overheard Merge, one of our people, lecturing the others and saying how noble and beautiful war was, just the way a warmonger would speak. This caused dreadful excitement. To throw this fellow out would have been terribly risky. He would have felt abandoned, and since he was mean, would have betrayed us. Originally I had forbidden our people to eavesdrop on each other, but now I too did it quite often. I would never have thought anything like this was possible.

This was the first great excitement in my circle. Oh, it is a difficult but beautiful thing to lead such a group of people whom one wants to save.

Chapter 4

We are getting more and more people. I cannot postpone the storming of parliament any longer. And so, on a day agreed upon, we set out. There was fighting right away, but then something strange happened. The enemy kept us at bay by taking my friend prisoner. If we attacked, there was the threat that they would shoot our friend. Parliament believed that they had us in their power now, and they made their second demand, namely that we disperse or they would shoot our friend. Now they were asking too much. We attacked suddenly and furiously, and succeeded in saving my friend. The man who was supposed to shoot him had laid his pistol aside and we managed to press forward and save our friend before the man could aim his gun. He did take one shot at him which, however, scarcely wounded him. In spite of the fact that it was a negligible wound, he couldn't manage to work his way through the crowd so easily, and by the time he got home, the wound was dreadfully deep. The fight resulted in fantastic bloodshed, and after a long time we stood there, so to say, victorious. It was a very sad story. A month later my friend died. Well, you can't let your heart take over in things like this. I am not lacking in heart, but my desire to free these people was so great that the death of so many people I loved could not drive me to despair. I toppled tyranny, but I felt no self-satisfaction then and I don't now. Now I stand here, the leader of these people, striving for ever-new and greater goals and acts of justice.

Chapter 5

A man can be happy only if he does good in the world and tries to improve it as much as it is in his power to do. And only when he is striving for something lofty can he be assured that he will never completely despair. And unless he is crazy, a man has no reason for suicide, as long as he is improving the world. The man who despairs utterly often only lacks the ability to lift himself out of great misery into the power that liberates, but instead, lets himself go. One could also call it a sort of lack of self-confidence. I had this self-confidence. In spite of my despair and sadness, I liberated myself from the business with my wife.

Editor's note:
Anna Freud's collection includes also an elevated, quasi-heroic and tragic poem on the same theme:

The Regicide

(1930)

In the club of revolutionaries
all spoke mightily of revolution.
But the old man (he really meant it)
earned only mockery and derision
with his burning speeches.

At dusk he put up a ladder,
climbed to the royal chamber.
He almost got there
when he heard the steps in the courtyard
and they pulled down the ladder.
But he threw a rope round a hook at the window
and pulled himself up, a panting old man.

Stood at the royal chamber
when he saw the light of torches
come up the stairway:
the guards!
He sneaked along walls,
held on with cramped fingers;
went on; hadn't yet crossed the hall;
when he heard their steps;
and ran along walls.

Suddenly, it was bright in the hall
and the old man was frightened.
A shot! From the old man's pistol?
The guards?—No one knows.
Even he doesn't know,
as he stares in the bloody face of the king.
He has done it!

Another shot and the old man falls
and his eyes are glazed.
Contempt of the club runs
once more through his limbs.
He won and paid his life.
He's our hero, they'll say.
He forgives them the mockery
of these last days. And dies.

In the club of revolutionaries
a shrugging of shoulders runs
through the rows.
There is silence in the great hall.
Admiration suddenly yields
to cowardly fear.
The crowds of revolutionaries find
it will cost them too high a price
to resist the guards
of a dead king.

Editor's note: A debased variant (written in 1930 at age 10) was included in Erik Homburger-Erikson's (1931) article on "Triebschicksale im Schulaufsatz" (Vicissitudes of drives in school compositions). *Zschr. f. Psychoanalytische Pädagogik*, 55: Jhg. Nov.–Dec. Heft 11/12), in which he analyzed essays by pupils of the Burlingham-Rosenfeld School:

A ten-year old writes:
Mr. Morgenstern was in a very bad mood. For his workers, he noted, demanded higher wages. While he was quarreling with his wife, a few street urchins were fighting in the yard of his factory, when suddenly one of them picked up something and ran away. The others went after him. After a while they sat comfortably on the gasoline tanks in the Morgenstern storehouse and smoked cigarettes. They thought themselves very grown-up and found that smoking cigarettes was a magnificent thing. Suddenly they heard steps in the yard. Quickly they threw the cigarettes into the gasoline tanks and ran away. After a few minutes there was a terrible bang, you could see a few walls fly up in the air. Then it was all over.

A few people came running. What happened? The Morgenstern factory blew up! Who did it??? . . . A young worker stands on the square. He reels back and forth and is white as a sheet. He did it, they all think. A few scream: He is the culprit!!! The young worker falls down on the ground. This is the proof: it was he!!! A couple of people go over to him. They say to him softly: "Hey, Fritz. I wouldn't have thought that of you. Did you really do it?" They look in the worker's face. It is still white as chalk. The two other workers leave.

At Morgenstern's door the bell is ringing. "Mr. Morgenstern, a worker is outside. He says he has something frightfully important to tell you," says the servant girl.—"I do not receive anyone at lunchtime. Send him away." But the worker won't leave. Mr. Morgenstern is getting nervous. But no, he thinks, my factory is safe; nothing can happen to it. Mr. Morgenstern goes outside: "Scram!" he shouts at the worker, "or else—." He opens the door; the worker leaves, and throws a dime over to Morgenstern. "You ought to be grateful to me, Mr. Morgenstern. You have less than I. Your factory went up in the air." Mr. Morgenstern faints. The worker runs down the stairs, laughing.

Little need be said about this story (Erikson continues), except that the father of the boy is—an industrialist; but, as one will readily believe, not of Mr. Morgenstern's kind. Only the embattled position of the boy makes him into that, in order to present the confrontation with the father in the guise of three distinct figures. As a boy he explodes the factory with a burning cigarette (the attribute of being already grown-up)—and disappears. As a worker he humiliates the father through the news: He proves to him that he is now superior to him. But as the younger worker, lying pale on the ground, he finds it impossible to rid himself of his guilt.

2. A Fairy Tale Without Meaning or Moral

[Written in 1931; see entries February 5 and 21–28, 1931]

I
Once upon a time there was a princess who was very beautiful. Everybody desired her, but she had all her suitors beheaded if they failed to answer three questions she asked. The questions, however, were so hard that not a single prince had yet been able to answer any of them. Ninety-one princes had already lost their heads. The princess was certainly not very humane.

II
Just when the princess was having the ninety-first prince's head cut off, nine princes and one nobleman came to the country. They wanted to meet the princess and perhaps marry her, but when they found that they first had to pass a test, they got angry. One of the princes was so furious over the meanness of the three questions that he felt he was too good to speak even a word to the princess, or "the beast" as he called her. He packed his trunk at once and left the city as quickly as he could.

III
The other princes and the nobleman were also angry about the beheadings and the three questions, but they did want to look things over first. They had themselves announced to the king and they were invited to dinner. When the king found out what the princes wanted, he looked pleased yet smiled scornfully. He was already looking forward to nine more heads that the princess would have.

Meanwhile the princess arrived. She was indescribably beautiful, and her face didn't show a trace of meanness, but it was there in her, buried deep so that at first you saw nothing but her beauty, only with the meanness hidden in her it was still there.

When the princes saw the princess, they were convinced that they had to marry her, and the nobleman was simply boiling with love. You see, he still had new blood; he didn't have a large family tree, so he wasn't degenerate yet. But I don't want to deal with the family now. I will go on.

IV
As I said, each of the princes and also the nobleman was convinced that he could win the princess. They forgot all about the three questions and the beheadings. It is

astonishing what love can do; and it can do even more than make a man forget his beheading. But that doesn't belong here.

In the house—or let's say in the palace—in which the princes stayed, it was very quiet now. Each one was thinking of the princess and of the three questions, because tomorrow the first prince would take his turn.

The first prince was a handsome man, but now he was somewhat subdued. He wasn't sure whether he would win the princess because he couldn't tell how hard the questions would be. When he reached the courtyard he became unsure. He saw the king's contented look and his scornful smile, and he saw the princess. Everything swam before his eyes. Now he heard the voice of the princess. Ah! Suddenly there was ridicule and scorn in her voice. She was smiling. Why did she smile so scornfully when a prince who wanted to marry her stood before her? Suddenly the prince saw it all clearly. He is supposed to answer the questions, and if he can't he will be beheaded. His head swims. The whole journey into the city is like a dream. He thinks: Am I not good enough to marry a princess without such a trial?! "I forego the princess, honorable king," the prince suddenly shouts. All he hears is scornful laughter. He looks around him, wanting to get out. He can't. Two armed men lead him back to the middle of the hall. He looks at the princess. It is all a terrible dream, and yet when he looks at the princess he is startled. A masklike face is smiling at him—and he thought he could fall in love with this mask? He is horrified. He stares at the princess's face and sees beyond the mask, right into the princess.

She begins to speak. She asks the first question: "Where have I hidden my ring?" This is too much for the prince. He had expected a scientific question and shouts furiously, "That is no concern of mine!" She asks scornfully whether he has anything further to say about the question. He says "No" and he has no desire to hear the other questions. He would rather be beheaded right away. The princess says smilingly, "Good. Take him to the prison. He shall be beheaded tomorrow." Then the prince is led away.

V. The Execution

The prince was suffering. Again it seemed to him as if he were dreaming a long, dreadful dream. Everything swam before his eyes. He tried once to flee, but he couldn't. Everything was swimming around him, and with his thoughts awhirl he went to the scaffold.

But then suddenly it was all real. His head was clear. He was standing in front of the scaffold. Was this his goal? To die for a princess who was nothing but a mask to him? The king asked if he had a last wish. Yes, said the prince, to speak to his friends. "You can't do that," the king said scornfully. "Anything else?" "No," said the prince. Now the executioner came.

He wasn't a coarse man, and he didn't have the bloated face and watery eyes one reads about. There he was, nice looking. A priest accompanied him and told the prince to say his last prayers. "I won't pray. I don't believe in God any more," said the prince. Many people got excited and wept. "He has even turned his back on our heavenly Father," says a fat woman. "The man blasphemes against religion. . . ." "What a beautiful face he has. . . . How bitter this great suffering has made him," an aristocratic woman remarked. Voices were heard everywhere.

Now the executioner takes his ax. The prince's whole life races by him. He screams but no one hears the cry. His head lies on the ground. Suddenly the executioner feels terrible. He stretches out his arms and falls down. He has fainted and has to be carried away. When they ask him later why he fainted, he is still terribly confused and says, "The prince's head screamed."

VI

The other princes didn't see their friend's execution. They were taken prisoner and brought to a beautiful but locked room. When they asked why, they were told: This is for your own good. Actually they were taken prisoner so that they would not be able to get away. And now it was the second prince's turn. He was carefree and didn't think of the execution. He thought only of the princess.

The second prince was led into the courtyard of the castle. Then they went into the same room where the first prince had been led. But the second prince was still quite carefree. Only when he turned away from the princess or couldn't see her he became uncertain. But when he saw her face he was again content and happy. The princess's face was so beautiful. When the prince looked at her he was entranced. Now she asked the questions. "Where have I hidden my ring?" she asked. "Perhaps in the cupboard," he said dreamily. Oh, the princess was so beautiful—"Take him away," said the princess. With his eyes on the princess, the prince was led away.

VII

Now came the day of the prince's execution. He was perfectly calm and looked only at the princess. The king asked whether he had a last wish. "To kiss the princess," said the prince. The princess went to the prince and kissed him. Then he looked at her. The prince found her so beautiful that in his love he no longer thought of death.

The executioner came and the same thing happened as the time before. He quickly seized the prince from behind and cut off his head while he was still looking at the princess.

The princess was just too beautiful.

VIII

Now comes the third. He had formerly been very stern and seemed cold to such as believe that a man's feelings consist only of a lot of emotional talk. And now it was this man's turn.

It was perfectly clear to him what was going to happen, and that was the worst of it. When he got to the courtyard, he became ever more agitated and the king smiled and this was the grinning mask of life and the princess was the puppet. And everything is burning around the prince, and grinning, and the puppet sits beside the king and makes a mockery of his whole life. And the prince is confused. Where to go? And the puppet smiles and the mask grins and that's the end of it. And everything is running around in the prince's head and he runs right along with his thoughts and the puppet smiles and the prince can't rein in his thoughts. The puppet smiles and the prince cries: "What is happening to me? What shall I do?" And everything is running and the prince is running right along with it and he runs around the hall and his thoughts scream. He runs to the exit and he doesn't hear the princess's question. He runs and can't control his thoughts and the mask is there again and everything is grinning and everything glows.

"Take him away," says the princess. Two armed men seize him. But his thoughts must out. The prince must run. The mask grins and the puppet smiles, and she is the mockery of his life. And everything is running around the prince as they lead him away.

And then suddenly the mask comes at him and the prince hurls himself on a lackey's upraised bayonet.

Still everything is running and still the mask is grinning. The prince must escape the glow and the heat, and he roars once more to heaven and then it's all over.

The prince died. And the princess thought: This was a change, to have someone throw himself on a bayonet. That was nice, she thought. The princess smiles and she is the mockery of life.

IX

The fourth prince comes. He was always very good natured and enthusiastic, but none too bright. He was madly in love with the princess and really didn't understand what the whole thing was about. All he wanted was to see the princess. That was enough for him.

When the princess asked, "Where have I hidden my ring?" he said: "Perhaps in the vanity table." He guessed wrong. But the princess explained to the fourth prince that she had had the ring embedded in iron. Just as she said this, something suspicious could be seen at the window. The ever-present guards walked to the window. Nothing to be seen. After a little interlude the prince went off to be beheaded.

He kissed the princess. Then the executioner came, took the ax, and in the prince's dull head everything becomes clear. Suddenly he is no longer carefree, nor stupid, he sees these humans as inhuman and only now realizes the dreadful thing that is happening to him. His head falls.

X

The fifth prince—yet another. He is in love with the princess and doesn't think of the beheading because as a pious man he does not believe that Satan could reveal himself in such a beautiful princess. And such a good girl as this, he went on thinking, could naturally never dream of the destruction of her fellow man. This was a good thought, but things don't turn out as well as good thoughts do.

The prince came into the hall. He gave the wrong answers, but he asked the princess to tell him what the answers were. The princess said she would do so, but first she had the room searched to see if somebody might be there. Nobody was.

The first question: Where have I hidden my ring? The answer: Embedded in iron. The second: How large is my palace? The answer: 700,000 cubic meters. The prince was astonished and said that couldn't be right. But it was right, because below the earth the princess had another enormous palace about which no one knows anything except me and the princess. The third question was: How many rooms has my smallest palace? The answer: Three rooms. But that can't be a palace, said the prince. Yes it is, said the princess. It was built according to the plans of a very big palace and every room is 60 yards long and 40 yards wide. But now that's enough. The guards led the prince away. In the night before the day on which the prince was to be beheaded he is perplexed. He thinks: It is impossible that I have been made a fool of for so long. "The princess is nothing but an image of the devil," something inside him tells him. Later he realizes that he is going to be beheaded and he sheds a few tears. But so pious a man as he is, is not afraid for long. There will be a judgment day, a day of justice, when some are sent to purgatory and hell, and others to paradise where only ardent longing can take you. The prince is calm and firm because his religion and the prospect of heaven support him. He goes to the scaffold, casts one reproving look at the princess who has sent him prematurely into the beyond. Once more he looks at the wide sky which he believes is going to receive him. He smiles with tears in his eyes. Then he feels hot as if the ground were burning beneath him—But already his head is lying on the ground.

252

XI

The last one is to come. It is the nobleman. He enters the hall with sure steps, laughs and looks straight into the king's angry scornful face. He walks very straight and upright into the hall and in a hidden corner of her heart, the princess thinks: A handsome fellow. What a pity. But with all her coldness she asks her questions. The first: Where have I hidden my ring? The nobleman thinks for a moment, then says: "Perhaps embedded in iron." The princess is startled. She thinks: Wasn't there something going on at the window, and wants to say so. But the voice inside her says more distinctly: What a pity, the handsome fellow, and she asks the second question. The prince has to think for a long time. "Well, let's say around 700,000 cubic meters." Right! And the princess pales and rejoices inwardly. Then she says, "Where have I hidden my slippers?" And is frightfully shaken that very moment, for this is a different question which he won't be able to guess. The nobleman pales. All he can do is whisper: "Perhaps in your night table?" Wrong! The princess almost cries. She turns away while the pale nobleman is led out of the room. Suddenly it seems to the princess that she is a bloody murderess. Then she pulls herself together and is just the way she was before.

But the nobleman has to fight a long time with his feelings. The beautiful princess, says one voice; the cruel beast! says another. This murderess! Her beautiful big eyes. She is the devil and she is at the same time the most beautiful woman and a murderess. But is it not right that I should be murdered?

Listening at the window to what one shouldn't hear! That must be punished?! Not so hard. I'm going to be beheaded. I am scared to death because of this cruel girl. She is so beautiful, she cannot kill. Oh, why did I listen? This is the punishment for eavesdropping. The death penalty for eavesdropping? Is there no God anymore, only beautiful murderesses? There is no God. The Bible is wrong; but I will go to her and—But the nobleman cannot move anymore. Only his thoughts race, heavy with insane force, through his brain. He hears them from all sides—the murderess—death—eavesdropper, eavesdropper! Who has the right to kill others? God, where are you? Punish the murderess! The murderess? She has beautiful eyes, but they are staring at me—is this the scaffold? Must I love her? What shall I do great God? God? Only a perverted justice! Where to! What is the Bible? What are the Scriptures? And so the thoughts race through his head as the day dawns.

"To the scaffold" says a voice. There stands Death, thinks the nobleman. There stands the princess. The murd—that's as far as he can go. She has such big eyes. She is so beautiful, so pale, yet a murderess. She ought to get an evil look from me, the murderess! But looking into her big eyes, my glance melts, and is gentle. Why does she enthrall me? Why?

The princess turns away. She can't listen any more. She doesn't want to see. Then she hears the word *murd*—. And the truth crushes her, but she does not lose her rigid composure.

The nobleman sees her big eyes. The murderess! The devil in the divine. All has been error. God was a fraud. The beautiful princess? The murderess! Everything goes astray, the lie rules the world. That is the reward of the eavesdropper. The murderess! God, devil, and beloved at the same time!

And the nobleman's head, seething with thoughts, lies on the ground. His eyes roll. His mouth wants to speak. Then there is one life less.

—Thanks to her resilience, the princess soon recovered from the love of the nobleman and was able again to receive other suitors. She had the nobleman's head placed in her room. She had it hollowed out and now used it as an ashtray. It was polished, and gleamed beautifully in the sun. But once she thought she saw the nobleman's head move, so she put his head with the others.

The princess still had a very busy life. She disposed of 400 more princes. All in all, she finished off 500 princes. After the 500th there was a big celebration and the princess (by then she was 40 years old) said now she could die in peace. But another prince came. He was number 501. This annoyed the princess, for she would have liked a round number.

She died at the age of 61. She was just about to count the heads. Just as she got to number 501, she died with a satisfied yawn. She fell over backwards and you can still see the place where she fell. The annoying part of it was that she was 61 and not 60, for above all else she liked things to go according to etiquette and to be orderly, with her heads as well as her years.

3. POEMS ABOUT THE END, ABOUT MAN, AND ABOUT THE WORLD

Poems about the End

[May 1931]

I

Rivers flow, men perish
In the unending current of life.
Where you believe to be
you are not.
Nothing stays with you.
Everything wanders, goes astray,
to make its own way
through the screaming crowd.
Everyone lives his own life,
believes himself to be alone.
Soon the end will come, death
letting you sink into blackness.
Dark is life,
dark the night;
and even day only appears to be bright,
can illuminate itself in appearance only.
In appearance only can life maintain itself.
What is true?
Death, Nothingness, the yawning Abyss.

II. Night

Gently she came to the village,
intoxicated we let life rush by.
The end will come, the end is nearing.
Soon death will rule upon the earth.

III. Answer

Let us raise the lyre,
let it resound.
Let us live in intoxication,
letting life rush by.
Come to me,
I will come to you.
Let us hold on to each other.
until death will take us.

About Man

Who is that hopeless power which created man?
To which of the gods came the awful notion
To perpetuate unhappiness in eternity?
You say, you are strong.
You are so great.
We rest in God's secure lap.
You say.
You:—a voice seeking in vain
to drown out fear
with well-meaning lies.
Useless effort!
What did it help!
You had to lie,
but to be drowned out by cruel fear.
Fear is so deep in you
and unrelenting.
As much as you scream,
all your good screaming
will not conceal
hard fear
and hard calm truth.

Poems about the World

[dated by A.F. Spring 1931]

1

The world is a lie.
Reach out, if you like it,
they tell you on your first day.
And you reach into
colorful rows.
And you reach into life,
reach for heights

they promised you in your youth,
if only you kept your word.

2

Thoughts are thieves,
make me reel,
steal my last strength
to lie to myself.
Monsters,
they tear down old walls
that enclosed me,
break into me,
glowing, destructive,
devour me,
live on me,
waste me.

3

The world is a lie.
Thoughts are only torment,
chase me through life's hallways.
They will kill me.
The beams are trembling
and thought screams: "Wither!"
and the beams are crashing.
Soon I'll be a corpse.
Be happy! But no, I am not.
I want life,
want the devouring thoughts.
I'm a coward in the face of death
and of life.
I am only a torment to myself
at the great feast
of drunkenness.
At last, I must die,
I am only torment!
What is death, which seizes men?
Him, myself, and you?
There he comes flying, to fetch me,
who was called a happy man.

4

The earth is a sphere
sinking into the ocean of devouring nothingness.
Only a few men
cling with their last strength on that round globe.
I myself am still trying
and do not know, whether I'll succeed,
to stay up on it for much longer.

Yet I am still on top and smile
about the dead devoured into nothingness.
I don't see the empty sphere
that has long lost its content.
I see the empty sphere still as earth,
my room still as space,
my fear still as fear,
the images of terror, I see them still as real and present.
And yet it is mere appearance, when I am happy.
It is mere appearance, when I mourn for the dead.
I see only appearance as reality,
never do I see truly
the essence of things.
Never do I learn, what space is in infinity.
Yet too many words have been spoken,
the sphere is too slippery,
it is easy to fall.
There I can see one:
he falls into unlimited space.
Suddenly I know how one falls.
I fall along
and all that was dark
before my eyes
as appearance, turns bright. Faces glow of blood,
stare out of green eyes,
Black cats pursue me,
glowing, glued to my steps.
And fear turns from appearance into reality.
Dogs with red eyes
race after me on huge tracks
The horrible, indescribable assumes a body,
becomes hard and stays. And yet cannot be grasped.
Horrible face! Ungraspable nothingness, which assumes a body,
and persecutes me. You glowing face, which is the truth!
Lie and appearance avenged by bloody nothingness.
I am sinking! Screaming, calm, persecuting nothingness
take me into you!

5

The world lies. Why does it stare at me
with its long face? It wants to choke me
and speaks so friendly to me.
But in its eyes I see flashes
of ghastly murder.

Everything stares at me, wants to seize me.
Everything wants to catch me.
In nature the trees stretch out their arms,
to catch me.
Me: who always lied to himself and was always lied to.—

I thought to recognize no trace of the danger
which now embraces me with iron arms.

Why does death
who rules the world,
have me seized by arms of polyps,
crushed by faces, by masks;
why does he let me be devoured
slowly, by lurking dangers?
Why do others go beside me
without feeling the glowing faces?
Why am I a victim of revenge?
Why was I born?

4. Ferdinand

[Written between October 1931 and Easter, 1932]

Small town. Schoolhouse. Poplars as tasteful background. Windows: First window
girls' heads; second window, again girls' heads; third window, mixed; fourth window,
boys; again mixed; a few closed windows; teachers' rooms and office; waiting room
in name only; gym and medical office; superintendent's room, a good man who got his
wife from a newspaper ad under the heading "Serious. No. 104." He took the first one
who came along. Why spend time looking around, one is as good as another.

Out of the blue, a boy between 11 and 13 appears, black hair, green eyes, yellow
teeth, slim, schoolbag with a hole 4″ across. The gatekeeper lets him in and the late
comer runs upstairs to a door. Then another boy. He has blond hair, blue eyes, is of
medium height; but things don't depend on height, as sly Greenspan always says. He
goes up to the gatekeeper and asks shyly how to get to IIA. The man answers and the
new boy goes away shyly. In general, shyness is his passion. Knows nothing, has had
nothing to do with anything; if need be, very stupid. That makes a good impression on
adults, who, unfortunately, must be recognized, but can be fooled. Upstairs, knock,
door opens, a fat face looks at the newcomer. "Good morning!" "morning—What do
you want?" "I want to go to this school, I want to be a pupil in this class." "Hm."
"Where is the teacher?" "Please say professor. Politeness is a duty especially for
newcomers." "I hope I know that as well as you. Is the professor coming to class?"
"Of course he is." "Then I'll wait here. Let me in." "Let you in?! Don't be
ridiculous." He tries to make a face and hiccups. "And why won't you let me in?"
"Well, who knows who you are. Maybe you have bombs on you." "So what?" "Don't
ask such stupid questions, or you'll get it." "Don't get excited. I don't have any
bombs. I'd be blowing myself up." "Leave him alone," yells the slim boy who came
in first. "You or me?" says the fat fellow. And without letting the other speak: "So,
that shuts you up, eh? The duties of my office would be too much trouble for you,
wouldn't they?" And turning to the new boy: "You see I'm Mecha and I'm in charge
here." And then with a sociable smile: "Come on in. You may sit down here." "The
chair isn't real, I'd fall right through it," says the blond fellow. "I seem to be among
people who want to shame me with petty matters, a gang of"—"Sit on the bench or

you'll get it," says the fat boy, reverting to his bureaucratic tone. And now the interrogation. The blond fellow is startled. Does he have to take this from a boy like himself? I'll beat them up! But the professor! What will the townspeople say? It's really not so bad but they're treating him like a dog. The walls tremble before the blond fellow's eyes. It is he who has been crushed by discrimination. Now the walls have got to stand still, because he knows why they are trembling. Otherwise the townspeople will speak, the town that judges everything. They will ridicule him—

The interrogation, he heard him say. "Where do you come from?" "Bitchville." "How's that?" "Bitchville!" "Oh, I suppose there are only bitches there." The blond fellow is about to hit his interrogator when, from the side, he gets a punch on the chin and one in the stomach. The whole class laughs. The bitch, as he is now called, is close to tears. He delivers one blow after the other, but in the end he does shed a tear. "The little boy is crying," someone yells, then falls down because he has been hit from behind, on the head. "The bitch is fighting dirty, give him hell!" — Steps in the hall. All dear little children are sitting on their benches as the amiable professor likes to say. A rather poor child is leaning, docile but completely confused, against the wall. The professor walks in, behind him the girls with whom he has taken an instructive stroll because they are so well behaved and obedient. The professor takes attendance. Apparently he hasn't noticed the blond fellow. The boys throw spitballs at the girls. Some of them look angry, some arrogant. Woe to her who dares to smile! Ten days' talk about why she smiled. It's obvious, but you can't say that. So they shut their mouths. My God, the implications! You don't dare to smile. And yet, it is not all that unpleasant to be considered daring and to provide gossip for ten days.

Suddenly they see the blond boy. He looks great. "A Bohemian ape," a boy whispers loudly to the girl sitting opposite him. She doesn't hear him very well at first, but then passes it on as quickly as she can. All of them now try to find something wrong about the blond boy. It hurts. There are tears in his eyes. If only he knew what this nasty smile means.

The professor is still writing. The mumbling in the class grows louder. "Silence!" The professor has stopped writing. He turns to the blond boy. Another interrogation. But much more silence, much more fear. Everybody wants to laugh at him. There are tears in his eyes. He alone is persecuted, he alone is miserable. The interrogation begins: "Family?" Mother sick, father at home but drunk, his little brother like a leech. That's what he had to think and would have had to say. Instead: "My father is at home, my mother works a lot. I have a little brother and we get along fine"—. As he says this he looks around the class. He is overwhelmed by a hopeless feeling which is replaced by helpless fury. The feeling says: I am alone among strangers! He wants to be sentimental, but everything in him fights against that. Hatred! Hatred! That's what one has to oppose to these fellows. How they stare at you with their stupid fat faces. How they stare at his clothes! They are making fun of his poverty. But they will see who it is they are reviling!! They will learn to respect him!!! His rage grows because the scorn of his poverty is scorn of his home and he has to defend his home. He has to defend it—because of the love he feels for it, and because of the fear of his father who is also poor. When they scorn his home, they scorn his father. And he is almighty! He will revenge himself. The professor is angry because the blond boy is pausing in order to think. He waits awhile for the boy to start talking again, to engage in an orderly school conversation, not to be mistaken for small talk. But when the blond fellow doesn't resume the conversation the professor does: "And you want to be a student in this class? Very good, very good." —Want? The blond boy thinks: *Must!* "What school did you go to?"—"I? In Bitchville" (muffled laughter from all sides) "in public school at Taubgasse 3, high school at Berggasse 13." "Very well. You'll bring your birth certificate along tomorrow. What's your religion?"— "I? I—I—" "Come on," says the professor impatiently. "I have no religion." On the girls' side excited giggling, on the boys' cold smiling contempt. They come from another world. The professor tries to get out of this delicate situation but only manages an embarrassed "Well." A pause.

The lesson begins. "Otto, where is Cairo?" Otto is one of the most faithful adherents of Mecha, although his high academic standing is not an advantage in the eyes of this great ruler. The yearning to be popular, the passion to see something bad as good just to be different, just because one is still so childish as to think that the compulsion and the punishment resulting from being a "bad pupil" is better than working steadily; the urge toward the "forbidden" which is in all of us:—all this is expressed in Mecha's dictum: "Teachers' pets are apes."

So: "Cairo is in Africa, on the Nile which overflows annually and makes the earth fruitful with its flood. Cairo is in Egypt and is its capital. The"— "That's enough," the professor interrupts. Otto is annoyed. He likes the sound and shape of his words. "Yes, you." The professor means the blond fellow. "Oh, I forgot to ask you, what is your name?" "My name is Ferdinand Heller." Ferdinand says this calmly because he knows that this name cannot be ridiculed by the others. In spite of this there is the same ironic giggling. Ferdinand would like to smile about it but it does annoy him. And that's why the others are laughing. "So, Ferdinand, where is Cape Town?" "Cape Town is in—in—in the South"—"Yes, that's right," says the professor, disturbed by Ferdinand's nervousness. "Africa is in the south—No Cape Town is in South Africa."— "Very undisciplined," murmurs the professor. But this is the very behavior one shouldn't give in to. "Where is the Congo, Ferdinand?" "The Congo? The Congo is"—. Disgrace, contempt for the *newcomer*.

The bell rings.

Recess.

The hall is wide. They walk around, argue, sometimes even fight. The guy from Bitchville looks confused and stares fearfully at the strange faces. He thinks of the countryside that now seems so beautiful and contemptible to him. With every look cast his way, he feels more and more dirty. His shirt is dirty, his pants are torn, but the others are in the same condition, only in their case the girls are impressed. What was that? The girls? How he would like to knock them down. Why are they so important? Oh, he does so like to annoy them. He likes to throw them on the ground and make them cry. Again and again he has to annoy them, and he doesn't know why. Oh! It's too stupid, why the many useless thoughts—

"If you fight any more, you'll get blacklisted," Otto says to the big youth with the slit eyes like a Chinese.

Then the teachers come. "Don't throw banana peels on the floor!" "No, of course not," the sarcastic thin boy whispers, "an old lady might pass by and break her leg." The bell rings. Not even half an hour! What a dirty trick. And again class—.

School's out! School's out! School's out!!!! Will Mecha, the fat leader, be picked up by car? Mecha runs downstairs: "Oh shit, nobody here again. I'm going to have to give them hell at home." The others look knowingly at each other. Only Mecha can behave like this. Mecha pretends to be furious: —So that they can see what I'm like. No! So they can see how I would like to be. Mecha leaves. Ferdinand walks home the same way. The others talk of rumors that their enemies are soon going to attack. The date hasn't been set yet. Mecha is afraid the enemy is going to attack them singly, and therefore there would be the need for a decisive defeat. Great excitement. Mecha scolds a great deal.

Suddenly Ferdinand, who is walking a little to one side, hears a voice behind him:

"Hey, atheist! Stammerer!! Get over here!" The blond fellow turns around. "You mean me?" "Who else? Don't look so innocent, baby, I'll get even with you yet, you Hottentot!"

The blond fellow is standing in front of Mecha. He doesn't know how he got there, but he knows that a circle of onlookers has formed around him and the fat fellow, trying to get them to fight: the two heroes, as they think. Some girls pass by. "You," the fat one starts, "look at me not at the girls." The blond one turns around. He doesn't move. He wants the quiet. . . .

5. ESSAYS

1. Long Live the New Generation!

[Written in December 1931]

We live in an agitated age. Everything must be quick, has to scream, or else it'll be drowned out. The man of today is the vitally healthy, strong man. Indeed, just look at their faces in the street, the large heads, hollow eyes, the tiredness, the weakness! So we live in the age of the strong!?

The head is filled with ideas: Revolution, hurray! A new world is about to be born! The head is empty, must scream itself out, must be pumped dry every day. Hurray! We sell the new world of tomorrow for a penny of today. We live in a healthy age! The stronger wins out, that's why you have to fight, oh you vital men!

I am my career, I am strong, I have courage in the marrow of my bones. Oh yes: the stronger wins out, the man with money, and if he is ever so small. And so you've got to go without food, or be quiet. No, this is not for me. I want to speak, I will write, I'll be in the movies, oh those golden opportunities for us vital men!

Art is just, art, at long last, is what I have been looking for. "No superfluous ideals, please. 'Homeland'—an outmoded concept, all is banal, a slogan." Let us simulate the simple, the naive! Let us say the opposite of the others, that will be original. Even the simple, the naive is played out. Whoever has something to say, is not allowed to say it. "Above all: nothing old!" Don't mix emotions into art, otherwise: "a cliché!"

The new world has been sold; the stronger man is the man with money; there is no such thing as art: "Stay current; don't say anything that is old fashioned; or suspected of idealism; otherwise: journalistic drivel; cliché!" And who is to blame for the fact that I cannot say what I want to say? Precisely the many eminent journalists who rule over the market of the arts. *The journalists are the strong; they are allowed to say everything, because they never have anything to say.*

2. We Must Study

[Written in 1932]

I go to a public "Real-Gymnasium" [high school]. The director is an intelligent Social Democrat. The school is located in a workers' district. We have 45 pupils in our class. A week ago I still had the intention to look upon learning as a useful mental occupation. I was free of the intention to see everything critically and wanted to work gladly together with the others. And now I am full of anger and criticisms. Under a varnish of knowledge and learning, the public school is a mixture of idiocy and compulsion. The only thing it gives to its students is a training in hardening and dulling.

I'll describe an hour: Latin: There is screaming and fighting. Suddenly the teacher enters: Quiet!! He passes along the rows of benches. Stand straight! What do you think a general would say, if the soldiers would stand up that way! (And that is considered a standard for a democratic school!) The teacher lets us stand up for a few minutes, then we are allowed to sit down. One pupil raises his hand: "Please, Mr. teacher, Swoboda is pushing me!" Swoboda must come to the teacher. "What's the matter with you, you damn lout!" The teacher grabs him by the hair (3rd class Gymnasium!): "You'll bring a statement from home with the signature of your father!" Now we are being examined: "Adametz, what is the main rule governing feminine nouns?" "The -as and -is and -aus and -es are called feminine." "Wrong! Sit down! F! I'll have your father come and see me." The giving of marks is the means for punishments and rewards. In order to make students achieve, a conflict with the father is produced. While the teacher puts down a pupil's name in his book of marks and reprimands, another pupil has to serve as watchdog and write the names of those who talk on the blackboard. (The pupils can be made to do anything; but the teachers cause these things to be done.) "Do all have their homework?" "Yes." "The one sitting next to you has to review the notebook with your homework and to raise his hand and report if an assignment is missing. Whoever fails to do so will get an F himself."

The teacher makes a few students change places because they talk too much. Some bawl. (There is crying almost every day.) The teacher shouts at them: "Crybabies! Go to a kindergarden!" In the last 5 minutes he dictates something that is to be learned by heart. Then the bell rings.

Judging by this description one might infer that the teacher is a cruel man who torments children. But in reality this is not so. In the eyes of our teacher the student who is incapable of something is a hindrance, an impediment which must be removed as quickly as possible. He does not consider that there will be a row at home. Talking during class is for him a disturbance. That is why he appoints an overseer. He does not consider the fact that he is educating pupils in behavior that is contrary to good comradeship, and disloyal. He gets his work done by giving us material to be learned by heart and examining us in it. And the attitude of the pupil toward the teacher is just as irresponsible. You cheat him whenever you can and often mock him. If one gets a bad mark, one rebels. When the mark is good, you find that he teaches well, etc. Yet one would assume that a man of 30 to 40 years might have more knowledge of human nature than a pupil.

Most subjects are being taught in an astonishingly dull manner: In History we have dates, in Latin little verse, in Physics rules, in Religion faith is required, and in Physical Exercise a military drill. Manual skills and drawing are the only subjects in which one is allowed to achieve anything. German essays must be written in the imperfect tense and in the style of our primers or readers; and the professor of mathematics writes formulae on the blackboard. The recess is full of secret activities and talk; loud conversations are being carried on only about football; and politics is meant for letting off steam. The political parties are divided into two large camps: (1) For the Jews (mainly Social Democrats), (2) against Jews (Nazis [above all], Protestants, and Christian Democrats [Christlichsoziale]). Big fights are rare. (The hatred between the political parties is expressed in bragging and telling on others.) No party turns against the teachers. There is no active opposition, only passive resistance, that is: by "doing nothing."

Editor's Note: The following is a continuation or a new attempt to deal with the same theme.

Football! Football! Horeschovsky, Hiden, Hiden, Horeschovsky, Hiden, Sinclair, Schall, Sesta. Müller, Smistik—Hiden—Horeschovsky—Sindelar—

But even the talk about football must end at some time. A chain of doing nothing is tiring. Suddenly, only in order to do something, someone gets a fixed idea: he must become a model pupil. The -as and -x, -aus and -is [are femininum generis]. For such monotonous babble one gets an A. Useless and boring drudgery. Those who refuse to learn this stuff get an F. One of the main reasons why so many intelligent children fail or get poor grade reports. As a main occupation school offers nothing, it does not offer intellectual work. But if one wants to work nonetheless, one writes poems or writes little stories. What for? For whom? Surely not so that relatives might be astonished what "the child" is capable of! Surely not in order to get into our newspaper, the "Neue Freie Presse," as a curiosity among pages of self-important posturing of the greedy children of the rich. You want to say something, show something, but there is no one who will listen to you. With painting, I understand, it goes the same way. So all that is left is "politics." But that is not for children. You should beware of politics as long as you are so young. Old men who have grown childish are to lead the state. They know how it is done.

But that is not so. The entire world is now a hodgepodge of words, opinions, and theories. One grows up in a certain political group. When the children are barely four years old, they are told already: "You are a German." "All men are equal." "You must go to church." And even these three sentences show different ways of looking at the world, which is what politics is about. A pupil wears the insignia of a party in school. He is kicked out of the school. Why? Once you can read, you find that every other advertisement is political, you see uniforms. How could one then be supposed to look on and think nothing of it? Every one of us has a definite picture. Every one of us wants to belong somewhere, and many are in political organizations. Indeed, they have been put into parties. Mostly their fathers told them, go to the youth organization of such-and-such. Another kind of parents are those who consider it premature for "children" to join such organizations. But they let them read political writings. A third kind of parents are those who say: Politics is no good.

The first two kinds of parents have their reasons. When a worker (for I believe the workers to be those who put their children into party organizations) has his son join a youth section, he will learn to work there and to live together with others, and he will know from early on where he wants to get. On the other hand, he will also learn to suppress every idea which would go against his party even if it were his own. He will never learn to look at a matter objectively and he will have difficulty in forming an opinion on his own. (When one joins a party as a grown-up, he is far less susceptible!)

The parents who do not give their children to a party but allow them to read about politics and to listen to lectures will only theoretically educate them in one direction. In practice this knowledge is never applied. You belong to no one, don't know what you want, and this is precisely what many of us miss so much and what could be supplied by a party. However it is true that one learns thereby to look at all things impartially and that one can later on take sides relatively freely without prejudices and imposed opinions. (Perhaps one will then be troubled by the fact that one has never learned to develop a sense of community.)

But what is surely wrong is to tell a child that politics is evil and that one should not be concerned with it. Sooner or later you are bound to come up against it, for in life you'll need a *Weltanschauung*, a way of looking at the world, an attitude toward the world: you'll need politics.

POEMS AND REFLECTIONS

1. A Dream

Someone is standing behind me.
I know it.
Run, run! it says in me.
Run from the night into the day,
where he cannot hurt you.
Run! He wants blood of you.

I run,
He follows,
Seizes me.
I run!
He throws me
—there—into the machine.
There—into that shaft.
He presses me down.
The wheels are turning.
I cannot run.
He presses me down.
What does he want of me?
Into the shaft . . .
Into the wheels . . .
A point races through the air,
The wheels turn . . .
Points . . .
Wheels . . .
A pit . . .
And he is pressing me down.

The point comes at me.
Run! Run! Run into the day!
And I cannot.
Points whirr.
Wheels turn.
The shaft . . .
And he stands behind me and presses me down.

Distantly, softly: voices.
Run, run, it says in me, softer and softer.
The voices grow clearer,
between them: wheels, points, still turning: blurred.
The voices now louder,
in between them still wheels and points.
The voices are loud.

I wake up,
I am told I screamed in my dream.
And meanwhile wheels and points are turning through the air.

2. The Murderer

Where shall I go?—I do not know.—It's dark everywhere, I must
run. There are faces, everywhere, angry faces

That is their revenge. They'll murder me, as I have murdered.
There flies a face and grins.—I must stab them, I must.
There he lies. The dead man.

Where shall I go? I must live and I can't.—I can't go on.
Faces fly in the air.—Die. Dying: that is the only thing I
can do.—And even that I cannot do.
And the grinning face comes closer. What does it want? To
murder me as I have murdered.

What is all this? Why do I live? I must die, then it's over.
—The face is coming at me. Living doesn't work and dying
doesn't either.—Where to?

There is the face. Now die!

3. Poem

Living,—living is only a dream.
We are living in narrow space.
In narrow space in a narrow mind.
All comes to a halt before the eternal, unscaleable wall.

What *do* we know? We know nothing!
Nothing gets out of the dark into the brightness of light.
What can we do? Forever only ask: Why?
Even the cleverest only skirt the questions.

4. Yearning

Life, where are you? Can it be called life, when I have to vent
my feelings on lifeless dolls! I want to kiss, but that can't
be, I can kiss only rag dolls.

I ask if she loves me. But it's only a rag doll I ask.
Am I really still too young, not to kiss rag dolls? Will I
always kiss rag dolls instead of girls?

Here I lie in my bed. I don't know the answer to the question I
ask myself. I must go to sleep now and the question will still
stay within me.

The light goes out, and I must again kiss my rag doll.

5. Five Poems on Life

Let's run in
Let's run out
And it all is just a dream.
And in the dream there are thoughts
And love is running past me.
And I run in
And I run out
And it all is just a dream.

A dream! Inside is fear!
A dream! Outside are masks!
Inside it's alive
And outside it's dead
And it all is just a dream.

A terrible dream
of life that grins in its iron mask
And I reach the edge
of the dream and the fear—

—No! Let me not lose the dream,
Though fear and the iron mask
press down.

The dream will pass—
And where then?—
The iron mask will be pressing down.—
And I will ask:
Where was life?—

It was that terrible dream!
And now I stand at the edge
And now the dream wants to end
And the iron mask is still pressing down.

And now the dream is gone
And now my life will be over.
For the iron mask no longer hurts.

Life was the mask and inside was fear.
It tormented you, it tormented you,
If you did not wrestle with life.
You trembled, did not know why,
called yourself coward and stupid.
But red blood wanted revenge.
That was the fear;
It wanted to kill you—

266

If you did not wrestle with life.
And the red blood flowed, and the fear came on.
Fear took your life, and stared at you,
stared at you with green eyes
as the blood flowed down the stairs.

So I ran and the red blood after me
To the very edge it ran after me;
To that edge where my life was over.

iii

Can you tell me where to go?
Everywhere life is so full of blood.
What shall I do, where shall I go?
Everywhere one has to see men dying.
What is the goal? What is the end?
Everywhere are the red hands.
And red with blood this glowing fire will finally stop.

iv

Let us run, let us run into life,
And what we see, is given to us.
Let us quickly take all in
In the frenzied ride
around life.

We live a short while, and we live fast,
but there is night,
In the frenzied ride
around life.

Briefly we are on this earth,
We leave no trace.
Come along
On the frenzied race
For life.

v

What is all of life about? It is a long dream
with a pretty seam.
The dreams we live
Is life that we dream
In our small spaces.

And life will be over
And I'll turn to earth.
And the dream will have died
and my gain will be little.

6. Two Poems

I

And so I must put on my mask again,—and sing a hit-tune—
I am to be happy again, and to lie to myself,
to live again without you.
Where have you gone? All over
I have looked for you—
But it's too dark to see.
And so I can dream you are here.
Come here—and if not
in reality,
Come back again
in my thoughts!

II

You are so far,
I am so far
And still you are so near.
Why don't you come to me when I even make poems about you?
Yet you are far and I am far.
Near only in thoughts.
I think you will never come
And still I love you.
Why is love a mere feeling that cannot be
guided?
Why must I love you?

7. Love

I am in love with you,
But in this love, there is no rhyming
As in verse.
I lie in bed, make a sad face, saying, and saying it again:
She does not love me.

8. A Life

You are so high
I am so low.
But there was a voice that called me.
And I had to go up and I had to succeed.
I had to see you again.

But when I saw you, it wasn't you.
You were only a face.
And I fell down
And I shall fall
to my grave
And there it's all over.

9. The Fairy Tale of Man

Big flowers fade,
So others can walk on them,
For whom the soil would be too hard.
But even flowers that walk on flowers
Must fade.
For they should not bloom forever
On the blossoms of the others.
They shall fade, and
Join the flowers
That have faded blossoms.
So they too will learn: there is a below
That is like the world above
And has feelings like those above.
But the corpses of the flowers become too many
And man is made of the flower corpses
With his below which is an above
And with his great yearning for the young fresh Above
That is nothing but an enslaved Below.

10. Piano Concerto ("The Emperor")

And it begins.
Upward races the tone,
to fall
to race upward;
the chord in pursuit.
It rises, rises, and reaches its height,
and falls,
and was only a whim.

11. Music

There was a sound and a yearning
And they became entwined in one another,
to rise, to fall,
To dissolve in the blue sea of sounds
Where everything rhymes and turns into feeling.

12. Death

This is war with its roaring
This is life with its quivering
This is death in its greatness
The greatest we know.

We tremble before him, shudder
That he should take from us our sacred life.

Yet he too is great wisdom,
we rest in his womb.

When he takes us, he surely knows why;
for he is never unknowing.

He would not be so terrifying if he told us what he is doing
with us.
As it is, all happens in terrible calm.

Can you see him standing there by the neighbor's side?
That man can now see into the beyond.

But we must weep
that he went to his kin.

We know not what Death will do with us.
Death, raging so, and yet so gentle.

13. To the Poets

You want to hover and float on air,
Yet with your fat poets' souls can scarcely get off the ground.
You try to capture feelings
bound prettily in a nosegay with red ribbons.

You always want to beguile men,
And when called to account,
claim: you wanted to teach them.

Poets, I am through with you!
You make the most beautiful things fall flat!

14. Defense

I have no use for your riches!
I have courage for better things

Though I know you won't believe me,
I scream into your faces!

You may never believe me, I know,
but neither will you ever

Take from me
My own sense of truth.

15. Song of Higher Beings

Rolling, rolling
The great wave devours
And man goes under

Time rolls on

To devour the world
The wave, oh the wave
has sung many to rest.

And many more will it sing to sleep
as they fight for a glorious
tiny
span of existence.

Rolling, rolling
The great wave devours
And man goes under

16. The Drives

The drives are the flowers
which grow in the depth of man
When man sees them, he is frightened:
They are too perfect for him.

17. Rage

Horses foam at the mouth
when they are enraged,
cats hiss, dogs
may bark; but man may
only subtly blush.

18. Life

The autumn wind blows through the leaves/ it is he who made me drunk./ I have seen her and laughed. / / / The autumn wind races through the leaves./ I felt burning lips and was happy. / / / The autumn wind blows through the leaves, / the dust beats my face. I have / expected too much of love. For I / had money and women want /money./ Burning lips have deceived me . . . / / / The autumn wind blows not in winter,/ in winter there is ice. There are poor men too / who are beautiful / and the women want all things beautiful./ I am not beautiful, I have no / money, all that is left to me is the pistol.

19. Spring
[Easter vacation]

I

Finally love is here,
It has made its entry.

She is now mine.
Finally I am alone with her under shady bushes.
No one disturbs me, quietly the trees wobble and sway

I am not sure that I am not dreaming.
She too is here and feels the same.
Feels me as I feel her
and know we are together.

II

Butterflies fly from flower to flower,
Crawl up on me,
While I look over at her.
Perhaps I can tell her what I want.
Barely know it myself.
I trust I will find the words.
Butterflies too find their way from flower to flower
And also the way to me.

III

But the two of us lie in the shade beneath big trees,
Look at the rustling stalks, which are all driven
By the joy that makes them bloom.
With dreamy eyes we look deeply
I into her, perhaps she into me,
And then look on, happy about the big trees,
At the birds.
We speak not of art nor of literature,
I do not quote from love poems
I only love her in herself,
And can only look at her
Drunk with the radiance of air in the spring.

IV

In the rustling grass I have heard too much.
I said too much about love.
Love is still far. I may not yet love.
I am too young and too small.
I can love with feelings,
in thought I can reach
but my body keeps me in iron limits.

Butterflies fly.
Trembling blades of grass before my eyes
hide the big trees in the distance
as they sway in the wind with outstretched arms.
My thoughts too are trembling blades of grass
hiding the great men.
And yet these thoughts, these trembling stalks know
they only seem to cover and conceal the great
but never reach there.
The blades of grass bend under the wind
And the big trees nod their wise heads.

20. A Plaster Cast

A youth stood on waves. A statue—of plaster.
Proud in itself, the wave rears up. A girl comes along, not
all that pretty, nor mighty. Yet the wave breaks, and the
youth lies shattered at the feet of the girl.

21. Forced Scorn

Let me be cruel, oh my pen, let me hate love. For I must
despise where I am despised myself.

"A girl stands on a meadow, stalking like a crow in
search of prey. A boy comes along. The girl, with a
pert glance, looks up towards the sky. He stops and wants
to kiss her. She refuses. And he walks away. The proud
girl follows him and finally he kisses her. Proud again,
the crow turns away. The young man leaves, still followed
by the crow."

It is written down, but to despise on paper is not to
despise in reality.

22. Two Poems about Nothingness
["Hunting trip with father"]

I

It came to me in a dream,
stared at me with glassy eyes.
It wanted revenge
for blood that had been shed,
blood poured into the sacred vase
of life.
It wanted blood;
it got blood back
from life's own body,
the invisible nothingness with the glassy eyes.

II

1

Man was a whim, created by nothingness
and as a whim still bore the trace of nothingness within him.
To fill the desert left by nothingness in him,
The whim called man invented whimsical reason
And with its cup filled up the desert in him.
But there remained a fringe that glinted, stared ahead,
empty and vast.

And once again, nothingness intervened in its whimsical game,
and filled that fringe with large, never-fading flowers,
which draw men to them, and are love.
And all went to that edge and to the flowers
And took them, putting them into themselves
Until no flower was left.

And so these flowers grow on the faded human beings,
whim, serving other humans,
other games of whim.

23. Circus Director's Speech

Honored Ticket-holders, and Patrons!
It gives me an immensely, unspeakably great pleasure to have the privilege of
presenting this circus which matches the most prominent undertakings, to so
venerable a public. No crass greed for money warms my heart at the thought of
full wallets! No! The pure passion for art burns within me. This purest of fires
consumes itself within itself, if it is not permitted to present itself most humbly
to a high and mighty and all-judging audience. Believe me when I tell you this!
Believe—that I have this ardent fire, read it in my heart, see it shine in my eyes.

Oh blissful day, for my wishes are fulfilled. Blessed is the circus director with
his jingling purse, commanding all; and the poor but creative artist who is
rewarded in cash. Blessed are they indeed.

But oh, be silent, fire of idealism! The earnestness of life calls the artist back
to reality in a warning bass voice. A poor circus director, the most devoted
servant of all those known as the public requests your most gracious ear. Our
artists do not belong to the greedy mob. They are without exception poor but of
noble descent. I myself, a ruined Baron, after a youth passed in sweet luxury,
have turned myself into a vassal through work, sweat, and zeal. I am modest, I
wish for nothing. God save me from being an autocrat, a tyrant, the great circus
director with the whip (he lets his whip fall from his hand). Much rather: the
small, self-effacing, ever obsequious, obliging—immediately sir, my lord, I have
only done my duty, your most obedient servant—that is all I hope and wish to be.

But now I have a great request at heart. Stoop to the romantic sphere (woe to
him who says romanticism has disappeared from our time!), condescend from
your height to the romantically miserable but adventurous existence of the circus
artist, to the circulating, eternally rotating life of man, try to immerse yourself in
it, to stay in it for an hour!

But I've got to go!
So long and cheerio!

The eternally servile artist

(The circus director appears on stage with a parchment scroll covering his
whole body.)

24. Waiting

'The stupid thing about it all is that I am waiting. You can't just simply 'wait' for years. You cannot consider a time of your life a waiting period and make no use of it. You have to do something. Otherwise the event might even disappoint me. Besides, it is just wasted time and wasting time is always terrible. So I am telling you, that is: myself, do something. Don't stand around so stupidly and whine. You are in good shape, accomplish something. You have been claiming that you can do things! So go to it!'

How would I like to live?—No: How *do* I live?—I live for many things, but they consume me. So I say: live more simply. But what does more simply mean?—Should I only eat vegetables? No! I should live life the way it is. I should not let myself be consumed by little things.—I like him—I like the other. I can like them all even though they may not like one another. I am not the slave of certain people!! The little worms which gnaw at my heart, destroy everything. I must be bold and generous: I must live life.

I talk too much. It is quite clear. I am preoccupied only with myself; but there are others. I must finally put my powers to the test, and not see myself as a sufferer. It is obvious. I am already so enraged at all this scribbling and at myself. Just what am I doing? What right have I to fancy myself to be something?—Show them what you can do!!!!!.

25. Something about an Anxiety

It is funny: I am afraid of death and I am 12 years old. I fear for my parents' lives. Why is that so?—It is not that this anxiety gently makes its rounds in me like a feeling you can regulate. It is oppressive, as all anxiety. Why? Who knows what thoughts wander around in me? Who knows if this compassion is not just fear of a thought that has arisen in me? That is likely. Today my father's life happens to be at stake. That sounds as if I wanted to kill my father. And I shudder at this thought; and I look at the window and think that any moment, a man will come through the window. The man takes revenge, it is my father. But why should I wish in my thoughts for my father's death? Because he has someone I want. Or because he has someone and I have no one. Because he can do something I can't do. Now I've got you, fear, now you must disappear. I say to myself: But it is nonsense to want a father's death. I simply have to wait a little, then I too will be able to do what my father can do. And again the fear appears. I know why: I fear the competition, the revenge.

26. A Life

Hours, long hours must I wait.
Days, long days must I wait.
Years, long years must I wait.
And I am still not a youth, not a man.

And again the waiting years
And at last I'm a youth, a man.

A boy with a slanted beret, and a girl,
a girl, that is happiness.

A day has passed; and I am an old man;
and may not wear a slanted beret;
again with no girl,
and the yearning again in my heart.

27. Time

Do you hear the storm blowing outside?
The cannon Time that blows you away?
You once had a home, now you stand alone
In the storm.

It's the times, people say. The upheaval.
It's the confusion; the agitation.
—Is it?

You think, you know how Time and Man,
and his mad brain,
circle around in space,
and fall.
You think *you* stand still.
But you will fall just like
the neighbor you have thrown down.
Meanwhile you've been preaching brotherly love,
saying it wasn't your fault.
It's the fault of the state, of politics, they don't do things right.
They govern badly.

But where has government come from?
The state was created by masses of men thousands of years ago.
And who are the masses? What are they made of,
if not of individual men?

So the fault is mine, after all?
Yes, yours, or perhaps your neighbor's, or perhaps
it's the fault of us all.

RETROSPECTIVE

RETROSPECTIVE

In working my way through Anna Freud's materials I proceeded as if I were in analysis and compelled to write down, without censorship or critical restraint, everything I recalled of those early times or connected with them in free association. Yet I came to edit what I had written in this manner in terms of style and could not help but suppress or reduce to a mere hint some details which, though few in number, were all the more embarrassing to me. Moreover, I had to curtail even this revision at the insistence of readers who objected to a lack of clarity, a confusing back and forth between Anna Freud and Peter Heller, then and now, or explanatory notes and later associations. To avoid this I separated the earlier materials from the retrospective. They also deplored the absence of a positive conclusion or purifying happy end. They expected, if not the wisdom of the man who had been healed, at least an integrated perspective. On this point I was less inclined to oblige. I pruned and edited but stuck, by and large, to my initial procedure. The retrospective remarks relating to the first sections of Anna Freud's record retain their original form. In reading them, as well as subsequent comments, the reader should bear in mind that the writer is taking up Anna Freud's collection of notes and materials bit by bit. He allows ideas to come to his mind which explain or amplify Anna Freud's record or are associated in his own mind with it. Passages designated as *associations* stem from the original continuous retrospective. I will be responsible for them only insofar as one can be held responsible even for thoughts or images that come to mind without premeditation or conscious intent.

PART 1

"Pavor Nocturnus" (see p. 3)

Associations

The stereotypical nightmare that brought me into therapy now reminds me of its opposite positive stereotype: A farmhouse looking out placidly from under its steeply gabled roof, surrounded by a meadow, enclosed by a woven wooden fence; behind it, over the hill to the right, a patch of forest, to the left the orange-red disc of the setting sun cut off by the hill. This idyllic picture I painted or drew again and again, even as late as my entrance exam into the public high school at age twelve, when an art teacher said to me disparagingly: "You probably always draw that."

The *anxiety dream*, however, went as follows:

I am walking on the grassy edge of white gravel, along the rondelle, the circular path round the big oval pond of the upper Belvedere Gardens, humming and whistling. A big blue-black machine with handles and shafts comes toward me. I cannot get out of its way. It seizes me, draws and presses me with its iron rods into its shafts and grinds me up so that I cannot stop screaming until, at last, voices from afar penetrate like drops, through a black, resounding thicket, calling my name, first softly, then louder, and I, exhausted by my highly dramatic performance, stand in my bed without allowing myself to wake up, savoring, it now seems to me, with some guilt and shame, the attention of those standing around the bed trying to calm me down.

This was the major screaming that did not occur every night but often enough. From the start one has to assume that it was a performance—though not consciously so—to attract, accusingly, the attention of my parents who were caught up in the vicissitudes of their separation and love affairs. And indeed, my being sent into analysis was, I think, partly due also to their own sense of guilt.

Associations and Explanations Regarding the Dream

The Belvedere Park was divided into a lower level and, near our apartment, an upper level where I played as a child. It was formerly the palace and garden of Prince Eugene of Savoy (later for a while my Austrian hero and ideal). What comes to mind? "Prince Eugene of noble class / through the window sticks his ass/ And his brother hardly quailing / lays his noodle on the railing." Never mind! Later still, I composed a poem about beauty, a hymn to the sunstruck flashing windows of the Belvedere palace reflecting the beams of the setting sun, dazzled and blinded by their radiance, seen from the very point at which the machine in the dream came toward me. The "Belvedere" is what is beautiful to look at, in short: beauty. Did beauty arise as a result of turning away from the horribly exciting, by lifting one's eyes upward, in order to deny the terrible and to embellish it, to gaze, blinded by the sun, as a protection, a glossing over, a palliative, into the sun-blinded, crazed, dead eyes of those windows? Even as I wrote that poem I did not understand why this dazzling light, blindly reflected by blind window eyes should be the epitome of beauty! Yet the complex of looking and being looked at which disquieted me again and again in later years (it was interpreted according to the psychoanalytic fashion of the twenties as having been derived from observation of parental intercourse) is clearly implicit in this scene of terror and beauty. And so it is in another, older memory: of the *Mopapa* or *mon papa* song and a game with a mirror which delighted me (I was told) because I saw myself in it; as well as in the memory of the song of the June bug: *"Maikäfer flieg, dein Vater ist im Krieg, die Mutter ist in Pommerland, Pommerland ist abgebrannt, Maikäfer flieg!"* ("June bug rattle, your father is in battle, your mother is in Pomerania, Pomerania's set afire. June bug fly!")

Playing with a mirror while singing the *mon papa* song or hearing it sung, I learned how to flick specks of light into distant windows, but was soon told that this was forbidden and (later) that you could blind people that way. Still farther back, yet also connected to the above in mysterious ways: I am lying somewhere "below," on the dark ground floor, looking upward toward a slit of a window, as if from a superintendent's basement apartment. I can see the feet, the high-heeled shoes of passersby. And then there is something blue from which a pinkish white thing emerges, just a corner, a little tip, a tail, looking out of pants; or a blue sea, from which a whitish knuckle with a slight pink tinge peeps out like a cut-off piece. Is this a fabrication? Are these fantasies made to order for psychoanalysis? Having read in the past a little about Lacan and the mirror stage, something like a fragmented ego comes to mind. But I should stop playing analysis—though that is more easily said than done. For what else is my current project about?

Concerning Fear in the Corridor (pp. 3, 199, 227, Figure 2.8B)

On a layout of our apartment drawn by me toward the end of the analysis (October 1931), the frightening places in the hallway are marked; immediately next to them, there is no anxiety.

Description of Our Apartment

In the apartment house at Karolinengasse 5, which decades later still smelled of stale soup as it did in my childhood, we occupied the first mezzanine on the left (on the right were the Portheims) which was reached by way of a shallow white stone stairway, easily overtaking the elevator rising in slow majesty in its elaborate wrought-iron cage. The vestibule with a little balcony looking out and down into a narrow, shaftlike courtyard, branched off on the left to the toilets—the brightly tiled "good" one for us, the "dark" one (with bare walls) for the maids and the cat. It then led to the bathroom where the serenely dignified Mrs. Brom appeared for mani- and pedicures, and the eloquently affable barber, Mr. Sedlaczeck, came, every morning, to shave my father. Following the vestibule further, and taking a left, one was led by a fairly narrow passageway to the spacious kitchen where I frequently visited the cook and the maids, because I was much alone (one of them slept behind the kitchen). But turning around and returning down the passageway one would now pass the dining room on the left where my father and I frequently had the main, midday, meal for which he came home from the factory before taking a short afternoon nap, in keeping with Austrian custom. Besides the long table and the carved sideboards, there was only the black telephone with its cylindrical receiver (44–4–16), where once, when I was very little, a man by the name of Löwy called up, which delighted me (I am told) because I thought that a little lion (in children's German: *"ein Löwi"*) was at the other end. The glass doors that opened from the dining room into the large drawing room had beige silk curtains which I pushed aside, spying, until my father had one of his violent fits of anger about that. Here, bordering on a corner of the big red Persian rug stood the grand piano, a Bösendorfer, on which I was taught by Mr. Weitzmann from Brooklyn, a pupil of the famous Steuermann, an excellent tall man with a big nose who used a strong perfume, presumably because he perspired. Later I took lessons from the dully bustling Friedrich Dührauer, initiator of a special day for the "cultivation of music." I remember his enraptured, brightly yellow face and wrinkled nose as he half spoke, half sung a lyrical song by Marx, drowned out by a noisy accompaniment, but culminating in presumably blissful "*Bienenge-summ*," a humming of honeymooning bees. An almost square, very wide, beige couch stood by the wall with a little cushion on it which I had had to embroider painstakingly (as a Christmas present) in cross-stitch. The angora cat (Niaunza) sat there. On that couch my father once surprised me trying to masturbate and said nothing, but later on told me that his mother once caught him and had frightened him with the threat of dire consequences.

Parties took place in this drawing room, the "salon," and spread into the adjoining library and study with its high, richly furnished, colorful wall of books, stylized in black and scattered red accents by my father's friend, the architect Franz Singer, who decorated this room with dark flat squares or glassy-black mirroring shapes and metal structures in the new functional Bauhaus manner. A little "alcove" door led to the parental bedroom which soon became obsolete and was used increasingly for Ping-Pong, since my father spent nights with others and eventually with one other, more often than with us. At first a huge double bed stood in there, or was it two singles pushed together? Blue predominated (blue sea out of which something pinkish white peers?). I recall nocturnal clanging and the shadows playing on the ceiling from the streetcars in the Karolinengasse below rattling by and sending off sparks. For once in a while I slept in that bed with my mother. On the opposite wall were gleaming cupboards for clothing and linen, with a smooth walnut veneer. Their doors, I believe, were fitted inside with mirrors. When they stood ajar and the door to the adjacent nursery was open, a child might possibly see, diagonally across in the cupboard mirrors, what happened in the blue semidarkness. Later on the big chests of drawers and cabinets were probably

284

removed from the wall; only one bed, I think, remained, and under the portrait by Egon Schiele stood only the green Ping-Pong table on which I achieved a certain virtuosity.

Finally, passing through the bedroom, one came to the nursery. On the right there was the tiled stove with round, semispherical protrusions, cold, warm, or hot to the touch, according to the changing seasons. From there I would move all over the room sliding on the smooth green linoleum; sitting, in early years, on the pot; or, stretched out on the floor, filling pages with scribbles in order to produce important work long before I could write, behaving, I thought, exactly like my father.

Windows, a door, and a short iron stair led from the nursery to a spacious, irregularly shaped, asphalt-covered sooty terrace of the old building, bordered on one side, at the height of a child's shoulders, by a gravel-covered surface stretching to the windows of the opposite apartment where sometimes Susi Portheim appeared. She liked me, but was a little older, and I considered her boring and grown-up, until, as time went by, I came to admire her from a distance. This was "my balcony" on which sparrows and blackbirds alighted. In prepuberty I felt compelled by an exciting and forbidden lust, to kill them with my air rifle. I lit small fires on the asphalt with similar tingling shudders of excitement, and a great sense of guilt about both the fires and the killing of birds at which I rarely succeeded. From the balcony one could look into the window of the tiny maid's room which was next to the nursery but not connected with it. There Tilly, our domestic help, slept together with the big black-and-white great dane, Bella.

I return to the nursery, or rather the crib that I loved with anxious passion until the architect Franz Singer took it away from me, to replace it with a convertible, red-lacquered, *Bauhaus* invention of his, which, like most of his designs, dramatized functionalism but failed to function. I cried and made a huge fuss about the loss of that crib, the same, I believe, in which I had sat as a baby, smearing myself with feces and eating them to the disgust and horror of my mother, who later mentioned this scene.

So much for the apartment; but there was still the dark passageway going from my room along the outer wall of the library back to the vestibule, the most uncanny place in the apartment. For sometimes there was a little child in a white nightgown there, floating in the air, waiting to pursue me along that dark corridor. I was told later that I myself was that child (see p. 223), but to this day I am not fully convinced of this and have reserved for myself a little faith in the possibility of evil, suffering spirits or ghosts.

Associations to the Two Dreams (see p. 3)

The interpretation of intercourse as quasi-deadly contest is relevant to the dream about the battlefield and the field marshal. The name of Goldscheider (a teacher at our private school) is made up of two parts. Is he the one who can discriminate ([*unter*]*scheiden*) between gold (precious fecal matter) and the vagina (*Scheide*), or unite the two: the fecal gold and the vagina, and thus prove himself to be the master of the field or field marshal? Or are such retrospective associations of an adult quite unrelated to what went on in the head of the child? In this dream I seem to be saying about the struggle of the sexes: "Thesi, let's go away. I don't want to see it" (p. 3). Yet this would be highly ironic. For according to psychoanalytic tenets I was all too eager to see it, to be part of the intercourse of my parents, the "primal scene," as a "laughing third." However, more strongly than all this I now feel a breath of death and the beyond, emanating from this dark battlefield. So many of the boys and girls, the men and women sitting and standing around there watching the battle, are already dead. They are the dead. But precisely this association may merely belong to the present, the retrospective after more than half a century.

The first dream seems to refer to my mother and her relationship to my father; the second is about my father, though it may also have to do with my relationship to women, German *Schachteln* ("boxes") being a derogatory slang term for females. It was characteristic of our assimilated family that we celebrated Christmas, but none of the Jewish holidays. (I was in a temple for the first time at age twenty-three in Canada.) My parents, convinced atheists, had registered me with the Jewish community only for my grandfather's sake. But Christmas was part of the cultural sphere to which we felt we belonged and wanted to belong. The Christmas tree, Santa Claus (though I almost recognized my father in his costume) played nearly the same role as in any other bourgeois Viennese household.

Now I also find the second dream full of irony. For it describes a hopeless confusion: how, if it was my room, could one see from it my father wanting to hold the door to this room shut from the outside?

Where was the governess standing who wanted to open the door my father held shut, if we had seen him before in the act of holding this very door? The lack of clarity in the dream appears to me as a sign expressing my worried bewilderment about our family situation. And it is characteristic also of my judgment that Thesi in her simplicity did not understand this situation, though, as I now reread the dream, it occurs to me that Anna Freud did not understand it either. Nor do I understand it. Moreover, it also seems ironic to me that my father—for he is the burglar (or isn't he?)—should have emptied boxes of candy. If there was anything he did not need to steal, it was candy. There was always candy in abundance, of which he would take a first bite only to spit it out after tasting it. (My mother also liked to eat half a candy and leave the other half in the box.) Or am I, Peter, the burglar after all? Or one who would like to break in, but can't, not yet? It is hardly surprising that I spied in the room where the presents were hidden. Who wouldn't have! But which room was that? My parents' bedroom from which, diagonally across, one could have seen after all that someone held the door to my room shut? How could there be any room from which one could have seen something like that? It's still a mystery to me, as is fitting for an absurdity.) Characteristic for me, it seems to me now, was not the spying but that I was sorry to have found two gifts meant for me: the concupiscence, the sinfulness, and at the same time the quasi-moralistic, pedagogical regret; and also that I often found it disappointing when I found something for me. Disappointing: like the empty cartons, those boxes in which there is nothing but emptiness (rek—Recha in *Nathan the Wise*—the woman is emptiness), as later, when I touched Mädi's genitals in the back of the car and there was nothing there and I thought: "Is that all?" But even long before this disappointment, I had invented my first story, my beginning as a "modern author." It was about a rabbit that fell into a pitfall meant to trap him, and made the greatest efforts to get out, and almost succeeded by desperately jumping and thrashing against the clay walls, scratching a step into them, and with redoubled efforts reached the top, only to fall back and die. Just as in the case of my fairy tale of the princes who woo the princess where one of them almost wins her only to be beheaded in the end like all the rest (see pp. 249–254). For I found such endings blunt in a cutting, modern, bitter way, which, from early on, impressed me as artistically valid, and as both sad and true. And who can say that this is not the way things go!

Who knows?! And indeed, such endings were also in keeping with my mother's taste. She declared her allegiance to the *râtés*, the misfits of this world, and all her life long read Flaubert as her Bible.

About Phase I ("Introduction")

Associations

Anna Freud impressed me right away as a beautiful and interesting grown-up, commanding respect; and I can still see her delicate hands and their rounded movements with my mind's eye, as we sat at a little table playing tiddledywinks by way of introduction. Pressing with a chip on colored chips, one had to make them glide or jump and land on other chips to cover them. For that counted as a conquest of one chip by the other. However, as it was not customary for grown-ups to have little boys come to them to play tiddledywinks, I should have noticed, at least from the uncomfortableness of the fragile table with a glass surface covered by a cloth, that something else was intended. At first, I recall, it was all rather pleasant: She was not one of those silly grown-ups, but natural in her ways, and one felt almost free in her presence without being encouraged or provoked to be naughty. But I also remember the disappointment, the irritation, the humiliation which I thought I felt for her and me when she began to aim at a subject that seemed quite improper and embarrassing to me. "How," she asked, "can you tell the difference between boys and girls?" "By their eyes," I said, to avoid the issue. (How could such a proper quiet woman seriously want to lead up to indecencies!) And as she now started to lay out round and square chips—"I am going to make two figures and you tell me which is the boy and which is the girl"—I knew she would put a square chip—actually it was too big—against the belly of one of the figures. And so, to prevent her from going that far, and since she had, carelessly, begun with the girl, I pointed to the first, harmless figure and intentionally gave the wrong answer: "This is the boy." Yet, she did not give up.

"*Play with Mädi*" (p. 5) refers to the fact that, in contrast to my modesty ("dissimulation") at tiddledy winks, I had been playing sex games for years with a pretty cousin with whom I had been taken out in a pram as a baby. My memory goes far back when the two of us, perhaps even sliding around on our potties, touched each other and showed ourselves and were discovered by adults, including Mädi's mother, Gabi, on grandmother Jenninka's veranda in the Hietzing house. (I remember the view from the windows into the dark brown and dark green crowns of chestnut trees.) This led to a big row, perhaps even slaps or spanking: an event which made me feel terribly ashamed, while my little cousin was calm, unabashed, and nonchalant, and certainly less cowardly than I who made a theatrical fuss in order to deny the obvious. I think this happened when I was about four years old, during the six or twelve weeks around New Year 1924, when my parents, still living together, traveled to Egypt, up the Nile (and to Jerusalem), and I stayed with my grandparents. In retrospective, it seems absurd and characteristic to me that a sexually hyperactive person like Mädi's mother should have been so scandalized by the sex play of little children. Later on, among the sparse shrubs in the garden behind the same yellow house, there was also play in which we tried to inveigle others, for instance the prim and dainty Lydia, who, with calm indignation, refused such entertainment to which we tended to resort when we felt bored. However, adults must have told A.F. about all this. For otherwise she would not have known anything about it. And perhaps this is why, even though she labeled the initial phase mere "play, transition, and pastime," she aimed, straight as an arrow, at my sore point with her question, to perplex me deeply, and perhaps to startle me out of a hypocritical pretense of modesty.

Regarding "Material in the Resistance: Poets, Book Titles, Comparisons, Comparing Opinions, Plans for the Future" (p. 5)

Even then I sought refuge in literature, knew names of poets, quoted book titles, and tried to find out through comparisons who, in A.F.'s opinion, was greater or the greatest, in order to compare my mother's or father's opinion with hers. The important thing was to quote and know—and compare the great. Thus I became an expert at playing the game "Great Men": a contest about who knew the greatest number of great men starting with a given letter, and could write them down within a set time; for which I had a great stock in readiness. The R's simply came rolling out: Rubens, Rembrandt, Rossini, Ressl (the inventor of the ship's propeller, standing in the Ressl Park), and more; and in the same way the S's were always present in my mind. My wanting to be a great man myself led to "plans for the future" which

I had for everybody. Nothing more dreadful than to go down into the nether world without glory. All must immortalize themselves, all become famous. However, as I made plans for those close to me, anxiously concerned that they too would work their way up to immortality, the tormenting question arose of who would be the greatest of all; and so I had to reserve the greatest greatness for myself. Never before or after me, let alone among my contemporaries, must there be anyone greater than me. And behind these plans for immortality for myself and others, and along with them, came the fear of death, to which I now admitted. It had often kept me awake; not because I was afraid of dying, but as anxiety and terror at the thought of extinction or nonbeing. There was the incomprehensible threat or certainty that everything that now is will then not be, that I and all who are with me here now, would be nothing or nowhere at all.

The "sudden disparagement" of my "parents as writers," as A.F. observed (see p. 5), stands in contrast to these efforts to provide immortality for all. My father's literary ambitions were focused then on the craft of writing. My mother's forte was the invention of stories, an astonishing gift which included a great variety of genres, ranging from dramatization of little episodes in her own life (and, unfortunately, a relentless examining of her own experiences for their literary potential) to the composition of elaborate and intricately intertwined plots, and grandly conceived events permitting the development of a character. She was drawn increasingly toward film, and to a visual dimension, a tendency which seemed also in keeping with her love for an architect who cultivated the visual arts as his own, proper domain. Then and later, Mem, as I called my mother, collaborated on scripts for a number of films, among them some German patriotic trash under the direction of Kurt Bernhardt (*The Last Company*), and, later on, in a lighter vein, *The Beloved Vagabond* with Chevalier. I mentioned my father's publications; a play of his was about to go on stage in Berlin when the Nazis came to power. The depreciation of the literary activity of my parents corresponded to my wish to be greater than they, which I suppressed, however. And indeed, the double curse of megalomania and the self-imposed interdiction of the very greatness which I desired all too greedily was to trip me up for decades to come, and to prevent me from doing all I was capable of.

What A.F. designates as "result of phase I" (p. 5) is plausible enough. "Most superficial relationship to parents" probably refers here to desire for the mother and rivalry with father. My *displacement* of curiosity onto the books, and the fascination with their titles turned into an enduring character trait. I still recall standing in front of the old bookstore, Lanyi, my heart beating with lustful guilt. The store, near the opera, had the most fabulous bargains. I recall (though I never read these books) staring at the *History* of Polybius and the, presumably erotic, *Skimmer* by Crébillon. It wasn't indecent books that particularly attracted me, certainly not at all at first. Later on too, I would dream about walking through stalls of old bookstores to which I had never been. For decades I spent many Saturdays among second-hand books, collecting a variety of them and could probably even now spend hours in this way with feelings of pleasure and guilt caused by the expense for books I would never read. And again I become uneasy at the thought that curiosity displaced onto books, the "Material in the resistance" (p. 5), the evasion or escape into literature, turned into my profession. But it also comes to mind that in my second analysis, as a graduate student, Ernst Kris, my analyst, took me to task because of the very sense of guilt (including self-reproaches of a Germanist for being in that corner of academia) which I experienced, for instance at Stechert's Bookstore in Greenwich Village, when I found Hettner's *History of Literature in the 18th Century*, and bought it. For this kind of indulgence, he thought, was quite legitimate, especially when compared to other, more questionable gratifications of impulse in which I suppressed all sense of guilt.

Anna Freud's opinion that I displaced my jealousy onto plans for the future of my father, Thesi, A.F., and so on, seems likewise convincing; particularly so, as my solicitude or constant concern for the future greatness of those I loved had assumed a compulsive character. Nor would I deny her contention that my fear of my father was displaced onto fear of death or the fear that he or I would have to die before either of us would have become famous. And yet I doubt that this was the only root of my fear of death. For it is a distinguishing characteristic of man that he is the animal that knows of the inevitability of death.

About Phase II ("Breakthrough to Spontaneous Communication") (pp. 5–15)

Again the focus is on greatness and smallness, glory and shame, being a genius and being a pig, but also on mind and body, purity and filth; and the increasing confessions move to the worst of all, the confession of the most embarrassing, humiliating, threatening, "piggishly" lustful compulsion.

Associations

The phase starts (p. 5) with my "worry about Thesi's profession" as a governess, and her future. My arguments, I thought, had "impressed" her (a word that elicited stylistic reproof from my language-conscious father); yet Thesi bore me out, decades later, by claiming I had been the architect of her profession and fame, even though A.F. had explained to her that my exacting concern for her stemmed merely from my concern with myself. Behind this theme and the argument about one of my mother's favorite expressions, lies the question: How does one "impress" Mem? And in the face of the separation of my parents (during my fourth year) which was denied yet known to me, there was always the appeasing response: "In a way Mem loves me as much as Hans" (p. 4, footnote 1). Sad irony: For what was the worth of such equal love, since she had left him as well as me! The accompanying piece of paper with its increasing and decreasing groups of musical notes suggests a play on the question, how many people I could count on: the three of the intact family; or the four (including my stillborn sibling of whom, however, I had no conscious knowledge at the time)? Or were there even six or eight: the men and the women my parents would choose as partners, and so on, ad infinitum!? As a result, however, only two are left: Thesi and I; or even only one (the quarter note): I—*solus ipse*. And from below a sad "shock-headed" *Struwelpeter* or naughty boy with mouth turned downward, watches it all, sadly, out of empty eyes; and this same fellow also has cause to worry whether he won't be laughed at.

Then follow the dirty words, beginning with a reversal of the dignified *Grosspapa* (grandpa) into *Graspopo* (grass-ass), a pun much favored by aunt Gabi; and followed by vulgar expressions, which fascinated me, as I was accustomed to a more refined conversational tone. Anticipating things to come, there is even an allusion, via Wedekind's play *Lulu*, to fantasies of a savagely orgiastic sexuality, which one would later try to dismiss as "Wedekindereien," infantilisms of an author obsessed with lust and murder. And now I am, or rather the little boy is, on the defensive: "fussing," according to the analyst, for the sake of resistance, by wondering how he was supposed to address A.F. Shouldn't he use the formal "Sie" rather than the familiar "Du"? And if she called him Peter, should he dare to call her Anna, which certainly would not do. Decades later I still hesitated whether to write *"Liebe Anna Freud"*—while she wrote *"Lieber Peter,"* or rather: "Dear Anna Freud" instead of "Dear Miss Freud"; and felt relieved at the thought that the English language did not distinguish between Du and Sie.

Likewise serviceable for resistance was the observation (see pp. 5, 13) that everything is "disgusting." For it effaced the difference between the general state of affairs and specific obscenities. If everything is disgusting, oneself is no more so than the rest of the world.

The dreams too, that follow (p. 7), belong to the same circle of conflicts. The enlightened "school excursion" through the gate of the Schönbrunn park to beautiful islands and phallic trees conflicts with the dream of the conversation about Christ and the steeply downhill road, much as the conflict between sensualistic Hellenism and Greek worship of the body, which my mother liked to speak of—in conjunction with her happy love affair with Fellerer—were in conflict with the Christian condemnation of evil sensuality of which I had heard earlier, particularly from Lilli, my first governess. For this pious Catholic who took me frequently into the quietly cool church on the Karolinenplatz, apparently felt threatened by diabolically sensual temptations in our non-Christian family—as I learned decades later from a half-crazy letter she wrote to one of my uncles (see pp. 305–307). On a more primitive level, the conflict between the Greeks and Christianity was also translatable into the conflict between the impure and the pure. But who was the pure and who the pig? The Christian who condemns playing with the body as the precipitous path of sin; or the Greek who remains pure in his devotion to the senses, as my mother claimed; and might even swim naked in the *Schön-Brunn* (the "beautiful well" or source of beauty)? The dreams deal with the hope of being allowed to discover the body as such a fountain of beauty, and the fear that this might be forbidden. Or, they deal with the wish to permit myself every freedom, as I did with Adi, the gardener's son, and the other village boys in Baden, who looked into each other's behind. But then there was the fear of being killed like the squirrel on the country road which my father shot, to our horror, being provoked by my mother's doubt in his marksmanship, and—turning halfway to passive surrender—to be run over, like Bella, our great dane.

What follows are again admissions of indecent, forbidden things: of looking and being looked at in the dream about sh . . . (pp. 7–9), of peeing contests at school, playing firemen; or of ridiculous, though tormenting, compulsive games in which you had to imagine you had to cut off with a knife or with bare hands everything protruding or upright as you drove by, and that you couldn't keep up with that cutting job and got stuck, or fell behind, while the car was speeding ahead.

Those were my *associations* to the key phrase *wire fence* in the dream of Ricki (p. 7), but in the analytic game of retrospection more came to mind, actually too much; my memory became garrulous:

"Around the playground of our school was a wire fence, against which we pressed our faces, gesticulating toward the people who were sitting in the garden restaurant of the Ressl Park until our director came by and said in pompous, didactic fashion: 'Leave them unmolested!' " The Evangelical School with its firemen game, rough ways, and foul language was for the protected and somewhat pampered boy the first experience of communal vulgarity and ruthlessness in a dully brutal atmosphere. I felt miserable in the face of coarsely authoritarian, threatening, and, I thought, stupid teachers. Unaccustomed to it at home, I could not speak the heavy Viennese dialect of the other boys who thought me merely snobbish. Every other word of theirs seemed to be "shit" or "lick my ass." In their own estimate, this made them appear quick witted and grown-up; but I was numbed by this monotonous use of filthy language as well as by their pushy, grasping, rude, and brazen manners. And so I was tired all the time, though I held my own by virtue of my readiness to fight and my high opinion of myself. And yet there were always boys like Pollak (p. 7) whom I could beat up once in a while, but could not prevent from insulting me, which he did by calling me a filthy-rich pig of a Jew. Neither could I prevent him holding against me the poverty of his unemployed father, which shamed me all the more as I considered this reproach to be somehow justified. I became even more helpless, though, vis-à-vis the streetwise, or the true street urchins who knew how to operate in a savage, raw, wide open world. I grew conscious now of my sheltered state as vulnerability and weakness, especially since the others,

294

thrashing about with coarse words and deeds, I thought, were surely in the majority. I heard it said that the Viennese were vulgar folk, and felt I could not be like them. But at the same time, I think, I was also disturbed and attracted by the idea that only a little below the surface, I was myself a vulgar Viennese.

On the way to school, a walk of fifteen minutes, accompanied by Tilly, the maid, or by Thesi, later alone, dawdling, sauntering, I sometimes bought honey cakes, or Manner wafers (not often, my father kept me on a tight rein with a small allowance, being extremely thrifty both as a matter of principle and by inclination, especially when it came to small expenses). And I began to acquire the habit of being late, which subsequently also served to build up petty guilt, especially when, on my way home I made a detour to accompany my girl-friend Lydia to her house first.

The compulsion to cut (p. 9), however, belonged to another sphere: when I was driven in the red or cocoa-colored, long, low Lancia by our chauffeur or my father, and was in an uncanny way "above the masses."

Such were the thoughts coming to mind, and in these associations, too, the issue is one of "high" and "low" status. Yet it seems to me that these retrospective recollections were singularly in tune with the circumstances, thoughts, and feelings of my childhood and the child analysis also in that they only served to postpone the confession of the worst. And worry or fear of confession was also in the dream-associations concerning the movie-wonder-dog, Rin-Tin-Tin (p. 9), a kindred spirit to me, both as poor dog and boy wonder. For in that dream I denied the wish for a giant *Spitz* (peak, prick), and I was similarly bent on denial in the dream about being run over by a train (p. 9), in which the forbidden games with Mädi met with a terrible punishment. For I conclude with the consoling thought that doing the forbidden will not cost me my life.

Finally, however, the *confessions* themselves come through (pp. 9, 13):

> "Tells me how he likes going to public toilets!" (p. 9)
> "(form [of communication]: writing)" (p. 13)
> "wants to kiss me" (p. 9)

followed by (see notes, pp. 9, 13, 119):

" 'gifted boy,'
read outside [the office]
would like to know about other children" (p. 9) and:
"reaction to confessions," (p. 13)
"reads to me poems for four days: Chinese Flute" (p. 119)
" 'doesn't want to know anything' " (p. 9)

Associations

"Wants to kiss me": as if, in the exuberance of liberating disclosure
and in its euphoric aftermath "the strictures of convention," as in
Schiller's Ode to Joy, were now to be abolished.

After humiliation, exposure, breakthrough to the wish to kiss,
follows as a reaction, a sense of shame, and, to support the faltering
ego, a flattering remark which I overheard or which I accorded to
myself, as if I were a grown-up speaking of myself as a "gifted boy."
What did I read outside? Perhaps A.F.'s schedule in which I figured
along with Bob, Tinky, Ernsti, and the other children of whom I
wanted to know whether they too had such terrible wishes, desires, and
compulsions as going to public toilets, and were therefore as piggish as
I. Reading, connected with not wanting to know indicates again a
flight into literature: poetry as embellishment and evasion, averting the
glance from the lower sphere to the higher: a retreat, in exhaustion,
after self-surrender and self-revelation, the great confession which
even in retrospect appears to me as something quite monstrous,
perhaps because this complex had to play its part over and over again,
even if in different forms and shapes. I decide to refrain from further
associations touching upon the "Chinese Flute," jade palace mirrored
in water, in poetry set to music by Mahler, and verses about death, via
"playing the flute" = masturbation and the image of an exhibitionistic
episode. "Doesn't want to know anything": one can empathize with
him, also with the fact that he wonders whether she whom he wanted
to kiss, still cared for him at all.

And so it goes on in a similar vein: There is the odd contrast between
shame in private and shamelessness in public toilets; the fact that a boy
who admits hanging about disreputable places in aimless lust cannot
bring himself to pronounce the "anal words" (p. 11). But breaking
through ineffectual shame, preferably connected with a sense of

danger, will turn into a fascinating game and compulsion, so that the never-assuaged guilt feelings and the avid need for punishment should not be short-changed.

The entire turn to a lower sphere has become, among other things, a habitual response, already well rehearsed, to being abandoned by the departing mother. It is a retreat to a safe position of defeat, the role of the loser to whom nothing can happen because he is at the bottom already, stuck in the dirt, and need not pay attention to time any longer, enjoying the abysmal advantages of infamy, behaving as he thinks the street kids do, and "bad" boys like Basti and the pale, handsome Ighino (p. 11).

And again A.F. notes incapacity to "verbalize" the "unspeakable" and the resort, instead, to writing it down, followed by periods of "literary" resistance (p. 15). Even at that time writing must have meant to me being permitted to say things which otherwise had to remain unsaid, a mode of confession, self-description, exhibition, and self-judgment.

The dreams reported in this phase now elicit associations which link up with the associations from a distant past, possibly only to maintain a fiction of identity.

In the dream of the war (p. 11), the lines "It's war, alas, it's war,/ and I desire to bear no guilt for it," were favorite verses of my father, who, like some other left-wing literati (though he otherwise preferred prose) had a predilection for a few very simple and beautiful poems by Matthias Claudius, on the moon rising over misty woods, and on the astonishing condition of man, "mysteriously conceived and nourished by woman." As for having seen him "naked" in the bathtub (p. 11), I still recall the scene which, on that morning, it seems to me, was attended also by Mr. Urban, the masseur. The penis, small and short, or possibly foreshortened, floated upward, which Dr. Kris in my second analysis understood to be counter to the force of gravity and therefore indicative of an erection, whereas, according to my memory, given the fairly low water level in the tub and the position of the man, it would seem quite feasible that the member in question could have approached the surface even in its relaxed condition. It is a moot point and will remain unsolved for all eternity. The position of "big Germany" vis-à-vis "little Austria" (p. 11), with feelings against and fear of Germany, was a frequent topic of discussion in my father's circle which observed the rise of the Nazis with concern. From the retrospective view of a Jewish emigrant, the identification of my father with "big Germany," as a kind of Goliath, might appear as an insult, though, given the context of the time, this need not have been so intended, because Germany was also admired in some respects by the grown-ups around me. Both of my parents went frequently to Berlin; they thought the theater exemplary. In leftist circles too there was sympathy and always appreciation for Germany coupled with skepticism vis-à-vis small Austria with its inflated, oversized hydrocephalic Vienna, which became increasingly petty, abstruse, and provincial.

Anna Freud interprets P.'s compulsion as compulsion to compare himself to the father, and derives it from the wish to take away the "big one" from the father in order to have it oneself; hence the fear of him, the ceaseless "measuring" of adults; the guilt feelings and fear of death as punishment for a criminal wish. But there was also in reality a lot of talk about war. Again and again my father told in a stereotyped fashion about the weeks he had spent at his observation post for the artillery in the snowy mountains above Rovereto; about the screams of the wounded who could not be rescued because they lay in the line of fire; about the cook, shot on the latrine, the first dead man he had seen, killed, absurdly, during a most harmless activity. But he also talked about the fact that the war had made a man of him; and that, at the end of the last war, the returning noncommissioned soldiers and workers tore the insignia off the officers' lapels. And there was also talk about the threat of war to come, much as I now also recall my sudden fit of weeping when, as refugees in London, we heard the announcement of the outbreak of World War II over the radio.

(Another, later *association* and postscript to the German–Austrian dream: My second marriage was to a German—hence to my "father"?—whose name, Chris, as my second analyst Kris remarked, was identical in sound with his own. In a poem I compared her somewhat grandiosely to a pageboy on horseback crossing the blade of her sword with mine: "boy and girl in one." And thus I came, as close as humanly possible, to my ideal: joining father and mother.)

On the Dream of Gabi (pp. 11, 15): *Associations*

The railroad station from which my mother used to leave was the junction for traffic between Austria and Germany. It was thus the junction at which the question was asked as to who was bigger. It became also, complementary to public toilets, a place of mythic–dramatic dimensions, though, to be sure, of "romantic" and tragic emotions. Indeed, in later years, we did not dare any more to accompany each other to railroad stations to say farewell. Did the comparison between Austria and Germany lead to further comparisons between my mother's lover in Austria, the architect, and her lover in Germany even at that early period? *Moncalm* comes to mind now, meaning: my calm, the peace my parents "owed" me, but never gave me. Finally, what role was played by Mädi's mother, Gabi, famous for her frivolity? She gave my father the key to her apartment, of which he made no use, and told me decades later that she and her second husband had a window made in the ceiling of her bedroom through which he could observe her having intercourse with other men, notably prominent actors and musicians. Thus, she engaged in a promiscuity of which I perhaps began to dream already at that time (taking it as a sign of being a truly great adult) and continued to dream in somewhat painful ways later on, with that larmoyant Austrian sensuality, in which lascivious promiscuity, tortured sentimental guilt feelings, and a melancholy sense of the futility of occasionally pleasurable gratifications coexist rather inconsequentially.

On the Dream of the Parkkeeper (pp. 13, 15)

The woman doctor = A.F.? The parkkeeper is not to be found in the dream, but appears in the associations, and provides a ready link to its interpretation: all will be permitted; there will be no guard any longer. And thus another bridge is formed to what I probably thought at the time; namely, that Socrates, I had heard, did not write down anything, yet took his place in history as a very great man. Given our cult of literature and writing as the royal road to immortality, this impressed me with a prospect of a new freedom in which everything could be obtained for nothing, or without effort: for instance, immortality without written works, precisely because everything is permitted. However, in retrospect these thoughts rather seem to lead away from the statement in the dream that my grandmother will hang herself; and thus to cover up death once again with erotic interests. Carrying out an intention nursed for years, she really did take her life, not seven weeks but approximately seven years later; and not by hanging herself but with sleeping pills she had saved up, just as later on my mother did, as the daughter of a suicide condemned to suicide. Had Mem mentioned her mother's threatened intention? Did the association with the suicide of Socrates (his voluntary death by refusing to flee was often understood as such) point after all to the other freedom, the freedom of death? Given A.F.'s avoidance of that topic, it is hardly a coincidence that her interpretation of this dream went somewhat astray.

A.F. notes: "Transference: wants to touch me, have for best girl friend (I shall let him do everything: dream of parkkeeper)" (p. 15.) Touching, animal warmth, physical motherliness were out of question. The impression of puritanical distance remains; as well as the suspicion that she who had insight into other people had little insight into their relationship to her, or was not quite capable of guiding such a relationship.

The "half-heartedly and reluctantly" given promise (p. 15) of the boy to behave decently during the summer vacation brings back the memory of the fear with regard to such promises. For I was only too aware of the fact that they aroused the impulse to desecrate and violate them. And this is also why I half feared A.F.'s cathartic, purifying influence. From an excess of purity sprang the wish to throw oneself back into dirt. Promises given for the sake of someone else or in a moment of moral euphoria, inspired by the wish to will at last only the good, gave rise too easily to a sense of constraint or the compulsion and the wish to put one over on himself and the other. In brief, it was the appeal of the forbidden which I mitigated or sought to mitigate by not promising too solemnly or firmly.

My *letter* (footnote 6, p. 14) contains a truth about my love relationship to A.F. and its disappointment, and perhaps, more generally, about the emotional tie to the analyst provoked in analysis and deemed necessary. It is easily said that the feeling of being in love aroused in analysis should be used as a vehicle and managed reasonably. A love manageable in this fashion would have to be either of a very inferior or else of a very superior and rare kind. Therapy may play a dangerous game with passion even when it does no more than erode the capability for passionate engagement and self-surrender.

About Phase III ("Fear and Competition.
Rivalry Mixed with Homosexual Stirrings")

I will try to retrace the line of interpretation of this *phase* which A.F. describes as "Fear and competition; rivalry mixed with homosexual stirrings" (p. 33). What is at issue is once more the wish to be big and fear of defeat; competition and the prohibition to compete. A turning point is described in the dream in which P. no longer wishes to be David slaying Goliath but rather attempts to slay the David in himself (p. 19), in order to be defeated; that is, to be passive, to let himself go, to wallow in dirt, and to want to be run over by his father.

The same dilemma is treated in connection with the dream of the officer (pp. 17ff) as a choice between begging and dying, where dying is said to mean being killed by the father, "begging" equals "scoundrel, public toilets, rivalry, homosexuality" (p. 33). However, it seems to me A.F. confuses crucial elements: The demonizing, sexualizing, or romanticizing of poverty à la Prince and Pauper seems characteristic for sheltered upper middle-class children like P. To be a ne'er-do-well seemed easy to me. In my second analysis, too, after emigration, there was the sense of safety in being defeated or in degradation. The association of poverty is with libertinage, self-indulgence, and exemption from all fear because nothing worse could happen to you; in short, the advantages of infamy seemed evident to me. In the dream, however, I do not choose the easier, "safer" way of self-neglect, wallowing in dirt and degeneration, but the nobler, more terrifying death; and as a reward I get a happy end. For this is how it seems to me now, even though the toy pistol resolves everything into a mere joke.

The monotonous concern with greatness pervades also the "Screaming dream about the castle moat" (p. 19), and I am wondering now what would have become of me without this lifelong preoccupation which was surely more expendable than I ever dared to think. In any case it establishes a continuity between the child and the old man. The worry about being great and grown-up connected with the dream of the "emperors" of Greifenstein is implicit also in remarks concerning the excursion during which one shouldn't talk about grown-up topics with other children. Even in retrospect I am annoyed at the solicitous dampening of the spirit of precocious intellectual superiority and uncommon talent, and I recall that not a single line by me, the would-be poet, was ever printed in the school paper at the B-R School. The mediocre ever want to mediocritize; to foster "democratically" feeble talents and to hold back the strongest. The gifted, which means in the present context the one who wants to become "great," has to defend himself against an unsettling tendency (often merely the mask of envy) to put in doubt his very claim to intellectual initiative.

In the associations regarding the reversal of the David–Goliath relation (pp. 19ff) which summarizes the dilemma about greatness, I accuse my father of putting me down, outsmarting himself by way of overly clever analyses, a psychology of suspicion (which was, indeed, characteristic of him). A little later (p. 23) there is a similar reproach leveled against my mother for demeaning criticism in connection with incidents involving rowing and a boy, Heinerle. For she trained me to swim long distances, rowing in front of me at a speed just fast enough to make it impossible for me to catch up with the boat when I wanted to; and she praised other boys, rather pointedly I thought, such as Heinerle, or the natural intelligence of my practical-minded cousin (as opposed to my book learning). She had a way of being sharply sarcastic, speaking in a low voice, and occasionally being exceedingly offensive, as, for instance, when she later said about my second wife that I would have found someone of "better quality" had I stayed in Europe, and the like.

My associations then and now seem to be accusing my parents and all the world for unjust criticism, holding me down, not allowing me to be "great," or truly grown-up.

By contrast, the *sexual enlightenment* by A.F. (p. 23) following the long overdue talk with my father, who enlightened me finally about the "parental *separation*" (p. 33) did appear to offer me an opportunity to take a step forward in the process of maturation. Although my parents separated when I was four years old, the implausible appearance of union was maintained for more than half a decade by all concerned, including the child who could not admit his knowledge to himself. Hypocrisy of this kind was and continues to be characteristic especially of liberal–progressive families in which supposedly "everything" is being discussed "openly" and with a great show of sincerity. But it was not only this enlightenment that I was resisting. For after A.F. had told me about sexual intercourse I put the newly gained information on ice by denying that my father could do any such thing (p. 119). Even earlier, my mother had, in fact, tried to enlighten me somewhat. For after little Reinhard Simmel, son of a Berlin analyst, had told her that it was "high time" for her "to educate her son about sex," she had described the business to me, with flowers, wind, and pollen, in a rather veiled fashion, which I did not retain. And even my immediate reaction to A.F.'s more determined effort at sexual enlightenment (p. 23) suggests to me some unconscious defense, akin to the way I recently told an astonished surgeon after a rather unsuccessful operation that it had "really been worth while."

Yet the satisfaction with the sense of sexual enlightenment did belong to a process of growing up. At the same time, one wonders whether such sexual enlightenment, including the intellectual interest it aroused, did not serve also to cover up the true emotional turmoil of the triangular situation, and a deep insecurity; and was thus subservient to another maneuver of displacement into an explicitly sexual sphere. In turn, to be sure, sexuality itself would then play a role of its own even to a point where one hardly knew any more whether one was to be *"ein Mandel oder Weibel,"* boy or girl, male or female. With regard to A.F.'s entry: *A shift from castration anxiety to wish for castration* (p. 33) formulations such as "radical ambivalence" or "paranoid notions of bisexuality" occur to me now as involuntary self-diagnosis, perhaps also because I dealt with these themes recently in an essay on bisexuality.

Concerning the "dream of the chestnut tree" (pp. 23–25), dealing with competition with my friend Victor as to who was the bigger or more grown-up, I noted in 1978 that he confirmed our "competition for Tinky," and, later on, in fishing. Staying with us at our house in the summer resort at Grundlsee, he presented us with a trout he claimed to have caught himself. I was consumed with envy, until he admitted that he bought it, as it was proper for a guest to bring a gift. He bet I would not jump off a boulder into the water fully dressed in leather pants and shirt. I jumped in; whereupon he said: "I wouldn't have thought you were that stupid." He and Mikey B. race on bicycles, timing themselves with a stopwatch. I want to do the same. My time is so much worse that I suspect them of cheating. Later on I find him enviable in his elegance, self-assurance, witty arrogance, while I am both hesitant and arrogant in a timid way. It satisfies me that his literary ambitions are not fully realized. It disturbs me that he makes more money than I, and achieves a brilliant position. We are in our fifties: my daughter Anne finds our constant competing insufferable. On a recent visit, he lent me his fishing rod and benevolently took me to places where he could give me an opportunity to get a better catch than he. And thus this early competition has continued over decades as the accompaniment to a most durable friendship.

In my child analysis the competition for greatness is invariably considered as competition with the father. "Peter's dream of the little bag" (pp. 27–29) likewise deals with growing up to be a man, the refusal of mere children's books (such as *Little Lord Fauntleroy*, recommended by A.F., or Josephine Siebe's *Kasperle*). For I want books that show I am big, a big man. And yet in retrospect, my associations become again ambiguous or bisexual. The rustic game in which men holding little paper sacks in hands clasped behind their backs, swinging them and challenging girls with candles to set their bags afire, was played at our home by our fat Hungarian cook who wiggled her behind shouting: "Set fire to my tail!" which neither Tilly nor I were able to do with our matches.

Another game is part of the interpretation of "Peter's dream about fleeing" (pp. 25–27): The first to see a man with a full beard has to shout "beaver" in order to win. Anna Freud connects this beaver game and the cutting or castration complex (p. 27). The interpretation of the dream revolves around the wish to cut off the father's penis, because mother lets him drive his machine (car) into her gate. Anna Freud notes (p. 27): He (P.) "confirms" (*bestätigt*), then crosses out "confirms," writes "says" "that he is especially fond of his father right now"; that is, she interprets my increased affection for my father as a confirmation of subliminally negative feelings. The emphatically positive veils a negative impulse. Perhaps so. Yet, in retrospect, it occurs to me that if practiced with tactless consistency, this kind of exegesis would indeed lead into a chaos of ambivalence or the mutual annihilation of the positive by the negative, the negative by the positive. And this consideration, temptation, or fear, which is characteristic for me, and for our age, appears here as another variation on the ambivalent wavering between an active and a passive role.

About Phase IV ("Return of the Mother")
(pp. 33–41)

After the relation to the father and the male has been considered, the relation to mother and women is being reviewed: first under the aspect of anger (the song of horrible Memka, the threat against A.F. with the knife (p. 35), reminding me of the story of a sex murderer, entitled

"Myself Revealed," which I wrote as a young man; then under the heading of the conflict between A.F. and Mem (pp. 41, 47) which I did not invent since A.F., it seems to me, reciprocated my mother's unquestionable antipathy, though she did not, of course, admit this in the analysis.

The history of my relationship to my mother and to mother surrogates at that time here speaks for itself.

Associations

Eye anxiety (pp. 35, 41). My fear of getting my pupils pierced corresponded to what my first governess, Lilli, did to her eyes in a photograph where she "did not like herself." As I mentioned above, she was a pious Catholic, a fair-haired girl from the countryside, who once gave me a beating and locked me in the servants' toilet because I had been bad in the Belvedere. Later on, I came to associate this, vaguely, with the screaming at night, the frightening places in the apartment, and, perhaps, also with a scene I can't place (though I may have observed it) in which a woman (on a beach or in the dunes) bends over the lap of a sooty tramp to take his hard white penis into her mouth, or else (in a corner of the upper Belvedere?) simply watches him masturbate, or does it for him with her own hand. As for Lilli, whose association with these images remains vague (she is certainly not the dark-haired woman on the beach), decades after her employment with us, on July 2, 1968, she sent a letter and parcel to the Heller firm in Vienna requesting that the enclosed handbag be returned to Stephen, that uncle of mine whom I hated most cordially because he had once been too curious about, and too friendly with, my mother. Lilli's letter reads as follows:

> Dear Madam Secretary;
> I courteously request that you give this red handbag to Mr. Stephen Heller or his relatives. It was not a hostile present to me, but a Christmas gift which he gave me in the presence of Mrs. Grete Heller, the mother of my little charge, Peterle, in whose house I was for close to seven years in the capacity of governess and kindergarten teacher, until 1928. I would appreciate it if the bag remained within the circle of relatives of Mr. S.H. Mirror and purse have become unusable.—I do not want to burn the bag, nor give it away. Nor leave it behind with my estate so that after my death nobody will speak unjustly or impurely about either of us.

When he entered the nursery for a brief visit, together with Mrs. Grete Heller, Mr. Stephen Heller's conduct toward me was very noble. I could look back upon my past with more satisfaction if all fat young gentlemen had behaved toward me in as distinguished a way as Mr. Stephen Heller.

The bag was once lined in red, and some colorblind person might have seen a diabolic combination of colors in it. Not so I. The pure white nickel of the handle and, likewise, the white nickel and white pure glass of the inner lining wove the angelic white lilly color into it. I carried the bag with a little paper and a note written on both sides which I left in the nickel powder box. This is because I wish to live as a virgin and therefore *nobody* may *secretly* mix love-potions into my food which are of exceedingly diabolic origin. Neither Aphrodite's diabolic love potion nor Jewish love potion. Possibly it was a colorblind woman who years ago shouted up to my window: I should give the bag away, a queen would offer me a handbag with silver lining. I do not know where I should have gone to get that bag. Also it would have been an insult to Mr. Stephen Heller, who never insulted me. Mrs. Heller gave me a mother of pearl rosary and a mother of pearl Saint George's medal which she brought back from Jerusalem as a gift for me because the child was in my sole care during the parents' absence. These two pieces I can leave to my relatives in my will. When Mrs. Grete Heller was moved by a pious, pure spirit she frequently sang the song: *Auf dem Berge da wehet der Wind* (On the mountain blows the wind). That was the spirit in which I brought up the child Peterle and experienced many a beautiful hour.

One year after I had taken leave from the family of Dr. Hans Heller, I had to run a few errands in Vienna's inner city (First District). There three Jewish boys behaved very unpleasantly and conspicuously, yelling at passersby. However, I did not have time to look at their faces more closely, because I had to catch a train.

Some time later I had the same experience once more. Now I took a close look at the children's faces, but none of them had the features of my former charge, Peter. I was overjoyed. Also, I could not imagine anyone would let a boy brought up painstakingly with the help of a concerned mother and *ennobled* through education, run around in town like a savage in the company of saucy classmates, boys and girls; without supervision so that he would end up by being summoned to the juvenile court *(Fürsorgegericht)* * along with anyone in charge of his education (educators = parents, being coresponsible, included). Some

---

*How far extends God's omnipotence? How great is God's omnipotence? How great the power of the educational milieu? The power of the educators?

people would have rejoiced over the child's misfortune; only I would not. Not I who treated him like her own child. A choleric temperament by nature. A choleric nature, difficult to tame, especially at an early age (infancy). One is simply not prepared for various contingencies and events that occur, suddenly, out of the blue, with a child of such temperament. One is faced with a riddle.

May I ask courteously to have Mr. Stephen Heller read this letter. I do not request an answer. I am giving you an address in care of general delivery, because I have an aged sickly sister who does not want me to receive letters even from my relatives. I live with her. She is a housewife.

Thanking you in advance for your trouble.

Faithfully yours
Virgin Miss K. Karolina [Lilli K.]

Lilli K.'s question concerning the relative powers of God and of educators now seems all the more justified to me, as it does not preclude the possibility of a certain limitation being imposed on divine omnipotence through the interference of educational personnel. Interesting also are the "choleric" disposition, temper tantrums, which occurred then, and occasionally up to this time. Lilli and I could still pray together: Lord! What a handiwork is man! The letter was forwarded to me by my father with the remark: "The combination of intelligence and mental disturbance is fascinating."

On: Wide Awake Screaming, "Young Pig" (p. 35), *"Repetition of the Original Hurt"* (p. 41): *Associations*

End of August 1978, Grundlsee: the water is greenish-blue today, and there is a feeling of autumn, as blue haze envelopes the dark, rounded Ressen mountain with its dense forests rising up straight across from our house. Only it is not our house any more. Again I recall how Thesi two years ago responded to my hint at remaining inner difficulties: "As they said in Grundlsee: Once a pig always a pig." How could I help being offended by her remark as a child! For a half-truth or even a whole truth is always more offensive than invention; and they all felt they had justice on their side against me. Later I thought they had made too much of the separation of my parents and above all of my being abandoned by my mother. Yet children, in such cases, did almost always stay with their mothers; and though she gave reasons for having left me in my father's care, the fact remained: she had abandoned the "young pig." What good was all the psychoanalytic talk about whether this had happened, as I apparently suspected, because I had "masturbated like a pig," or for any other reason! All reasons became pretenses, what remained was the emptiness: abandonment, being forsaken. Though at the same time an intense, almost passionate love relationship was maintained by the very same mother who did not renounce her claim altogether, by staying away permanently, but preserved her son for herself and herself for him by sudden return visits at three- or six-month intervals terminating in wrenching departures with a maximal expenditure of inner turmoil and an inflated sense of tragedy. Am I being too harsh? In later years, after my divorce, when I did not see my daughter for several years, I failed in the opposite direction from my mother's and perhaps caused greater damage through continued absence and indifference. As for my mother's behavior, I think in retrospect that it corresponded also to something of which she was to become fully conscious only later on, namely a hatred of men which she seemed to have taken over from her mother who herself hated her husband, and partly developed on her own, especially in her relationship with her own father. And indeed, Leopold, in turn, did not seem particularly fond of his daughter or to respect her, insofar as one could infer this from his festively solemn or serenely pompous manner. Decades later, in a depressive, half-mad state, the deepest inner truth came to light when, couched in the rhetorical suada of the women's liberation movement, she would engage in endless denunciation of the tyranny, stupidity, brutality, incapacity for love, and viciousness of her father, her lover of many years, her two husbands, and, indeed, of men in general.

Where was one safe: with one's father, who perhaps was guided only by his own greed for power, or with a mother, who hated him and all men, including me, her son? I see her with my mind's eye now, as I saw her for the last time, at night, at the New York airport, walking in the spotlight toward the huge shadow of the airliner that was to take her back to Switzerland, her no-man's- and nowhere-land, and to the suicide which she had been planning for so long. She was a woman on the threshold of old age, abandoned by her second husband, and by her only son after an unsuccessful attempt at living with us in the United States. And I can still hear her say (in a pitying, disparaging, tenderly disdainful tone of voice) that I was a good boy. A good boy? This was the last time she left me, not without guilt or blame on my part, and the final repetition of the initial injury, hers even more than mine, which she was destined or compelled to reenact until her self-annihilation.

About Phase V ("Transference to Tinky") (pp. 41–45)

Returning to my manuscript I am wondering whether a scrap with scribbles and the words *blotch on the ass* refers to the "dream of the pig wallowing in mire," and again I find it embarrassing and ridiculous to produce this kind of antiliterature. What would the Viennese critic Karl Kraus have said to that? Or a respectable German citizen? How could I justify, or rather reconcile, to my own satisfaction this painstaking collection of unattractive, pettily intimate details, this plaintive and smug attention to self, with the fact that only a few years after this child analysis millions of my kind were murdered in Nazi factories of death? But even though I do not know *how* or whether these things fit together, I do know that they do coexist, like tragedy and sniffles, earthquake and indigestion. And the aesthetic objections of respectable folk who might as easily be neurotics themselves as they might be healthy, reality oriented, and job conscious instruments of genocide, or its neurotic or healthy victims, should bother me as little as the posturing of critical *arbitri elegantiarum* in a realm of words defined by conventions of literary propriety. For my present labor I have to follow the psychic realities and nothing else, to the extent possible for me, and must not allow my own cowardice and conventionality to intimidate me, which, to be sure, is more easily said than done.

I remember the atmosphere of the Christmas vacation of 1930—I was nearly eleven then—in the winter resort of Breitenstein (p. 41): the walks in the snow; the peasant boys teasing and insulting me; skiing, which I loved above all; and writing in the snow—not "LTT," as A.F. has it (standing, possibly, for love-theater-Tinky [*Liebes-Theater-Tinky*], that is: my dramatizing of my love affair), but "PLH," which stood for "Peter's-love-hatred." And I recall the talks with confidants, who were at the same time rivals, carried on with a false friendliness, a thin veneer barely covering the hostility against me, the boaster who made himself ridiculous. Reinhard, always in his speckled, dark brown and beige sweater, snot-nosed and snotty, debunking my pretensions in his Berlin manner, was actually rather well meaning but despised me nonetheless for the affected and tormented comedy of love which I performed. Victor kept or feigned ironic distance, while I, overzealously and obtrusively, criticized myself in the service of self-exhibition and self-damage, analyzed the sympathies and antipathies of all concerned, and bothered Margot—the governess of the Burlinghams, who was in charge of us—in a spoiled, fretful, half-angry, half-lamenting or miserable manner with my moods and fits, knowing full well that it was her job to cope with us. I had worked myself up to a fever. The others went to the Christmas celebration, but I lay upstairs in my room with its dark wooden paneling, in bed, in keeping with the requirements of my romance of love spurned.

And now I am compelled to imagine again a fictitious German reader or an Austrian of my generation, disgusted by this account of the children of the wealthy going on vacation, these Americans, this Jewish boy who fifty years later still takes his little woes so seriously while people like us— Ah yes: prepared for the conquest of the world! However, the determination to do great deeds and to inflict great woes was hardly more productive than the dwelling on little difficulties; and there is consequently no need to justify oneself to an imaginary protagonist of pseudo-health or Nazi-syntonic criticism. And yet it is I myself who brought up this "Nazi criticism" of myself. And perhaps there is something to it, insofar as a private filigree is examined here under a magnifying glass, ambivalently, caught up in bourgeois egocentricity. While in other spheres of reality poverty and misery prevailed, mass movements exercised and provoked compulsion, violence, and harsh discipline aiming at goals, which, to be sure, were no less crazy and no less influenced by self-destructive tendencies than what is manifested here in minute repetition compulsions and self-tortures.

Are the above reflections, more than half a century after the events concerned, still turning around the theme of self-punishment out of a sense of guilt? Anna Freud derives this guilt-feeling from masturbation (though this is denied by the cunning child [pp. 43, 45] who claims that numb friction yielding scarcely a feeling and no forbidden pleasure should not be considered "bad"). Apparently, the "Nazi" who just now appeared in my thoughts to condemn me as a soft decadent rich boy and Jew was the imaginary agent of self-punishment. And thus, it does seem that I am repeating, fifty years later and on a lesser scale, the very pattern enacted at Breitenstein, in the repetition of failure with mother, which I transferred to Tinky, to bring myself to the point of half-faked despair, with rivals and being unloved and harming myself in the eyes of the beloved—all made to order. For all this was done, at least in part, to stage a self-judgment and to satisfy an unsatiated sense of guilt in a suitably distressing and painfully embarrassing manner.

Anna Freud's characterization of my early love for Tinky is, nonetheless, too harsh. The girl, with her fairylike charm who kept escaping me, came to be and remained closer to me than A.F.'s term *Verzettelung* (distraction, dissipation, waste of time) would allow. What is the status of such judgments anyway! Unlike the repetition of the initial tragedy of abandonment, the transference of affection from a hopeless love-object like the mother who abandoned me, to a less hopeless one could hardly be considered objectionable per se. The love affair, it seems, proved a distraction above all in terms of the therapy on which the primary interest of the therapist was focused. But love affairs, even when they are childish, juvenile, and silly, have a worth of their own, and appear even in retrospect mostly as the kind of distraction or "waste of time" that one doesn't really regret and would not want to have missed.

About Phase VI ("Masturbation")
[p. 123; see pp. 45–83]

Preliminary Remarks

The full title of this phase, which I find particularly distasteful, reads: "Masturbation as discharge of oedipal excitement" (p. 83). Decades later I had the notion that a fellowship already confirmed by a government agency would not come through because they knew that I was a "piggish sort of a man," and called them to be reassured that everything was all right. How tenacious this insatiable guilt-feeling is! Again I wonder whether some perverse velleities of mine did not merely serve to feed it so that the guilt feelings would no longer be the consequence of certain semifantasies but the latter would rather serve the purpose of maintaining a sense of guilt. Someone once claimed that I thrive on my bad conscience. Similarly this guilty conscience was said in my child analysis (see pp. 43, 45) to hold masturbation responsible for my mother's leaving. But the guilt feeling had still other functions. It could provide or rather impute a reason to everything that happens. It could eliminate the merely accidental, and, above all, make failures and renunciations palatable. And so there would not only be the possibility of evasion into semiperverse sexualization but also evasion by way of the mobilization of guilt feelings capable of rationalizing and exploiting whatever might happen to the individual as well-deserved punishment. Everything in this world would seem to be in order, albeit in oppressive and painful ways, at the same time satisfying a masochistic need.

Associations: Dream of the Wallowing Pig (p. 45)

Anal-paranoid? The pig remains my favorite animal: "dirt-love" as *character indelibilis*? And later, satirical imagination of a society ritualizing collective defecation, making it a cultural occasion, as we do eating, which they, however, would desocialize as a low private matter. And the incessant questioning seems also anally compulsive.

Concerning the fear of the peasant boys: "Struggle in the snow": they come running, throw snowballs, threaten, challenge me to fights, and I cannot fight them (though I am sure that I could throw them into the snow because I am stronger than they), and my fear of them is compounded by a Prince and Pauper complex, as if one was not allowed to defend himself against the common people, the poor, and had become an outcast and contemptible due to one's privileged status. Whinily anxious I react, half-faking it or playing at it, in the role of the "cowardly Jew." I see myself on a snowy path, skis on my shoulders, trudging along in a sweat, helplessly anxious, tears in my eyes, trembling inwardly in front of these boys who tease me during the winter vacation. Yet I play and fight in Grundlsee in the summers with the same kind. Anna Freud notes (p. 83): "Fear of peasant boys (homosex.)," and finally (p. 121): "Fear of peasant boys [changes] into active behavior [toward] boys, homosex[uality]." She considered the fear and the wish to get rid of the cowardliness as preliminary stage of attraction: The fear of the seductive or of seduction is projected onto the boys who appear as persecutors. Later, in puberty, it was, indeed a peasant boy (he looked like a young Bacchus or melancholy Antinous, with hazy brown eyes) with whom I briefly fell in love. Draped in a blue bathrobe we played together on a veranda over the lake, for hours on end. And similarly, at an earlier stage (see p. 45) there was the fear of inviting children, allegedly because Thesi would scold us for the mess we would make, but in reality to avoid the temptation to join in intimate play.

Fighting of a different sort is again at issue in the following: as a dispute for and against Freud's antireligious perspective in his "Future of an Illusion"[1]; as fight with Tinky, A.F. thought, by speaking disparagingly about her nephew Ernest, although I think this was meant rather to hurt A.F. herself. Finally, as conflict between A.F. and Mem, and as discord I invented between A.F. and my father by claiming that she disliked him too (pp. 47, 67). The "dream of Herod's hall" (p. 47), which seemed at first strange, then prophetic to me, makes me now think, contrary to tradition, that he had the boys killed because they had done something forbidden (as I thought I had). I thought of Herod—mistakenly—only as King of the Jews, rather than his being also their enemy, and I had an inkling of the murderous antisemitism which was rapidly gaining ground. The woman with the blue train is an angel of death. The discussion of socialism, anxiously taken back right away, also points to a forbidden sphere ("not that—"). For socialism would do away with rich manufacturers like my father, in spite of his socialist opinions. And perhaps this too is a reference to National "Socialism," though, to be sure, these are belated interpretations; ex post facto, from hindsight.

In the associations to the "dream of candy" (made by my father in his factory) (p. 47) condensations seem to occur similar in meaning to me as my conception of Herod as both Jewish king and child-persecutor. Again the figure of an enemy is constructed out of apparently contradictory material: a combination of the father with the persecutor of Jews, Hitler, the "housepainter with a barber's face," in analogy also to the dream of the battle between Germany (father) and little Austria (me) (p. 11); and I find the same duplicity also in the reading of Goethe's *Prometheus* hymn (p. 47) directed against the celestial father, which was at the same time a favorite poem of my father's.

In the series of drawings which follow (see Figures 1.4A to 1.4J), I am, of course, the harmless, pensive pilgrim (Figure 1.4A) who is hardly troubled by the awkward, scrawled jumping-jack hanged man

---

[1]Freud, S. (1927), The future of an illusion. *Standard Edition*, 21:1–9. London: Hogarth Press, 1961.

who I am also. On the reverse side (Figure 1.4B) a coffin, a lizard, semen with d-shaped tails, a round candy with a black spot in the center (graffiti symbol for vagina), a penis rearing up and bulbous testicles, all represent the conception of P.H. in "Vienna," with the syllable "Hel" relating to both hell and light. I appear only floating over the lizard's body as a ghost-child, who also follows, on the next sheet (Figure 1.4C) the strange virago or man-woman in twilight breezes, just as the ghost-child in the white shirt followed me in the hallway of our apartment. On the next sheet (Figures 1.4E, 1.4F) the upper and the lower spheres separate. The seraph and the host of angels who look quite dull belong above; the condemned man with the penislike tongue (as if swallowing a penis) belongs to the nether world; and so does, probably, the man between the angry woman in the upper region and the jolly devil (Figure 1.4G); but certainly the powerful villain with plumed hat, a truly imposing fiend of hell (Figure 1.4H). In Figure 1.4I the woman (my mother, also the woman in twilight breezes) stands before God and a heavenly tribunal to bring charges against the man on whom she has evidently squealed to the angels. He must be my father, I suppose (the dream of the yellow candy signified, according to A.F., that he had stolen her penis [p. 47]); or I, the all-too-innocent, all-too-pious pilgrim. At issue in all these instances is the reason why my mother left my father and me; that is, the guilt of men, of my father, of myself. Are all of us guilty, or only he, or only me? Seen in this perspective the thoughts about heaven and the heavenly tribunal only pass on the question of guilt to a higher authority.

One more association occurs to me to all these arguments and accusations: The fear of intimacy so evident in the fear of the peasant boys (with the idea of throwing them into the snow, like man and woman) or the fear of inviting children, is less obvious in the half-imaginary *conflicts attributed to the grown-ups*, notably *between A.F. and Mem* from which the others are mere derivatives. To be sure, the two governesses, the shy Viennese Thesi and the brash Berliner Margot of the Burlinghams, were not particularly fond of each other. Nor was there any marked cordiality between my parents and Dorothy Burlingham. My erotically restless, lively, unrealistic, avant-garde, financially dependent mother and antimother, and the aristocratically desiccated, wealthy, puritanical Dorothy, who was a conscientious and caring mother, were clearly opposite types.

But A.F. was right. The imaginary conflicts were my own, and the fear of seduction did arise, in part, from my being undecided about whom I wanted to tempt or seduce me. If I shifted to A.F. and was seduced by her in a sublime way, I betrayed and abandoned my mother. And I was also afraid to leave the plump and cozy Thesi though she appeared plain and less attractive to me than Margot, who was closer to the revered Burlingham children, more bold and impertinent, and told funnily confusing, risqué, if unappetizing stories. For instance, she told how she and some other young girls drank actor Moissi's bathwater hoping to find a hair of his in the tub, found one, put it on a slice of bread, and ate it. My parents seemed to have proven themselves to be "bad," especially my mother, who left me in spite of her turbulent love for me, while my father, though attentive to me, looked around for other women. Who then, did I want to be with most? And didn't I often want to shift altogether to the other family, the Burlinghams and their reliably present Mother?

However, the relatively harmless explanations of my fear of temptation and seduction as a consequence of my indecision and fear of being unfaithful to my own folks do not suffice. As I thought that my parents' separation occurred as a result of my own mysterious sexual transgressions, I also thought myself the cause of other conflicts and even suspected myself of a mysteriously vicious, cold capability to cause conflicts everywhere, between A.F. and Mem, Thesi and Margot, my parents and Dorothy. And why would I do this if not because I *wanted* to cause these conflicts? I myself was the guilty devil, the wild villain, fiend of the underworld, the tough guy with the broad shoulders (for which my mother always praised me) and the hat with the Mephistophelian swashbuckling feather.

Yes, I was, I am the devil whose capacities for negation and disintegration, based on the guilt of his own misdeeds, empower him to sow strife and discord all around him. However, while the idea of such devilish power in me to cause conflict amounts to a glorification of my notions of guilt, another aspect emerges from the fact that temptation and sexual play were always close to conflict for me. For quarreling or fighting presented itself to me also as an expression of sexual union; that is, sexual interaction or intercourse appeared to me always in the form of strife (conflict, struggle, quarreling). Thus what is brought to light here would be not only fear of temptation but also participation in it.

In the case of the fear of inviting children (p. 45) quarreling appears only marginally in the notion that Thesi would be angry and scold me because of the mess we would make. In the fear of the peasant boys it is explicit as fear of fighting or wrestling; that is, doing what appeared to me as specifically sexual. In the imaginary conflicts (Mem–A.F., Thesi–Margot, parents–Dorothy [p. 67]) fighting itself is the theme. The fantasy that they were fighting with one another contains the temptation itself or the acting out of the temptation. To be sure, the whole delusion, as may befit a delusion, appears illogical in its structure. For the defensive "projection"—the fantasy of the fighting pairs—which occurred as a result of the fear of temptation appears to be, at the same time, a partial fulfillment of that very temptation; namely, through watching what the fighting pairs are doing to one another.

Associations: Resistance, Blinking, Reading Catalogs (p. 67)

Blinking makes me think of a later, somewhat unintelligible poem of mine on the letter G, dedicated to the inventor of this letter, one Spurius Carvilius Ruga, who also introduced the institution of divorce in ancient Rome. Abounding with Gs (Grand Hotel, Goethe, goose, and gullet-cutting cut-throats, Guglhupf and gonorrhea) it describes a wealthy crook (gray bird's claw/ circled by gold rings; ruddy gray pigment, glistening, redolent of Eau de Cologne), a speculator, and his yellowish rimless blink—vaguely connected to an uncle of mine, the associate and enemy of my father, who in fact considered him to be cowardly clever and crooked. In short, the blinking crook, the enemy of my father, is I.

And then, "after much urging" (p. 67), that is, on the part of A.F. again in writing, for writing is the form in which one can confess, surrender, say the unspeakable, I finally admit to the "harmless" form of masturbation (p. 67): the play with the penis which doesn't excite much feeling, as if it were anesthetized, but in which it can be smelled. The shame because of smelly feet, which gave me trouble as a boy, is understood as resulting from the displacement of feelings of shame and guilt caused by masturbation. On a sheet of paper the drawing of a clown with rings under his eyes and a wide mouth is placed next to the words *because of smelling*, and the penis which could be smelled at the indentation between the glans and the shaft where there was sometimes a small accumulation of excreted whitish matter. Also the "hole in the stocking" (p. 86, footnote 46) bringing the naked foot in contact with the shoe belongs here. As an older man one cannot help thinking: was there really so much to be so very ashamed of? And yet in coming to the daydream (?) of the dogs, where one of the protecting dogs is against me (p. 67), I do understand why that dog could very well be A.F., the analyst, who forced me to admit so many embarrassing things.

I include here also the unnumbered drawing in which a grim-looking woman strides along with something floating in front of her that does look like a cut-off penis (Figure 1.4K). Who is this stern virago? Tinky's mother, Dorothy? Anna Freud? Or all the grim women, the dogs, the bitches who are against me though they protect me? Or does this woman belong to the dream of Wolf (p. 67) with the interpretation: " The penis will jump out (fall off), then he is a woman," much as one feared of masturbation ("jerking off") that it would emasculate you? Finally, the interpretation of Peter's advances to Tinky (reaching down with the hand) as an attempt to spoil his relationship with her emphasizes again guilt or a need for guilt, and for repeating the trauma of separation, the prototypical pattern initiated in the relationship with mother; namely, offending the beloved by sexual transgression and being abandoned as a consequence.

The atmosphere changes with the hour overshadowed by the death of A.F.'s relative (p. 73), Tom Seidmann-Freud, the illustrator and author of uniquely original and attractive childrens' books. Characteristically, the things which can only be expressed in writing include not only embarrassingly "low" or humiliating matters of the nether world, but also those that are embarrassing in a sublime or holy or "higher" sense, such as condolences; and hence the oblong roundish shapes on the added paper of February 10 (Figure 1.5A, p. 72, footnote 34), which elsewhere signify semen, stand here for tears. On the same sheet the words *dignified tone of voice* suggest worry about finding that tone proper to the occasion, and even the handwriting on that page looks to me now as if couched in an attitude of mourning.

In connection with death, the theme of religion reappears (p. 73), in which A.F. took no interest. Later on I tried to settle it in a radically atheistic manner; then, together with the rebellion against psychoanalysis, I went in the opposite direction, and ran the risk of claiming more faith than I had a right to. This in turn moved me once more to assume an attitude more favorable to atheism. Yet I did this without ever again abandoning in principle the affirmation of God, though that word left me uneasy, as it seemed to bring in its wake so much that was impossible to believe in. And even here and now, in formulating this banal statement, the writing of it serves to touch on a sensitive nerve, the confession of the embarrassingly essential.

Again and again I am concerned here with "high" and "low" spheres, the genuine and the phony or artificial, the pure and the impure. My mother criticized me for not being genuinely myself, but imitating the Burlinghams. Absurdly, I turned this around, claiming that she, who was utterly unlike the Burlinghams, also imitated them. But my real objection to the artificiality of some of her self-stylizations, which I often felt so strongly, I never wanted to admit even to myself. The juxtaposition in my mind between purity and impurity or "high" and "low" spheres, is illustrated by the juxtaposition in a sequence of drawings and scribblings of 1) the heavenly host and 2) farting ("passed a sound") and obscenity ("You can tickle me in the ass") (see pp. 73ff, and p. 78, footnote 36). And my concern with my relation to the pure is also expressed in the fear of having to love Tinky's older sister Mabbie (p. 79), a grown-up, responsible and superior model pupil (we teased her with this) who represented to me an all too good—or goody-goody?—sphere of virtue.

But perhaps I myself am at this point turning into a model child in analysis, through collusion of the wishes of the patient with those of the therapist, by confirming all too obligingly the *disappearance of the fear of the boys* through insight into its irreality. I certainly did want to transform or rather overcome my fear of them by the wish to arouse their admiration for my skiing (see p. 79); but I doubt that I really succeeded in this at the time. I noted as current associations: Further modifications of the paranoid delusions of reference? The wish to be admired by the boys, in turn, also leads to the tendency toward exhibitionism as an attempt to overcome anxiety; which fits later episodes of play with hostility to transform it into its opposite, but also to provoke it masochistically.

About the End of Phase VI

In retrospect it seems to me that in this phase the boy I was "winds" his way between and around everything and everybody in a triple sense (not quite convincing in English paraphrase) of twisting one's way around everyone, passing wind, and being a windbag. He feels attraction and fear everywhere—with peasant boys, other children, the analyst, his mother, the governesses who substitute for her, his father. Attracted to and fearful of everyone, he neither wants to fight nor to side with anyone wholeheartedly, and retreats into sexual fantasies of which he is frightened at the same time. Characteristically, the discharge of the excitation through masturbation serves as means of "abreaction" to get rid of fear, but equally for the benefit of anxiety, to create a cause or reason for it, as masturbation itself leads to fear; for example, of becoming a "lame uncle" (pp. 79, 81).

That dream is charged with aggression. After her separation from my father, my mother occupied an apartment in her parents' house which, in this dream, displays the nameplate on its door reading "lame uncle" instead of "Dr. Heller," as my father was called. Evidently, *he* is the lame uncle who could not keep his wife. Did I hear of someone being a "lame uncle"? There was always talk of impotence, and at times, impotence had been one of my father's problems.[2] The theme of the dream is failure with women. Did I fear the same fate? And did I want to show in the "dream of the masseur" (p. 81) that I would not be a lame uncle as I walked toward him with an erection? What is at issue here are fantasies of failure, castration, or punishment for forbidden masturbation which serve simultaneously to show off, to

[2]As he himself (see John Heller, *Memoirs of a Reluctant Capitalist* (New York: Abaris Books, 1983, p. 44) states: ". . analysis did not cure my neurosis," he observes, "I admit, however, that it was only by means of analysis that I was able to begin to overcome my fear of impotence. But what about Gretl? I was able to function well enough to my own satisfaction; but not, I think, to hers. And there lies the root of the failure of our marriage." My father's analysis with Ludwig Jekels started some years earlier than mine: I do not know exactly when. Nor can I say when the theme of impotence was more or less clearly or consciously associated by me with my father. There was a lot of talk about sex and impotence in my childhood, on the part of my mother as well as of Inge, my father's second wife, and among the Grundlsee crowd. I recall in particular my mother talking about a left-wing sculptor-friend of my father and her, who was said to suffer from impotence, wherefore his wife had begun an affair with a "potent proletarian"; and since this talk (which puzzled me) is associated in my memory with the dining room in our Viennese apartment in the Karolinengasse, from which we moved away in the early thirties, it presumably dates back to the period of my analysis with A.F., but I am not sure to which year. The questions this theme raises, must be left largely unanswered. I have no doubt, though, that, as the dream of the lame uncle suggests, I did associate "impotence" somehow with my mother's leaving my father and me.

prove, and to damage oneself. (And so I had an ugly fight with my [second] wife after finishing my work on Phase VI, and though we have had other fights during four decades of marriage, this too, it seems, was due to a repetition of old motifs and miseries which are still somehow capable of being activated.)

About Phase VII: Relation to Father

The topic of this phase is treated by A.F. in terms of fear of and inclination toward homosexuality, which was already implicit in the dream in which I denied myself the role of a young David fighting against a Goliathlike father (p. 19).

Associations, Memories

The alleged infantile notion of intercourse (p. 85), alien and unpleasant as it is, evokes thoughts of "periods of flatulence" as possible, later "relic," and the suggestion of a connection between this notion and the "windy" *Zobeltitz project* (p. 83). I see myself writing on sidewalks with chalk, imagine myself affixing posters to pillars, and, as a painter, painting *Zobeltitz* on gigantic walls, though I never put such ambitious projects into practice. What is evident is the proximity to mass movements which manifested themselves with proclamations, insignia, shouting and smearing of names and "brown" slogans (Heil Hitler!) onto walls. The grotesque idea, however dimly perceived by me, was to build on nothing to the greater glory of nothingness. For the declaration of allegiance to a mere word—akin to the alleged "centrality" of language—is the emptiest form of nihilism. Anna Freud's untranslatable slip of the pen—"Ansprechen auf der Sprache"—substituting language (*Sprache*) for street (*Strasse*), an accosting of or speaking to strangers on the thoroughfare of speech, is to the point. And it does seem to me now that there is an essential similarity between such empty, quasi-Dadaistic or absurdist, nihilistic wit (a sterile sense of humor pretending to inflate to gigantic importance the near nothingness of a name) and the faddishly refined poststructuralistic metacriticism which currently proposes to reduce all literature to an autonomous verbal web or network, a kind of Zobeltitz project without reference to anything beyond it. My resentment of this movement (as distinct from the reasons for my opposition to it) may well be due, at least in part, to the fact that the tendency toward sterile nihilism and aggressively sterile games, which are also akin to some forms of homosexuality, always held some seductive attraction for me. Yet these are again rather far-flung speculations on the connections between now and then. According to my retrospective associations the "dream of the coal" (pp. 85, 87) contains a justification for my father's actions. For in "purchasing" seducers (coal deliverers), Mem also purchased, earned, or deserved the kilometers; namely, my father frightening her by speeding. Mem got involved with men; so he had to say to himself: If she buys coals (seducers), then it's every man for himself; and finally, had to turn his back on her. And thus my current chain of associations meets again with A.F.'s interpretations. However, though the *sauve qui peut* leads to a fear for my father's well-being, it may well be that I also wanted something to happen to *him*, since he too had abandoned me. Again and again, while describing the world of my feelings and thoughts, I discover how uncertain and shaky all these relations were, and how easily, even in the associations to a dream, fear, affection, and aversion could shift their reference between mother and father. And thus I am led to think: this was truly a child who did not quite know where to turn.

Associations to the Dream of the Pond With the Frogs (pp. 87ff)

Tinky said that Peter Blos took a shower in the nude in front of her: *bloss* = naked, showing himself. The principal idea is this: The snake attacks; that is, one is made into a woman castrated by the father, the man with the snake, or else one must have been a woman (i.e., castrated already), in order to be attacked by the snake. Anna Freud too sees this (p. 89) as a kind of double bind ("castration" both as consequence and as prerequisite).

Associations to the Dream of the Train and the Episode in Cannes (p. 87)

Some of us were in the train, others were not. The train seemed to start moving. I was afraid we would be separated and could not continue the journey together. Only out of fear of staying alone with father? The memory of Cannes is also the memory of sewers emptying into the ocean, big round fecal sausages floating up and down the Côte d'Azur—which bothered me less than it did the adults. In the morning

I went down by myself to the veranda of the hotel, ordered café au lait, s'il vous plait, and felt or hoped my parents on the balcony above were watching me prove myself a man of the world. Then one had to go down to the desolate beach, build something in the sand when you didn't feel like it; and once my father lifted me up and held me high against the sky.

The mood was oppressive, tormented, not just because of the dirt on this elegant coast, or its emptiness. The journey—two or three years after their initial separation—was a last experiment of my parents to be together. The fear of remaining alone either in the train, separated from my father, or on the platform, separated from Mem and my governess, stood for the fear of my parents' renewed rift which was merely patched up for the present occasion.

This same trip to Cannes when I was six or seven led to my first literary effort. I wanted to record it, to hold on to it in the shape of a laboriously typed travelogue. Later on, too, it was the problematic or unpleasant experiences which would move me to endeavors as a writer.

The fear of missing departures, or of departure "by mistake," also stayed with me. How easily someone might be caught on a train: Seeing off a friend, entering the compartment, he would be forced to jump off or ride along when the train had started to move! And similarly there was the fear of being late, of barely missing or barely catching a train as it started. This happened to my young cousin, Tommy, and me in 1938 (I was eighteen then) in a critical situation when, leaving Hitler's Austria as refugees, with all we had in two trunks, on a train from Vienna to Paris, we got out for breakfast at the Salzburg station—I showing off, assuring my cousin nonchalantly we had plenty of time—and saw the train move and ran for it. Luckily the conductor opened the door of the last wagon lit, and we were able to leap and climb in. Moreover, as mentioned above, through the frequent arrivals and departures of my mother, railroad stations had taken on an aura of excitingly traumatic or fateful significance. But, oddly enough, my father was subject to a neurotic anxiety about departures and arrivals to a far higher degree than I, so that he was always too early, never tolerated standing in line, and took excessive precautions in all his travel arrangements.

The relationship to father and thus to homosexuality remains unfinished business; the fact that nothing follows after A.F.'s note "result of Phase VII" (p. 89; see p. 88, footnote 51) thus takes on symbolic meaning. Regarding the fear of departures, another memory comes to mind. When, as a little boy, I traveled alone to Berlin to see my mother, my father ran for a little stretch alongside the slowly starting train, which excited me terribly, as if he could end up running all way and so come with me. Further associations lead to homosexual opportunities in railroad stations, and generally to the recollection that centers of traffic are usually connected with possibilities for intercourse of every kind. Travelers cannot be stopped or stayed.

Associations

After working on Phase VII, an annoying fantasy that I am a woman with black silk stockings, spreading her thighs. Unresolved, unfulfilled homosexuality, like Schreber, extending to paranoia? An emotional and erotically sexual relationship to men, a real love affair, would always have been impossible for me, as distinct from (rare) sexual experiments, or from friendships in the ordinary sense of the word, and the experience of occasional fleeting, adolescent, playfully amorous flirtations in puberty. Passivity and activity, ambivalent indecisiveness, the oscillations, which a friend of mine considered characteristic of me, between *neque-neque and et-et* (the neither-nor and the as-well-as), I sublimated, perhaps, into academic fence-sitting, the ambivalently engaged or voyeuristically disengaged neutrality of the academic writer. And thinking about that, I say to myself: "You are such a scoundrel that even if you could sublimate yourself into martyrdom for a wholly worthy cause, you would savor, in dying, the applause of the angels; and indeed: this very thought itself, which satisfies a greedy ethical masochism. Weird saint! But that too is exaggerated, a self-dramatization. You are enjoying yourself, aren't you, as much as you can? You are no saint at all, nor all that weird—"

Postscript to "Relation to Father" (August, 1978)

After many years I am again in Grundlsee, the summer place of my youth. I spoke of my parents to old acquaintances and questioned them. "You will dream a lot here," L. said. "People dream a lot here." The following night I had two dreams:

1. I am driving with my father. He complains that I can't drive, that I drive badly, until I say: "The hell with you. How can I drive if you

323

keep bugging me!" I tell him that he unsettles me, makes me insecure. Then I am sorry to have scolded him that much. A gap. And now *he* drives, and somehow all is blue around us and ahead of us. He puts his arm around my shoulder. I almost believe he understood that my anger at him was really a request, my way of asking him to do this. Everything is sublime, almost as if we were merely two triangles floating in air. We are, we exist, only high above. I feel very happy. At last. Almost too happy. I awake with the feeling that this was a dream of pure wish fulfillment such as are usually given only to children. Now I recall that L. said: "Is your father still so mean to you?" alluding to his selling "my" house in Grundlsee decades ago, which, though it was not "mine" at all, I thought at the time I would "never forgive" him for. Dark matter, black and base, enters from "below": murder, death (the thought that he will die soon, he is in his eighties). And now, as if in mockery, words from his last letter: "The love of my family sustains me, helps me over the horror of getting to be eighty-two years old." The all-too-idyllic covers up such darkness by excessively serene elevation: "we exist . . . only above," in the upper sphere. With the blue color in the dream I associate the blue texture from which a knucklebone, a white and rose-colored piece of flesh peeps out like a bit of penis out of blue pants. I think to myself: "So you dream of being fucked by father *and* of killing him? Would that be the consummation, the fulfillment dreamed of by this kind of dreamer?" And I recall that I have had the feeling of my "kindness" and my guilt in and around the dream from the start.

2. After having made a note of the first dream, I have another dream: We are at home again in the States. My wife tidies up the very bright apartment (but it's the one I had in New York decades ago during my first marriage). I say to her: "Don't busy yourself with so much tidying up; be with me instead." After the second dream it occurs to me that I evidently also want the woman (as I wanted the man, the father in the first), and, incidentally, that I really was angry because it seemed to me that my wife did not occupy herself enough with me.

And now, relating to both (1) and (2): My former fear of driving = that someone will hurt me (bump into my car) from behind; that only a "real man" can drive well. One doesn't want to be a man, is afraid to be a man, is not allowed to be a man. Only the father is, who always drove so fast in his Lancia, too fast for my mother on our trips through Switzerland (in the same year as that stay in Cannes), when I began to write. For writing and being unable to drive or being driven belong together. Not wanting to be a man but instead to embrace and to be embraced by the father in the heavenly azure, that is one dream. The other, however, is about wanting to be a man, giving orders to the woman: Take care of me, and to be young at the same time, as we were when we had the apartment of my first marriage, where I lived (later on) with my second wife. In short, to have two wives, as seems to be quite the custom here in Austria, according to friend Victor (the same who appears in the child analysis).

So I want both to be no man at all *and* doubly a man. It is ironical that my old friend, Mumi, to whom I showed part of the present work, thought that I, unlike the children of today, though a neurotic little boy, did know limits. With the bisexual fantasy that includes everything, I am surely an extreme case of wanting to eat my cake and have it. I want everything, especially the mutually exclusive advantages. And yet my predilection for interpretation testifies also to a radical tendency to self-abasement and self-destructive self-criticism; and thus, perhaps to a consciousness of limits after all. For we differ from one another not so much by subliminal or manifest fantasies as by the way we control them or yield to them. But even this consideration is by no means conclusive. For it is that very self-criticism with its moral pretensions which may, in turn, be all too heavenly blue as well. Behind and beneath it lies darkness, like the dark universe beyond the blue sky: the dark eye of space watching in silence this entire spectacle as it rises up and gets entangled, dual in gender or opposition, a syzygy, only to consume itself in the end. A melancholy thought? But that is the way it appears to be; and presumably what matters is how the cadences, the rearing, and the receding are enacted.

Among other things, the sky-blue dream is one of a relationship without a "lower" sphere, and therefore too happy and too good to be true. At the same time both my father and I are, in the dream, two floating triangles; that is, triangles hovering between male and female. He too, as he appears to me in this context, has experienced this bipolarity, as indecisiveness and ambivalence toward man and woman, being married and living with me, or rather his two sons,[3] as conflict: wanting the woman and not wanting her, seeing her as a blessing and

---

[3]His second son, Marc, by his third wife, Helen, and myself.

a curse so that the ambivalent relationship to the woman may be counterbalanced in him too by an inclination toward men.

Enough! Now that I have left behind the retrospective immersion into stages associated with anxiety about masturbation, the attraction of the homosexual, and the fear of homosexual seduction, the worst, it seems to me, is over. The next phase brings a decisive turn from homosexuality to the opposite sex, leads to the high point of the analysis, and the prelude to the termination of what A.F. considered the core of the therapy, insofar as she divided it into phases. That thought relieves me. For in becoming engrossed in this material, the self reexperiences every phase of the child analysis, or at least of the child that continues to live on in the man.

About the First Part of Phase VIII (Attempt to Seduce A.F.)

Attached to the original of A.F.'s notes of March 6 (p. 89), there is a piece of paper (described on p. 88, footnote 52) with two figures constructed out of four letters and musical notes plus a bass clef, and the confession, connected with music in the low register, "I made some air behind just now" (p. 89). All this serves to confirm the anal part of A.F.'s interpretation: ". . . he made a twofold attempt to seduce me, at first *genitally*, then *anally*" (p. 89). Her gradation (genital, anal, spiritual; p. 91; *"geistig"* meaning mental, intellectual, as well as spiritual) is illustrated in the summaries of this phase (show penis, dirty competition, literary activity; see pp. 99, 123). Since the attempt at genital seduction does not succeed, the anal one (wind) follows regressively, and after both fail, there is an attempt to compensate by using impulses on an intellectual plane—reading aloud Meyer's ballad "The Feet in the Fire," which had already at an earlier session led back from the genital to the anal realm via reference to castration anxiety (feet = penis). It is an odd gradation or progression, though, leading, as it does from the higher to the lower sphere, then back to a higher sphere in which much can be utilized but nothing in the primitive yearnings can be satisfied. The apocalyptic poem "The Storm Roars" (p. 91; p. 90, footnote 53) probably can also be considered a confirmation of A.F.'s interpretation. The storm brings about the triumph of the small (leaf) over the big (tree), but in an overall landscape of gloomy destruction which intimates that too striking a triumph of the little one over the big ones is not permitted, after all, and thus suggests a pessimism born of faintheartedness. It seems to me, however, that a sense of threat also comes from the larger context of the times, which, incidentally, also put its imprint on the subsequent games of the two boys who, simultaneously serious and frivolous, alternated between reading Tolstoy's story "Strider" with tears in their eyes and spitting from the window with the aim of hitting the heads of the passersby.

The dirty masturbation fantasy in Cannes (pp. 93, 99) makes me think that in the place of my parents' last crisis, two attempts of mine to master calamity were begun; namely writing it down and sexualization (the attempt to make something excitingly pleasant out of catastrophes and evil by way of regression into the "lower" sphere, the dirty, obscene, disreputable, and forbidden).

The passionate love for A.F. reaches its first culmination point here, intervenes everywhere and mobilizes everything.

About the Second Part of Phase VIII (Solutions)

Forgetting the Enlightenment About Love (see pp. 99, 101)

It often goes with analysis as it does in Kafka's aphorism of the path in autumn—no sooner is it swept clean than the falling leaves will cover it again. All that remains is a sense of vague memory about insights which cannot be maintained at the surface. Moreover, an enlightenment as encompassing and perfect as the one concerning twofold love from above and from below and the preceding outburst—for the two belong together—leaves, so to speak, no remainder, and is so complete in its way that it, in turn, induces forgetting.

Associations

The dream that "Peter doesn't have a chance" (p. 101) is reminiscent of the above-mentioned earliest story of mine: the hare valiantly trying to leap out of the trap only to fall back again, because he really hasn't got a chance (see pp. 287f).

Associations to April 1 (p. 103). This entry reminds me of the previous sexual enlightenment (pp. 23, 33). Again I have the impression that A.F. was astonished about the fact that a neutral description of sexual intercourse should not have had an exciting effect. Nor, it seems to me now, did she understand that my appreciation of the discrete way in which she speaks of my parents is based on my own tacitly negative opinion (partly shared by them) that they failed me.

To the *"solutions"* offered in the second part of Phase VIII (p. 105) the following should be added.

Concerning Fear of the Football, Ego Restriction, Ego Expansion, and the Ideal of Integration, or Love from Above and Below

In chapter 8 of her book on *The Ego and the Mechanisms of Defense* (1936; revised edition, 1971[4]), Anna Freud cites the dream of Sigurd to exemplify restriction of the ego. She writes:

It would be a mistake to suppose that such restrictions are imposed on the ego only for the purpose of avoiding the unpleasure ensuing from a realization of inferiority to others, i.e., from disappointment and discouragement. In the analysis of a ten-year-old boy I observed such restriction of activity take place, as a transitory symptom, for the purpose of avoiding immediate objective anxiety. But this child had the opposite reason for his anxiety. During a certain phase in his analysis he developed into a brilliant football player. His prowess was recognized by the big boys at his school and to his great delight they let him join their games, although he was much younger than they. Before long, he reported the following dream. He was playing football and a big boy kicked the ball with such force that my patient had to jump over it in order not to be hit. He awoke with feelings of anxiety. The interpretation of the dream showed that his pride in associating with the big boys had soon turned into anxiety. He was afraid that they might be jealous of his play and become aggressive towards him. The situation which he himself had created by being so good at games and which had at first been a source of pleasure had now become a source of anxiety. The same theme reappeared soon afterwards in a phantasy which he had when going to sleep. He thought he saw the other boys trying to knock his feet off with a large football. It came hurtling towards him and he jerked his feet up in bed in order to save them. We had already found out in this little boy's analysis that the feet had a peculiar significance for him. By the roundabout way of olfactory impressions and the ideas of stiffness and lameness they had come to represent the penis. The dream and the

[4]Freud, A. (1936), *The Ego and the Mechanisms of Defense*. New York: International Universities Press, 1966.

phantasy checked his passion for games. His skill diminished and he soon lost the admiration which it had won for him at school. The meaning of this retreat was, "There's no need for you to knock my feet off, for anyhow I am no good at games now."

But the process did not end with the restriction of his ego in one direction. When he gave up games, he suddenly developed quite another side of his powers, namely, a bent which he had always had for literature and for writing compositions of his own. He used to read me poems, some of which he composed himself, and he brought me short stories, written when he was only seven, and made ambitious plans for a literary career. The footballer was transformed into an author. During one of the analytic sessions at this point he made a graph to show his attitude to the various masculine professions and hobbies. In the middle was a large thick point, which stood for literature, and in a circle round it were the different sciences, while the practical callings were indicated by more remote points. In one of the top corners of the page, close to the edge, there was a tiny little point. This stood for sport, which but a short time ago had occupied such a large place in his mind. The little point was meant to indicate the supreme contempt which he now felt for games. It was instructive to see how, in a few days' time, by a process resembling rationalization his conscious evaluation of various activities had been influenced by his anxiety. His literary achievements at this time were really astonishing. When he ceased to be good at games, a gap was left in the functioning of his ego and this was filled by a superabundance of production in another direction. As we should expect, analysis showed that a reactivation of his rivalry with his father was responsible for his acute anxiety at the thought that the bigger boys might revenge themselves upon him [pp. 98–100].

In the analysis, however, there is little discussion of all this. Why? Anna Freud herself emphasizes the difference between neurotic inhibition and restriction of the ego:

. . . A person suffering from a neurotic inihibition is defending himself against the translation into action of some prohibited instinctual impulse, i.e., against the liberation of unpleasure, through some internal danger. Even when, as in phobias, the anxiety and the defense seem to relate to the outside world, he is really afraid of his own inner processes. . . . In ego restriction, on the other hand, disagreeable external impressions in the present are warded off, because they might result in the revival of similar impressions from the past. Reverting to our comparison between the mechanisms of repression and denial we shall say that the difference between inhibition and ego restriction is that in the former the ego is defending itself against its own inner processes and in the latter against external stimuli.

The restriction resulting from realistic anxiety (concerning a source of unpleasure or pain) is not considered a neurotic symptom and thus appears to fall outside the pale of the primary tasks of analysis.

> . . . in its pursuit of [pleasure] and its efforts to avoid [unpleasure] the ego makes what use it pleases of all its abilities. It drops the activities which liberate unpleasure or anxiety, and has no further desire to engage in them. Whole fields of interest are abandoned and, when the ego's experience has been unfortunate, it will throw all its energies into some pursuit of an entirely opposite character. We have instances of this in the little football player who took to literature and the little dancer whose disappointment led her to become a prize scholar. Of course, in these cases the ego does not create new capacities; it merely makes use of those it already possesses.
>
> As a method of avoiding unpleasure, ego restriction, like the various forms of denial, does not come under the heading of the psychology of neurosis but is a normal stage in the development of the ego. When the ego is young and plastic, its withdrawal from one field of activity is sometimes compensated for by excellence in another, upon which it concentrates. But when it has become rigid or has already acquired an intolerance of unpleasure and so is obsessionally fixated to the method of flight, such withdrawal is punished by impaired development. By abandoning one position after another it becomes one-sided, loses too many interests and can show but a meagre achievement [pp. 102ff].

Restriction of the ego is thus not without its dangers. "Such measures of defense . . . represent the infantile ego's prophylaxis of neurosis—a prophylaxis which it undertakes at its peril" (pp. 103ff). The "protective measures which it adopts," such as "flight from physical prowess to intellectual achievements," may not, in fact, save the developing ego from confrontation with demands in the very field from which it has defensively retreated. The restriction harbors the danger of impairment once the protective environment is no longer there, which allows the child to get away with such maneuvers more easily than in the unforgiving exterior world of later years.

What Anna Freud describes in the book does not coincide entirely with my memory. The game in which Sigurd throws the ball so vigorously was not soccer but a kind of dodge ball (*"Völkerball"*) in which you have a choice either to catch the ball or to avoid being touched by it, frequently by jumping (as the ball was preferably aimed at one's feet). It hurt to catch the balls thrown by Sigurd, who was anyway the most threatening of the big boys. And yet, A.F. is right. I was afraid to play too well—especially later on in the public school and in particular at soccer, to be hit in the ankles, so that I never became a good soccer player but concentrated my ambition on *Handball*, skiing, and so on. In the same way, I took up fencing instead of learning more thoroughly how to box after having been hit hard on the nose by my boxing instructor.

Moreover, in retrospect it does seem to me that the mechanism of ego restriction has been, unfortunately, somewhat characteristic of me, though it certainly did not work smoothly or without conflict for me. I accused myself almost always of cowardice and failure in the field from which I withdrew. Nonetheless, a defensive tendency to avoid a success which might endanger me, or simply, to spoil my success while somehow sparing myself, prevailed all too often. How interested I had been in politics in earlier years, only to withdraw from that field, to be sure in the wake, first, of disappointment in Russian communism and subsequently of the refugee experience of complete powerlessness and helpless dependence. Yet others sharing these experiences did not react by withdrawing from this sphere of frustration to the extent where they would hardly look at a newspaper. And perhaps even my professional academic involvement with literature could be considered the result of a restriction, or of a withdrawal from earlier notions of active aggressive intervention, leading away not from soccer but rather from the ideal of revolutionary activism and scientific curiosity to the wish to become a poet or writer, and within that field to a further retreat into academically critical and, occasionally, uncritically learned scholarly studies, into theory and mere footnotes!

Perhaps my whole life up to my sixtieth year bears the marks of a restriction of the ego, perpetuating a self-imposed immaturity or dependency. And perhaps I also included in this mechanism analysis itself which is anyway always in danger of serving the restriction of the ego by way of an excessive concentration on miseries of childhood; and has always been under suspicion of legitimizing a self-protective withdrawal from the world to contemplate one's own navel, a flight from the social domain, in favor of an egocentric concern with private spheres and the past.

However, these considerations lead on further to the problem of reflection and the achievement of awareness, or of making a given content conscious (*Bewusstmachung*). For this principal means of ego expansion serving at the same time self-monitoring and self-surveillance, may serve almost equally self-restriction and inhibition. Inevitably, I am also led back to the present task of transcribing this autobiographical study where the charge of ego restriction gets inextricably entangled in my mind with that of exhibition in the service of self-description and masochistic self-impairment.

And yet positive voices make themselves heard arguing ego expansion. Certainly, reflection inhibits; cognition is an endless screw; and he who distrusts himself in everything he does will always have reasons to continue to do so. But the very restriction discussed above, namely the retreat into literature, or the withdrawal into the academic reservation, contained and contains in itself possibilities, in turn, for expansion and advance. This may appear, for instance, in the form of an attempt to conquer new fields of interest, of gaining more freedom and a wider horizon than would be attainable by the soccer player or even the mere writer or literary man. Moreover, I must note now that by thinking within a framework of analysis, I left out value judgments which have been, after all, of decisive importance for me. For I never seriously questioned the notion or prejudice that for me at least the profession of an academic intellectual and teacher was preferable by far to that of the sportsman involved in play, or of the active profit-oriented businessman (which would have been a more obvious choice for me than politics). And I was convinced of this especially since a writing career seemed to have been blocked off by the loss of my mother tongue after age eighteen when we emigrated to English-speaking countries. Moreover, I also note that with all this indulgence in psychology, I have disregarded the fact that thinking and reading give me pleasure, and that I always had more talent for these pursuits than for sports or business. The part played by ego restriction in my motivations and choices could thus be assessed correctly only in a context with other factors.

Another theme of Phase VIII running counter to ego restriction is the soothing prospect invoked by A.F., of a love in which everything would not just come ever so nicely and sweetly "from above," excluding "low" impulses, but rather in natural and harmonious collaboration with the nether sphere (p. 99). And now it seems to me, contrary to the suspicion I just voiced regarding the present enterprise, and even though I cannot resolve this ambivalence, that my present work serves ego expansion. For it continues along the same lines as the hope of the child, never quite fulfilled, to bring together the superior and the inferior, the high and the low, and to make them one; and it does so (as most of my writings) in the hope of contributing to a just and comprehensive image of man in which neither the lower nor the higher needs would be silenced in favor of one or the other.

To be sure, such sets of opposites as high–low, superior–inferior may be empty forms to be filled over and over again. Indeed they demand to be filled in. The roles of "superior" and "inferior" are played by changing protagonists. Anal needs are considered inferior to genital ones; the merely genital inferior to those combined with tenderness; and the erotic may, on occasion, assume the lower part compared to spiritual claims. The ambivalent person's need for synthesis, the all-too-abstract games with polarities, which assume ever new dimensions, are somewhat suspect. And yet, there is a legitimate need to become aware of the simultaneity, the possible interplay, and the counterpoint of the voices from different spheres or agencies of self and mind. And at the very least, these reflections illustrate once again continuities of motifs from childhood to old age.

About the Third Part of Phase VIII (Beginning of Termination)

The theme is separation, parting, and giving up the advantages of being ill (pp. 105–111) as well as the most positive gain due to the illness, namely Anna Freud, for whose sake I wish in the dream (if her interpretation is to be trusted) that my mother should die so that *she* would be in her place (p. 107). That far I went! And yet A.F., as she suggested later, wanted me to omit and thus slight this happy episode of a boy's amorousness or rather of true love and passion, in the reconstruction of my childhood! Parting and sadness, it seems to me, are also the theme of the dream of the birds which fall dead onto the ground wrapped in flowers (pp. 107–109), an image that strikes me as mythical and mysterious, pointing to a sphere of representation and imagery which my child analysis did not acknowledge.

Associations

Decisive at this point is the threat and temptation to turn "bad" again if I were left, and at the same time the anticipation and provocation of the abandonment by being bad so that it wouldn't really seem to happen to me, instead of my being able to blame myself for having caused it or brought it about. It was one of my basic perils: this tendency to bring about adversity out of mere fear, and eventually to find pleasure in inducing misfortune, with a mixture of gratification in self-punishment, anxiously prophylactic testing of the pain and unhappiness, and a greed for catastrophe, an addiction to catastrophe, a pleasure in sharp excitation, all coupled with repetition compulsion.

And in the context of leave-taking and *loss*, the theme of losing appears quite appropriately. In the entry of April 9, 1930, *taking* stands for being a *man*, *losing* for being a *woman* (pp. 109–111). And I now recall that during a visit, around my sixtieth birthday, I lost the key to the condominium where my father and I stayed together. In my childhood I used to lose things on a large scale (a fact which is not apparent in the analysis), so that decades later, when I visited A.F. and Dorothy in Walberswick, A.F. asked: "Do you still lose so many things?" adding that I simply left behind whatever did not please me, such as, for instance, three schoolbags in a row. The above-mentioned incident notwithstanding, I have pretty much given up the habit of losing things; but not the troublesome, if lesser nuisance of worrying that I might lose things or searching for things stupidly misplaced (glasses, wallet, manuscripts, etc.) in keeping with the stereotype of the absent-minded professor. Such is the progress one makes in life.

Regarding the Fantasy of a Relationship Between Father and A.F. (p. 113)

Oddly enough my father told me decades after the analysis that his analyst, Ludwig Jekels, thought he should marry A.F. My notion therefore was not as absurd as it appears. The couple on the balcony (pp. 111–113) still touches me as something eerie, like a vision, but now of a young couple I saw over twenty years ago, on the balcony of a Frankfurt hotel. At the same time it is as if this image was conceived after a scene in Thomas Mann's *Felix Krull*: The two at night on the balcony in the radiance of youth, a symbol of the passage of time, and the spell of precarious, exhilarating high spirits, appear with deep shadows in the sockets of their sparkling eyes in floodlight, artificially illuminated from the garden and fountain below them, though there was no such garden at the Frankfurt hotel. Again, this is a mysterious image, like so many others in reported dreams and fantasies, which strikes me as if it belonged to unexplored, "mythical" or "prophetic" realms.

Concerning Entries Up to April 30 (Father's Lover) (p. 113)

Then, as later, I apparently alternated between dark, depressive and excessively light-headed or euphoric moods, wherefore the analyst Heinz Lichtenstein classified me as "cyclothymic." My rather low opinion of my father's relationship to Inge was shared, as indicated above, by most of my father's friends. My claim that he did not do *anything* with his lover, "not even kiss," which I also maintained in a conversation with my mother later on, when I feared that Inge might be pregnant and I would have a sibling, appears like a fitting commentary on the theme of precociousness; that is, its lack of homogeneity and solidity. My mother, who had already turned me, on occasion, into a kind of confidant, was utterly astonished when I told her it was unimaginable that my father would engage in an activity so unworthy of him, and replied with some consternation: "You are often so wise and insightful, and then again you speak like a small child. How can you seriously maintain something like that?" But I held to it desperately.

Regarding Tentative Termination

Bashfulness concerning private and hurtful matters prompted me to ask A.F. in writing whether she was crying on account of the severe illness of her father whose constant care was, at that time, the central concern of her life. The lack of response to this kind of question (see p. 114, footnote 74) may well have contributed to the absence of reality in the relation between her and the little boy. On the other side of the appended notepaper is the familiar wild hunter, possibly father in his deadly, dangerous form, who, though no *Freischütz*, was a passionate gentleman hunter. Among the accompanying, grotesquely pitiful figures, two stand out as mirror image: He and I? And am I also the second, sadder wild hunter? In any case, the devil is raising his head again and is obviously linked to my attempt to identify with my "bad father" through being indecent and naughty. And if matters had stopped there, perhaps something like a happy end would have been achieved.

PART 2

I. Grundlsee: Summer Vacation 1930

Associations

In connection with the mention of the missing letter from Dalmatia (p. 125), where I stayed with my mother, I recall a snapshot of myself as a boy standing naked on a cliff ready to dive into the ocean. "How handsome and slim you were then!" my mother would say appreciatively of that picture. Much as she supplied fuel to my aspiration to greatness, genius, fame, she rather reinforced voyeuristic–exhibitionistic tendencies, which also found expression in her own need for or addiction to confessions, her interest in film and indiscreet accounts of the behavior of actresses (Marlene's performance with her legs), or encounters in woods and parks. None of this, however, appeared to be in conflict with her intellectual interests, her subtle sensibility, or her ethical claims to genuineness and integrity.

And especially at Grundlsee im Kreuz, a small settlement midway along the lake, where I spent the rest of this summer and the following summers, the grown-ups indulged in a voyeuristic–exhibitionistic fashion of semipublic love affairs, dramatized promiscuity, risqué parties and playacting, and bathing in the nude. Our house on the lake shore, in the shadow of the towering, craggy Backenstein, and opposite the rounded, woody Ressen, stood next to the houses of Mädi Olden and the Bernfelds where the avant-garde of the twenties—writers, actors, painters, journalists, politicians, musicians, adventurers, scientists, physicians, and, above all, psychoanalysts of the left-wing liberal-to-radical observance—circulated on their vacations and tried to mix with the astonished, cordial, subservient, participating, profiteering natives, without ever bridging the distance to these farmers or peasant petit bourgeois whom the leftists liked to stylize as true proletarians.

I always thought of Grundlsee im Kreuz, perhaps another "bad mother" like my own, like Austria who rejected me, or Europe which I was forced to leave, as my only "homeland." That same summer of 1930, A.F. and her aging, ill father, had rented the spacious, elegantly upper middle-class *Rebenburg*, near the issue of the lake into the Traun river. It represented, whether A.F. wanted this or not, the orthodox and proper psychoanalytic establishment, guardian of convention and morality (though also suspected of cultural pessimism) vis-à-vis the clique of progressive socioutopians and sexually superfree protagonists of the psychoanalytic left *im Kreuz*. The latter were a *Kreuz*, "cross" or burden to bear for A.F., not merely in the context of my analysis, wherefore, I suppose, she committed a slip of the pen, writing *Kreuz im Grundlsee* (cross in Grundlsee) instead of *Grundlsee im Kreuz*.

About Frank and Fishing (p. 125)

Karl Frank, later known as Paul Hagen, the other, additional lover of my mother, was, in contrast to the conservative Christian Democratic architect, Fellerer, a professional revolutionary and widely appreciated ladies' man. He preached to me on my father's and my pastime of fishing, calling it sadistic–capitalist exploiters' and hunters' pastime. Hence the conflict between the pseudo-"Communist" doctrine against fishing and my mindless passion for this "murderous" pleasure and vice in which I imitated my father with feverish competitiveness.

According to A.F.'s notes, I was surprised how married couples in Grundlsee did not act as if they were in love with one another but were friendly with other men and women they didn't "really care for" (p. 127). And again I am struck by the child's unawareness of the vehemence of sexual desire and the attractive power of lust. Yet that Grundlsee "freedom" made a lasting impression on me.

In the following, A.F. gives illustrations of my *antagonism to her* nourished by the Grundlsee experience: My projected letter to her father was to say that she was famous and sought-after only because of him (a statement also made by others at the time), and that he should give her more freedom. Another form of opposition, offending against the ground rule, was to talk about analysis outside the sessions or to quote the analyst's opinion, such as A.F.'s remark about reading Dumas' *The Count of Monte Cristo*, then my favorite novel, which I did not interrupt even during meals alone at my table.

Rejection of mother's affectionate gesture "because Hans doesn't like it when she is like that with him" (p. 127). Anna Freud seems to doubt my words here. My father, however, was indeed indignant about my mother's physical tenderness toward me and called it seduction, then and later. In her attempt at interpretation A.F. only takes *my* jealousy into account. She thought and said: Instead of being jealous of my mother who became involved with the communist Frank, I was jealous of her; and in order to save myself from jealousy, I tried to justify my mother which I always felt compelled to do. For I did consider my mother guilty but didn't want to admit it; and now, as a result of the Grundlsee style, Mem's behavior seemed to be justified by fashion. Moreover, A.F. explained my renewed fear of my father by the fact that new aggression against men in general had built up in me, particularly because I was jealous of my mother's obtrusive lover, Frank, who, in a puerile kind of revenge on capitalism, tried to turn me against my father by sermonizing against the fishing capitalist. The conflict was probably sharpened by the fact that I still seemed to believe that my future profession was determined by our factory (p. 131), a thought that soon became foreign to me, even before the temporary expropriation by the Nazis.

Concerning my mother's conversation with A.F. about her relationship to Frank (pp. 127, 131). Mother tells Peter about Frank but conceals the fact that she goes to Berlin to be with him. This mixture of exhibitionistic openness and secrecy, or of modernity and convention, was peculiarly effective in transferring to children a self-dramatizing confusion as well as the incessant and incessantly thwarted attempts at clarification.

In retrospect, the memory of a girl nicknamed "The Worm" seems to me characteristic of the progressive libertinage and ideologically grounded promiscuity which made so great an impression on me. She was exceedingly pretty, well built, and graceful. I still see her naked on the beach from the lake, stepping daintily on a stony path along the shore leading into the low shrubbery near our house. She lived next door, was the lover of one of the Schrecker brothers (the philosopher and Leibniz expert? Surely not the dentist! Or, perhaps, the atonal composer?). She was considered a "simple soul," and silly, or even fairly dumb, but in an endearing way, to be respected; an "Aryan" working-class girl, of the people, who spoke the Viennese dialect. It was said of her that she had worked the streets as a prostitute. To have been a streetwalker, and to say so, as much as the fact itself, was suggestive of a prestigious disgrace. It was not designated as such, of course, as everyone was ever so progressive and enlightened, yet it could be relished in a modern matter-of-fact style, partly for its (denied) haut goût and partly because one's frankness was a proof of freedom from prejudice. Certainly, one could not admit to romanticizing the status of whores, which was to be blamed on bourgeois exploitation. And yet, by a bourgeois velleity perhaps, that status was surrounded by a certain aura; and eligible to be invested with a pseudoproletarian Käthe Kollwitz pathos.

Do such memories merely prove my frivolity and limited grasp at the time, or even now? I doubt it. These people acted out and dramatized their sexuality, and let themselves go, in order to parade their opposition to convention rather than for the sake of sexual enjoyment, though it is to be hoped that they also took pleasure in their erotic exploits. The boys, Herbert, Hartmut, as well as some adult natives, rowed out on the lake with binoculars to observe the nude sun-bathing on the beach. They also observed Bertl Bornstein (B.B.), the analyst, when she disappeared in the bottom of the rowboat with the art historian Dr. Ernst, in the course of their short-lived grand passion. B.B., incidentally, was a somewhat shapeless person with a noble Jewish profile. The professional cheeriness and a soft and gentle Polish accent with which she pronounced her psychoanalytic comments on everything and everyone somehow reinforced the certainty of her severe judgments. Her habit of stepping into our boats with her full weight, like the proverbial cow into the bucket, upsetting the fishing rods and nearly causing us to capsize, provoked my father into teasing her. And she, as I said, was the one the boys spied, as she disappeared into the bottom of the boat with her friend (who soon after became a sycophant of the Nazis), somewhere toward the middle of the lake between Im Kreuz and the darkly forested slope of the Ressen. "Why?" "Well, to you-know-what!" "No, what?" "You know nothing!" "What do you mean?" "That you can do it by yourself too." "How?" "With your hand, jerk. You rub it." "And what is it like?" "It's good. It tickles. And then it squirts." This enlightenment, for which I was indebted to one of the boys, took place near the boathouse sometime later than the season of 1930, after we had been wrestling. I had defeated my opponent (pressed both his shoulders down on the wet pebbles of the beach, according to the rules), but it proved a

Pyrrhic victory, which he more than made up for by his superior knowledge. We boys also swam, casually, as if by accident, to the solarium of the Olden house where the house guests were lying in the nude. There the fat analyst Hanns Sachs, dubbed in a bogus contest "the ugliest man of the year," spoke wittily, or "the females" merely rubbed one another down with suntan oil and "gossiped about affairs," and Mumi or "das Mummerl" taunted us, saying with harsh justice within our hearing that we swam over to get an eyeful but were too hypocritical to do so openly.

Mumi, that is, Edith Kramer, who later became a painter and therapist, the author of *Art as Therapy with Children* (New York: Schocken, 1974), was the daughter of the unhappy Peppa Kramer, who attempted suicide in Grundlsee (and later on succeeded). At the time, she was about 15 years old, terribly intelligent; and drew caricatures and posters for the festivities of the Bernfeld–Olden circle. She had already decided to become a painter and was consequently herself drawn to the visual, but reacted defensively to the flaunting of sexual freedom by isolating herself in a kind of hermit's existence. However, we communicated, as friends. Being older, she was also friends with my mother, who, in turn, talked to me about Mumi's developing breasts. With some condescension and reserve of the more mature, feminine personality toward my frivolously hyperintellectual precociousness and the capitalist milieu which, in her opinion, had to have some corrupting influence on me, she cultivated together with me the game of "Cleverspeak," which consisted in talking nonsense on a nonsensical topic in the most pretentious and complicated arabesques of empty verbiage. "Do you still write books on German literature?" she asked me recently when we met at Grundlsee im Kreuz, now in our sixties. And indeed, even Liesl Bernfeld-Viertel, now in her eighties, still bathed nude in the lake not far from the old solarium. But Mädi Olden and Brassi Bernfeld who used to play God or the Emperor Francis Joseph—one made affectionate fun of both—died long ago.

Few of them are left. As a result of the emigration, I now belong to an elusive segment of a lost generation. Whatever can be objected to in that Grundlsee clique or its individual members who experimented with themselves and their modernity to the point of self-destruction, their heyday in the late twenties and early thirties marked the belle epoque of Grundlsee im Kreuz. Many gifted intellectuals gathered there, and without lacking in seriousness and self-engagement, attained even to a rare kind of high spirits and exuberance. Their style, new at the time, spread later on throughout the Western world in a somewhat modified form, especially in the America of the sixties, when it was made more explicit and flattened out, and new ingredients were added. For sex as the preferred terrain for the dramatizing of compulsions and liberations was replaced by the quest for "identity," the expansion and overcoming or transcendence of self, along with drug addiction, which altered the emphases and accents in an otherwise familiar idiom of rebellion.

I might add that Mumi (i.e., Edith Kramer), who still spends a third of every year in Grundlsee, confirmed and commented upon these Grundlsee memories and impressions of mine in 1978. The atmosphere in that bygone era, she observed, had been too seductive for children: "That makes for difficulties; one becomes either instinct-ridden or inhibited" (or perhaps both). As for Frank, over whom the Bernfelds' marriage collapsed later on, he was an adventurer, a "Robin Hood" with a great deal of personal courage, Mumi said, and, at that time, an anti-Stalinist of the radical left. His relationship not only to me but also to my mother, Mumi thought, had in it something of revenge on capitalism; "and A.F.", she said, "whether chaste abbess or not, was certainly right in rejecting the flight into uninhibited sexuality: the boy needed to work through his problems." So much for the opinions of Mumi, who has remained an admirer of the heroic Anna Freud—the care she gave her father, her courageous activities in wartime London in her nursery, and the establishment of the Hampstead Clinic which made it possible for lay workers to receive solid training in child analysis unavailable elsewhere. And much as Mumi kept her faith in analysis, she retained her loyalty to Grundlsee by continuing to paint, tirelessly, the lake, the mountains, the clouds, and the seasonal flowers. I acquired a painting of hers of water and shore in the morning mist which appealed to me as a fisherman.

II. Relapse and Breakthrough

1. Events Leading to the Relapse

It seems to me that everything here presses toward a crisis, *Fishing=murder* (p. 133) again brings to mind the quasi-confessional story ("Myself Revealed") I wrote at age twenty-two about a fisherman sex murderer. The sexual interpretation of A.F.'s weaving by little P. makes one suspect that the routine of sexual interpretations induces the all too accommodating patient to offer to the analyst what he thinks might meet her expectation; and I also find myself wondering now what kind of "masturbation" (p. 133) there was at this time when there was as yet no possibility of physical gratification. The sexual element is here all too readily overemphasized by the analyst as well as the patient and his environment. The attempt to banish anxiety during the night by an imaginary speech addressing my mother's lover ("I am not doing anything to harm you, so don't you do anything to me either"; p. 133) seems hopelessly "reasonable" to me, as if he hadn't done enough already by conducting his affair with my mother as publicly as possible and trying to create a conflict between my father and me with his sermon against fishing.

No wonder A.F. thought it would be better to remove me from this milieu (pp. 133ff). According to my father's recollection, it was she who suggested that I be sent to boarding school where I would be sheltered from my parents' conflicts, and, above all, the "homosexual" bond to him. This, he said, annoyed him, as he did not want to give me up, and I myself anxiously sought him out imploring him tearfully not to send me away. No doubt, this was so, even though I was tempted and attracted at the same time by the thought of a "free school" community, including the liberty in associating with girls, who would surely be there, and, generally, its aura of autonomy, freedom, and unhampered self-reliance.

The parallel to the lure of Communism (pp. 127, 131) is of interest. Kris too, in my second analysis, thought doctrinaire opinions were seductive to me, especially a strict Marxist determinism whose coherence, collectivism, and appearance of inescapable rigor at the same time provoked my opposition. As a result of Frank's influence on my mother, my concern with politics now intensified and continued into my late twenties when it waned, partly out of despair about the alternatives to fascism, not only in the guise of Russian Stalinism but also in the far more viable shape of American capitalism, which I preferred, but without enthusiasm. Both seemed to stink, and I proclaimed this opinion in my thirties in the form of uncompromising short stories for the benefit of no one and without eliciting any response at all.

On the Dream of Fare Beating (p. 135)

Mumi often indulged in this; much as she engaged in petty thefts which she justified by her anticapitalist convictions opposing profit-making department stores. Bernfeld, who acted as a father of sorts to her, talked her out of it: If she were to be arrested, he said, it would be detrimental to him who advocated a free socialist upbringing. People could say then: "You see where such education leads!" A rather circuitous pedagogical admonition against stealing, but symptomatic of a typical conflict. For with their reservations about and opposition to the "establishment," many "radical" liberals were and are in a comparable position when they want to teach their children civic virtues and obedience which, inevitably, must be exercised above all in relation to an existing establishment.

Thus a new freedom, suggested by the Grundlsee experience, threatens and beckons everywhere. "Every anxiety" (here, the fear of being definitively abandoned by the mother who left Vienna and moved to Berlin) "can be transformed back into a thought," said A.F. (p. 135). How nice if that were so! In the fantasized story, P. becomes Frank, the revolutionary and defier of prohibitions, hero of the novella *The Revolution*, written long before, which, incidentally, testifies to the fact that Frank only reactivated my interest in radical politics. The penchant for leftist revolutionary ideas, inspired, among other things, by guilt feelings on the part of the children of well-to-do bourgeois parents, as well as by the resentments of the children of the struggling petit bourgeois, plays a crucial role not only in my imaginary story but also in my mother's real love affair with the flamboyant antibourgeois ex-bourgeois Frank.

P.'s exclamation: "I have suffered immensely!" (p. 137) is both true and false. In self-dramatization and distancing myself from myself in a pose, I wanted to reap, as a kind of compensation, the advantages of self-importance and alienation. But then I console myself quickly and write my list of Christmas wishes. This, then, was the mood prior to the "relapse," an event of crucial importance, it seems to me, as a breakthrough into deeper layers.

Anna Freud, however, appears to assume in this context a palliative stance. She furthers the aspirations of the "writer," for which I was (and am) grateful; transcribes my "collected works" (p. 137); and I recall that she even encouraged me to think about publication. (To be sure, the quality of the "Dream" poem about the pavor nocturnus may have suffered from these literary intentions. (See p. 264.) And I am also thankful now for the fact that, unlike a number of analysands of my acquaintance, I was never brought to a point where activities, especially creative endeavors, were valued only with regard to their usefulness in the conduct of a therapy or because they were themselves therapeutic.

The suggestion made to my father, to keep his lover at a distance (p. 139), was likewise of a palliative nature; and as he was willing and wealthy, he did so by maintaining separate households for Inge and for me.

The new fear of becoming a woman confirms A.F.'s concern about the "homosexual" relationship to the father and suggests increasing agitation (p. 139; note also her reference to Schreber).

Associations about this: Paranoia after all! Struggle with, fear of, homosexuality at the bottom of this character who felt tempted, always, to change back and forth from male to female, to realize a kind of bisexuality; or was plagued by uncertainty about the question whether he should replace the woman for his father or play the man for his mother, or do both or neither.

"Restlessness, excitation, especially in the evening when father is in a room next to his" (p. 139). *Associations*: Memory of father improvising on the piano in syncopated minor seconds at high pitches and extreme intervals, which frightened me. "Disturbed about not seeing Inge any more. Dirty, forgetful (piano keys)": Not just the ivory keys got black edges; and not just my schoolbags got lost. And surely it is no coincidence if together with increasing agitation the memory of the old nightmare (although distanced by being turned into the artifact of a poem) now reemerges, before the augmenting tension leads further to the involuntary outburst.

2. The Relapse

The first Attack (p. 141): Associations: The vacation in Steinhaus gets mixed up in my memory with the love–hate episode in Breitenstein (pp. 41–45). I probably called Margot for help as one person who did not seem disloyal to me. The dream of the sleds was to the point: My parents were, in fact, like two colliding sleds in danger of falling into an abyss; a collision, interpretable, of course, also in sexual terms.

In a much later dream, shortly before my mother's breakdown, and a couple of years before her suicide, I was to dream again of a sled speeding along the sharp icy edge of a precipice, gliding over it, racing down the steep slope toward rocks. I connected that dream with the catastrophic developments in her life as if it were prophetic, though I already knew about her distressing insomnia, her isolation in a desolate marriage and sterile setting, her lack of money, and her sense of social *déclassement*.

Second Attack (p. 141): *Associations:* "At home Mem and father in the house," and each with another partner? They believed in this kind of modern "cameraderie" which, nonetheless, became increasingly a burden to them. Did I really think of Memka as a "monster" in this situation? Did I do so for my father's sake? It is as if I betrayed her to him on his return. But above all, I think, I was fearful of her bleeding. In later years, she often talked about it as dreadful, dramatizing her unhappiness, though her dilemma was essentially a product of her own hysterical or neurotic entanglement. For it was no one but she herself who forced her to live in intense psychophysical intercourse with two men, shuttling back and forth between Vienna and Berlin, and to ruin herself. Yet where did I see the blood? In the bed? Later I wrote poems in which it flows and drips down the stairs. The exclamation: "books fall on me and kill me" strikes me as a concession to my mother. For she liked to polemicize against my exaggerated absorption in books, to emphasize "natural intelligence," and to disparage the merely theoretical mind or cold, unsensual intellect of my father. (He had an extensive library, cultivated philosophical interests, and had earned a doctorate.) This was in contradistinction to both her Austrian architect and her revolutionary eroticist in Berlin. Moreover, she saw herself at that time as an intuitive person of "vibrant" sensibility open to visual, sensuous, aesthetic experience, and in sympathy with "Life."

The two exclamations: "The books are falling on me and killing me!" and "Memka . . . monster!" thus seem to point in opposite directions. One is a concession to my mother who is against books; the other a *captatio benevolentiae* in my father's direction, so that even the screams of anxiety illustrate my quandary.

The sketch on the note about the second attack shows a little man with raised arms standing between two closing book covers about to fall shut and to press him together like a leaf. I was afraid, it seems, that the two, who fall on or collide with one another, namely, father

346

and mother, might slay me or squeeze me to death between them, like two halves of a closing or closed book, as we did with flowers or leaves which we inserted between the pages to press them for our herbariums.

To be sure, these interpretations are contradictory: In one the mother is opposed to books; in the other the father and the mother fall upon or hit one another like the covers of a closing book, or two books put side by side. But contradictions do not exclude one another in such associations, and both of my parents could well be represented by books. For even my mother's tirades against books were, after all, a literary pose, inspired to no small degree by books.

The Third Attack (p. 141) attempts to mobilize the legitimate "natives," mother and nurse, against the intruder, Miss Schön. *The Fourth Attack* (p. 141) was an attempt on my part to save myself from the domestic entanglement by turning away from all that belonged to the higher, grown-up sphere; namely, Hans, Inge, my mother, and their relationships, and by turning toward those who were not part of the primary conflict but stood outside and seemed reliable (i.e., Thesi and Tinky). Basically, Thesi, as I saw it, was the only one who had not abandoned me. My father had left me for Inge, my mother for two or more men. So there was only Thesi who could help, and, as a hope, my own beloved, Tinky, thus already appearing as my future bride.

About the Subsequent Material (p. 141): Anna Freud's surmise that my notion that "Hans and Frank are really one person" was taken over by me "from the mother's ucs" is strangely plausible. What took place within her at that time were not simply love affairs, but just as much a continuation and intensification of her campaign against men in the form of affairs. For even before she was abandoned by her much younger second husband (whose name, Jeanpierre, she pointed out, combined the names of Hans [Jean] and Peter), the resentment of men, initiated in her embittered relationship to her father, increased within her, though she was still far from the final stage in which she seemed to hate far more than love The Man in all men. That two men are one and the same became, incidentally, an idea of mine for a "detective story" which has surfaced, irrelevantly, in my mind occasionally, as does the complementary notion of one person splitting up into two. The thought: "She hates men," however, leads to the following entry (p. 141):

"I see Mem red. Is she bleeding from down there? Hans shoots it off her"; an all too vivid interpretation of vaginal bleeding as a consequence of castration perpetrated by the man on the woman. I thought of Memka as a monster, I suppose, because she was, in my mind's eye, the castrated one (cf. also castration anxiety connected with seeing Ruth's foot injury [p.139]), and because I was afraid of castration myself.

However, as I now pursue this reconstruction, it is immediately accompanied by guilt feelings: "Memka," I say to myself, "comes off worst here. She has suffered most, she is suffering a breakdown; she is, in addition, accused and abhorred. Insult and condemnation are heaped upon her injury." And yet I want to blame the self-dramatizing ways of my parents, and in particular, my mother, for this entire relapse, reminiscent once more of the autumnal path swept clean only to be covered right away with more leaves. I imagine A.F.'s disappointment at finding again the old misery after all the work done on clearing things up. However, the last entry, that is, the notion of being a woman with the mouth suggests as another possibility, a desire for the role of the woman, not merely out of guilt, inclination, or fear, but also because I felt so close to Memka that I could not and did not want to give her up but rather wanted to and had to *be* her in order not to lose her.

Further Associations: In my associations connected with the preceding record of breakdown appears again the memory of the hazy scene with the dark woman going down on a man, perhaps at a beach among the nude bathers in Grundlsee? Was it Frank whose penis was vaunted among the liberated ladies? And thinking of Grundlsee, I recall the exhibitionist who is (according to Musil) a figure of extreme alienation. He wants to produce an "effect at a distance" (see Goethe's poem, though with different content); or rather, he recognizes distance as a necessary condition and wants to force closeness, overcome isolation and indifference, but not by eliminating hostility. He has nothing against hostility as long as he can turn it into pleasure. It is a kind of harmless sex murder to which he invites and wants to be invited; in which it remains uncertain who murders whom, and in which, ultimately, nothing has happened and fundamentally nothing has changed. Infantile pleasure in looking and showing oneself comes into play, reactivated into a compulsive method through the experience of unbridgeable, ineradicable alienation. It is an attempt to bridge or

348

suspend unbridgeable alienation, but an attempt which is itself part of the very experience which establishes alienation as the basic condition. The perversion, in short, represents a compromise between the recognition and the suspension of alienation. It plays with the thorn of displeasure, or, rather, of pain and despair.

And now, in contrast, the recollection of my Grundlsee poem: "Hand in front of your eyes—conceals,/ Melting wave—shatters / Image of woods of mountains.// Thank the mountains,/ the woods, beyond/ in circling mists, breathing,/ unmoved—// Think how your hand and eyes/ the wave, the mists,/ the woods and the mountain/ will fade and vanish.// Give thanks to the hand in front of your eyes,/ the image of woods it conceals,/ and the woods that rise beyond them./ Give thanks to the mountain in circling mists, /its image deep in the eye of the lake,/ and the wave in which it is shattered./"

It is an embellishing, perhaps an all too pretty thanksgiving address to the round Ressen covered with pines, looking blindly across over the smooth, dark-green water which I compared, on another occasion, to an eye into which a suicidal alter ego is plunging. This plunging into an eye to kill oneself is connected with my exceeding love of Grundlsee: its meadows, flowers, fragrance of wood, the feel of the air. The truth may be: "I have been wounded by one who awoke me!" That is, by the love of a bad mother. Wasn't Grundlsee a catastrophe for me?

The breakdown, starting with Grundlsee, of what seemed a terminated analytical purification and instruction, that is, of the healing process, was connected with something more than my person or my parents' condition. A pointedly exhibitionistic society or social group met there to play the games I described above. These culturally elevated liberal avant-garde circles, liberal Jewish intellectuals, or radical leftist rebels, were surrounded by hostility. And the "Jewish" and non-Jewish "impertinence" they displayed was, among other things, an exhibitionistic self-dramatization and a game with a hostile environment, a society, a nation, increasingly drifting toward murderous hatred. It was as if they said: "We are not ashamed, we show ourselves; we are not afraid of anything, on the contrary we are impertinent, superimpertinent." And, in a way, it was an attempt to seduce and to challenge the others, a game played with the threatening powers by the threatened, who were the weaker by far, though, as yet, not fully conscious of their weakness. At that time, sexuality was often referred to as "courageous" (as in "daring exposure" or "courageous frankness"). It turned into a seductively aggressive, exhibitionistically provocative gesture, in part, because of the threatening conditions of hostility and on the basis of the status of semialiens and of alienation. The latter also gave a peculiar spur and sting, an overheated, disturbing, even perverse appearance and appeal to this sexuality. This was not, I think, simply due to a particular erotic disposition, or to a "racially" or ethnically determined character, but rather to a sociocultural exposure and vulnerability to which the exhibitionism corresponded and which it expressed. Thus the sexual exhibitionism dramatized in Grundlsee does seem to me to have been connected with the rise of National Socialism, the intensification of the political threat which had become manifest also in my private sphere through Frank. This was so, notwithstanding the fact that fear or the reaction to a threatening environment full of distress and hatred were frequently expressed in playful or silly behavior by actors who didn't know themselves what they were doing. And these agitations also continued to ferment in the fantasy world of the sheltered child of a cultured bourgeois industrialist.

My image of that scene in which a woman goes down on a man on a beach may refer to something I saw in Grundlsee where I also imagined white threads of sperm drifting down to green moss through clear water. I remember a couple on our veranda, the man sitting next to his girl-friend with his erect penis under a towel. And yet there cannot be any question of a real memory. The scene is imaginary, dunes by the sea, the man with bare feet in a black suit and a top hat, a kind of clown, with an open white shirt, and his gaze on the flowing hair of the theatrical female. "The woman, however, at nine,/ laughed wildly and drank red wine!" was perhaps reminiscent of red-haired Inge, who was then still a blonde. Savagely exuberant she is, ragged, in a smock, as she bends down.

At any rate, the appearance of order which prevailed in my parents' arrangements prior to Dalmatia and Grundlsee, to the Menga–Frank episode, and the now public affair between Hans and Inge, had been relatively reassuring. With Menga's breakdown, everything reached a crisis, like a witches' sabbath, almost con amore. That is how it appears to me now in a reexperiencing of a distant past which, however, produced again some negative side-effects on my present marriage (such as occasional quarrels, impotence, and a slight temporary estrangement).

3. Breakthrough

The relapse and attacks were followed, I think, by a breakthrough to a deeper layer, in particular of images which remain mysterious to me, while A.F. was interested in them only insofar as they seemed to confirm the complex of themes which she considered to be essential.

In the drawings of this period (Figures 2.2A,B) the first picture shows a blind visionary of introspection to whom nothing more can happen as he is castrated already. He looks like Frank even though, or perhaps because, Frank was so eminent as a lover in a setting where multiple sexual activity was glorified as an expression of the full life. However, he also appears as a revolutionary confronted by figures of misery. In the second drawing, the visionary "I" resembles another role model, namely, the analyst Siegfried Bernfeld. The claim on the reverse of the sheet, that I am a famous man, is connected with these drawings by the thought that one has to make a sacrifice for one's fame, genius, talent, or power, like Oedipus, or the emasculated magician Klingsor (in Wagner's *Parsifal*), or the ailing savior, "God–Freud" (see p. 143).

Not just in the interpretation of the "screaming dream of the bull" (p. 149), but throughout this phase, one gets again the impression of a monomaniacal transposition into the sexual sphere, which is also confirmed by A.F.'s insistence on the search for the postulated "*vision*," the primal scene observed by the infant. But perhaps translation into the sexual idiom is appropriate. Concerning the pages on which, as once on Lilli K.'s photo, the eyes are pierced, P.H. himself claims (see Figure 2.3) that the nose means to him at times a penis, at times a vagina (a hole), and thus plays the game of being both man and woman, or of having a penis and being castrated. The image of a tree-lined trail (the interpretation is [pubic] hair [p. 149]) reminds me, to my surprise, of a poem composed decades later, in somewhat hymnic praise of traffic, the flow of cars glittering in the sun, through trees of an avenue, seen from the window of my room in Montreal, which again suggests a sexual interpretation (German *Verkehr* being a word used for both "traffic" and "intercourse").

The "screaming dream of the bull" also brings back the memory of hours of walking behind Hans and the forester, old Grinner, of whom my father said that, like the declining Emperor Francis Joseph of olden days, he was farting all the time as he could no longer control his sphincter. How careful one always had to be not to tread on crackling twigs. Only Thesi never went with us, as she does in the dream. The entanglement of both entrails and dream makes one think of a text beginning to interpret itself. I do not recall when the frightening encounter with the exhibitionist took place, but I remember where, and that I said to the man as he reached over to me: "We didn't bargain for that!" and ran off.

And so again sexual matters are brought up, as they are in A.F.'s interpretation of the "screaming dream of the globe" (p. 155) and the "screaming dream of Tinky" (pp. 151, 155) in which the ruins where many emperors are buried hint at the wish that the father were dead; a gold-brown stone stands for making money; and failure to remember that I did *not* spend the night with Tinky for the wish to have done so.

But perhaps we get closer to the core of my concerns at that time in the passage where I accuse myself of being egotistical because I don't want to allow anyone to get married, and where I ask whether people knew in earlier, preanalytic days that human beings were that bad. This then was my self-accusation and self-blame following upon my accusation of the all-castrating blood-king-father and the faithless, whoring mother. Günther Bittner, in his commentary on the German version of this text, thought the essentials for the boy were not sexual but human relationships, illustrated, for example, by dilemmas in which he was advised "to ask Hans" whether his mother's excuse of a merely professional trip to Berlin wasn't a lie (p. 151), and later on, is referred back to Anna Freud with the same question by his governess, Thesi (p. 175). It is finally decided that his father should give him a "half answer" by pretending that his mother did not go to Berlin because of a lover, but for the sake of her analysis with Hanns Sachs in order to gain clarity about herself (p. 175). The spying too was reactivated in the context of these impasses and entanglements, though the memory images now emerging of the glass doors between living room and dining room, with mauve silk curtains stretched at half height above which I could barely reach and behind which I wanted to hide, suggest a much earlier time of spying when I was still very little.

Among the relationships with which I was most concerned were also, I thought, the tensions between A.F. and Menga, rather than "jealousy of Thesi" or of my father's analyst, Ludwig Jekels. The hint at Menga's "secret chambers" (p. 155) refers to a conflict I felt, because my mother did not like H. G. Wells's *The Secret Places of the Heart*, which A.F. had praised. Painfully, I now had to inquire into further opinions, and to evaluate them; of course, without knowing the book myself. What troubled me was that I thought that either A.F. or my mother had to be wrong.

Associations to the "ununderstood dream of sledding" (p. 157) conjure up the lake, my folding canoe, and dark-green water around a densely crowded school of white fish chased by a salmon trout. Lasker's humorous painting of St. Anthony's Sermon to the Fish in the scary corridor of our apartment also comes to mind, as does a poem which I wrote decades later, impressed by a song from *Des Knaben Wunderhorn* ("The Boy's Magic Horn") set to music by Gustav Mahler. The fish are listening to the saint to no effect. The cowl of the monk above them is bulging upward like clouds of white bread; the positive gospel resounds over troubled waters, while they, insecure near the shallow shore, breathe deadly air. And after the sermon, appreciated, dutifully, by the fish, there is the blessing of flowing silence. Thank God, all remains the same, excepting, now and then, the croaking of a critical frog. Apparently, "understanding nothing" is part of the very message and substance of a dream which thereby turns into another variation on my basic motif of the rabbit that could *almost* get out of his trap or deep hole, but was fated, to fall back, to "relapse," after all. (Association: like Moses who never reaches the promised land.) A great deal is offering itself (many fish); yet nothing happens. There are many possibilities, but none of them is realized, either in fishing or in sledding. And as I go through these notes now, I have a more acute sense of the little boy's unhappiness than ever before.

The following dream gives rise to similar associations. According to A.F., it says: Even castrating myself for Hans won't help. There are no possibilities. Castrated or not, it is as if I were ground to dust between the two big grown-ups. And this is also what the drawing (Figure 2.4) says of the little frog raising its head between two giant faces confronting one another.

Suspicion seems also to be expressed on another sheet on which, as always, "unspeakably" embarrassing matters are consigned to silent, written communication. Hans said he had heard from A.F. that her father had said there were no neurotics in his family. Why did I consider this embarrassing? Perhaps because if A.F. had *not* said this, such gossip would annoy her; or because the content of the statement seemed too intimate; or, possibly, because I felt, even then, that this was a pretentious and deceptive boast and misrepresentation. Again drawings follow, punctured with holes.

Perhaps my compulsive and bothersome self-identification with the smugly smiling creep (pp. 157, 161) came also from a kind of despair. The "smug smile" recalls once more my verse about the letter G and the unidentifiable, self-satisfied crook (see above, p. 316) associated vaguely with my dwarflike, innocent-looking, likeable uncle whom my father considered crooked for having insinuated himself into the family, and the firm, just as I had ingratiated myself with Hans on our ski trip on the mountain? Again, it seems, I suspected myself of being the crook, the smoothie, and far too well off, considering the subliminal anxiety, the hatred, the yearning for surrender which were hidden under my deceptive, hypocritical surface.

Associations to the "Dream of Sesostris" and Mary Stuart (p. 161). Our neighbors, the Portheims, were truly refined ("more refined than we," I suspected); one could not have called on them in shirt-sleeves. And now someone enters who is not awed by Hans; who could, in fact, be his enemy; and he intends to call him to account, comparable to an Egyptian pharaoh, the enemy of the Jews, who put them in bondage. Yet, lo and behold, my father remains unimpressed. It is as if an avenger had appeared; but then this image or apparition is canceled, or retracted, nixed by a mere smile of Hans saying "Oh well—Sesostris." And Mary Stuart, too, is a royal figure and subjected to a radical devaluation. At issue are king and queen, and thus the evaluation of my parents. Who is nobler? Who can take liberties? Who is to be preferred to whom? Who to be punished?

The "Fairy Tale Without Meaning or Moral" marks the onset of disenchantment (pp. 169, 249–254). It renounces a happy end with mother, instead of reconstructing one in the way the analyst does by declaring "everything is dirt = wish fantasy = everything is love" (p. 169). And in connection with this antifairy tale in which no one wins the princess, I must think again of Menga's later hatred of men, aimed at my father, her ex-lovers, her unfaithful second husband, her brothers who were no good and neglected her, and, finally, at all men as exploiters of women, including, in her tragedy of *Xantippe*,

Socrates as the wisest and greatest of men. And the sobering end of my story without meaning and moral follows once more the disillusioning pattern of a Peter Rabbit who could not succeed; and thus the prototype of modern, *non*elevating tragedy, or tragic futility.

However, in the "second dream of Sesostris" (p. 169) and the drawing of the levitating, torerolike "performer" (Figure 2.6B), a positive elevation occurs. I appear both as a great king and as a marvelously potent and capable man who rises high above all others. Ill-humored discontent in artificial playacting would then follow, almost necessarily, as self-punishment with a feeling of unreality for the forbidden fantasies of self-aggrandizement. The uncomfortable sense of phoniness and of playacting is anticipated in the drawing itself that depicts a stage and the actor making a show of himself. That he is also supposed to be a teacher makes me think of my later attempts to realize notions of grandeur in a profession which, however, also tends to frustrate a somewhat sublimated exhibitionism.

Yet I was not the only one meant to be great and a genius: hence the concern about the competition between Erik Erikson and A.F. which I anticipated, and my criticism that she would be a genius if uncritical devotion to analysis did not prevent her self-realization. Did I threaten to reduce her, who writes only *g* and not *genius* (p. 175), to another *g*, meaning governess? Anna Freud notes the criticism under the heading *transference*. Associations: *I* am the one who feels injured when someone is or gets to be bigger than I. I am the one subject to frantic self-seeking fed by fear of being small, a negligible nonentity, a fear of nonbeing. And the disastrous thing about Grundlsee was the fear that my anxious megalomania would now combine with the enjoyment of the exhibitionistic sexualization of fear and aggression, or exhibitionism, as play with or dramatization of alienation. The compulsive need to be bigger, to show oneself as bigger, as a further motive in the exhibitionistic complex, must always lead to self-punishment since it represents a forbidden attempt at doing away with the other or others.

Anna Freud's remark: "*Bleeding as consequence of intercourse, lies ahead for him too*" (p. 177) strikes me as oddly excessive. Is it a bitter comment on defloration, justifying the imaginary connection between intercourse and blood? Or a comment made out of "virginal" fear of this connection? My visions of blood were probably based on some observation of my mother's vaginal bleedings, the major symptom of her breakdown in the wake of her life with two men. And this thought now brings back the memory of furious remarks she made later on about A.F., calling her cold, self-enclosed, without an inkling of what it means to be in the erotic "frontline" of life, to struggle with one's men and to be exposed to vital, sensuous experience: "And a frigid woman of that sort *dares* to pass judgment on one who feels and is alive and open!" It almost seems to me now as if the little boy broke down just as his mother did; and that he did so, partly out of a kind of loyalty, or simply because he *must not* be better than Menga. Everything here, at any rate, seems to be still in the shadow of the events at the turn of the year.

Then come poems, drawings or doodles, postscripts, repetitions, and attempts to work through what had happened up to that point, but also to avoid it by playacting. Increasingly, A.F. attempts, or prompts me to attempt to reconstruct, by hook or by crook, the postulated "vision" of observed or overheard parental sexual intercourse.

The drawings, listed on p. 177, again suggest thoughts of paranoia: There are pages on which Tinky's name is repeated constantly with modifications, as if I was unsure of it, or her: Katharin, Ketherin's, Katherin'so, Katherine, Katherins, Katherin, Katherinne, Kathe, Kater, Katherino, Katherin's House, Katharin's House; a pierced sheet with many D's (against Tinky's mother, Dorothy?), and the word *tedeum m m m m m m* as if one were humming it; followed in (c) by male and female shapes of noses and mouths (cavities, protuberances), some penis- or vaginalike, others castrating—hard, sharp, cutting, knife- or axlike. Concerning (h) *Elisabeth as half man, first Egyptian*, it seems to me (again "paranoid," cf. Schreber) that the Egyptian may be an androgynous Pharaoh with a stiff beard, and with curls as in the picture of Inge (Figure 2.6A). In a drawing about the quarrel between the women ("Stuart," "Elisabeth"; see dream p. 161), Queen Elisabeth, in keeping with Schiller's conception of her as virago scheming for power, watches in apparent anger the embrace between a bearded man and a delicate woman whom he lifts up to him. The counterpart of the virile woman would be Sesostris as woman; and I recall that Menga did say about herself that she was "built like a man, with broad shoulders and narrow hips," and that she felt herself to be an "Egyptian princess." It seems odd: this identification of assimilated Jews with the Egyptian as anti-Jewish nobility (ever since Moses? "If

Moses," to quote Freud, "was an Egyptian— "?).[4] What is obvious here is the confusion about the sexes.

The addition to the Fairy Tale Without Meaning or Moral (p. 179) of a noble suitor scurrying by the window and learning the saving solution to the princess's deadly riddles is introduced to heighten suspense and to accentuate the disappointment, to sharpen, so to speak, the dull edge of the ending (see pp. 252–254). For despite his advantages and virtues, even this noble and clever eavesdropper or aristocratic spy will not gain the one desired by so many.

The outstanding example of avoidance of analysis through playing at analysis was my Oedipus poem (p. 179) which paralleled talking analysis to death by discussing my father's Oedipus complex or Tinky's "resistance," advising that she and A.F. should discuss this some time. The way I understood it then was that A.F. considered my poem as an artifact imitating analysis in order to show off and put on an act (she refused to type it for me); and to me too it appeared contrived. However, it seems that A.F. saw in it more than just playing at analysis which got in the way of analytic work. For she interprets the playacting and the self-mirroring themselves as "continuation of the vision" (p. 181); that is, of the observation of the adults' sexual activity though by a reversal that turned looking at into being looked at. But perhaps my attempts to become the codirector of my analysis were also attempts to expand its scope; to get A.F. engaged in a dialogue with Tinky, and above all to introduce myself into it as the third party. To be sure, this kind of à trois would again reinforce the notion of the "vision" or primal scene composed of the two parents and the child.

The collection of ugly "human animals" (p. 178, footnote 28) brings to mind that this (namely, *Menschentiere*) was the title of a collection of verse I published some forty years later, treating still the human conflict and dilemma between "low" and "sublime," "noble" and "bestial" spheres and impulses.

In the passage concluding with being "very angry with Thesi" (p. 181), anger is considered the transposition of love play and a substitute for it—as, unfortunately, was the case all too often even later on, in marriage. The choice in favor of being observed (instead of observing)

[4]Freud, S. (1937–1939), If Moses was an Egyptian. *Standard Edition*, 23:17–53. London: Hogarth Press, 1964.

can be regarded as an attempt to solve the dilemma between watching, wanting to do it oneself, and not knowing whether to be the man who should eliminate the other man, or the woman who should take the place of the other woman. And it also might be interpreted as an attempt to avoid the danger of being crushed between the two, which of course could not have been the case in the alleged primal scene itself, but was a threat on a more immediate and "real" psychological level. This is what the nightmare and screaming were about. And in this situation there might actually be four "solutions": be a man (take the place of a man); be a woman (in place of the woman); look on; or participate as the third party. That the à trois would be eminently desirable, that it would be pleasant to seduce others into it, or be seduced by them, was one of those sexual fantasies which preoccupied or tormented me later on, without being acted upon. And, additionally, it occurs to me with regard to the above, that this might be an attempt to derive the complex of exhibitionism–voyeurism purely from the experience of the primal scene, the "vision" and thus to consider voyeurism (rather than exhibitionism) as the primary element. However, this appears to me also as somehow questionable, possibly "melioristic," a tempering down or "euphemization" of the aggressive element.

March 11 and 12, 1931 (pp. 181–183): The "big events" from which P. now wants to recover are, presumably, his mother's breakdown and his own attempt to overcome his relapse, and its shattering experiences, also by using them in writing.

March 12, 1931: "Rows with Thesi," Acts the Big Man: Again wavering between self-deprecation and self-aggrandizement, acting humble, and acting, rather more unpleasantly, the part of the braggart or show-off. Beginning of the need to establish independence from Thesi, which soon becomes stronger and probably contributed to Thesi leaving us around 1932, when, to be sure, Hans and Inge got married and moved to a house in suburban Hietzing with me. Again there is something of an attempt at solution in this; namely, the idea that I can perhaps get along without any of them. For I am a big man myself now and will show off the way the other grown-ups do. At the same time, however, there is the feeling of the hollowness of such gestures.

What follows, rather like a painting by Munch, are visions of demons (Figures 2.7A, B) probably meant to represent the society in which we move. For these "demons" are masklike grown-ups, people wearing masks. In a corner of the second drawing is a person who is helplessly perplexed, and since a single head encloses all other figures, it seems that the many demonic creatures are inside him. Even then the contrast between a smooth, friendly surface and what lies beneath it were all too evident to me in myself as well as in others, in the city, in all humans. Nor did I get very much farther in the way I felt about life later on. The whole gamut was now in place which, subsequently, I learned to play on more or less well, and with some variations.

4. Disenchantment

My disenchantment or disillusionment seems to have begun with the wish to leave home. I let myself go, became negligent, "wayward," and somewhat self-destructive, in order to "show them"—a familiar game also in later life, used to hurt others or pay them back by one's own failure.

Accompanying the "dream in hexameters" (pp. 189–191) is a drawing of a virago with whom I am fighting. It is, at the same time, A.F.: "I always feel as if you were my wife and I quarrel with her." I remember owning as a child a sturdy picturebook, like the one in the dream, and its thick cardboard pages including my favorite verse: "*Das tut man nicht!* (This is not done) or possibly: *Das ärgert mich!*" (That makes me mad) /*So spricht die Gans*/ (Thus spoke the goose)/ *und wackelt zornig mit dem Schwanz*/(and wiggled angrily her tail). Anger, prohibition, and tail-waggling fit with the infantile vision of a struggle in bed. The angry goose too seems to me a kind of mannish woman or virago, the tail (German *Schwanz*) being at the same time her ass. The fury in the dream, "a female—half man, half animal"; that is, a frightening woman who appears as man, touches upon my own quandary in choosing between male and female, and becomes the personification of guilt feeling, as an avenging woman who is herself a man and castrates men. And so does the funny angry goose with the tail, who represents again fear of the woman appearing as a man, and again belongs with my conflict—whether to be a man or a woman—in which I leaned now more toward the passive side (as A.F. stresses in emphasizing the danger of homosexuality) (p. 191, see also pp. 179 and 189 [Basti's remark]).

The notes on "how to become unattractive and disagreeable" (p. 189) focus on being "bad" or acting the part of the bad boy. Steep mountain chains connecting pointed peaks accompany the writing, as I myself tried to elevate myself to a high vantage point of contemplation and self-criticism. Characteristically, a typical German-Jewish inflection in the use of German was severely rejected by us "assimilationists." Similarly, the gesture of sticking one's thumbs in between shirt and vest near the armpits seemed to me the height of Jewish mercantile vulgarity, so that I was shocked when my father once stood that way in front of me. And again it was typical of our culturally self-conscious milieu that Karl May, a favorite author of innumerable juvenilia on the "Wild West" was considered, somewhat severely but not without justice, to be trashy reading almost on a par with cheap magazines about Tom Mix or Buffalo Bill.

As mentioned above (p. 343), A.F.'s plan to get me away from a problematic milieu, including the danger of my homosexual attachment to my father, and into the more aseptic environment of a boarding school, was thwarted both by my father's angry reluctance and my own ambivalent anxiety about leaving home. Ambiguously, in begging him not to give me away or in clinging to him, I wanted to flatter him with my love, and win him over, but also thought I was acting in this manner "for his sake" as well as being prompted by my own cowardly fear of being among unknown, ruthless people to whom I would be just anybody. And yet I wanted to be free from the domestic bondage and the playacting of conflicting roles in a conflict-ridden, split home.

Next are *poems* (pp. 269–271) which A.F. typed for me. Emulating my first favorite, Goethe's "Song of the Spirits above the Waters," in the Avenarius anthology which I had ardently wished for as a Christmas gift, I aimed for a kind of philosophical poetry with my "Song of Higher Beings." And when I read this poem to my grandmother Jenny on her veranda, surrounded by the rustling foliage of mighty chestnut trees, pretending that it was part of the printed anthology, she reacted to it, perhaps to encourage me, or because she only listened with one ear, as if it were the work of an established grown-up poet. "Not bad," she said, "but not quite as good as [Goethe's] 'Wanderer's Nightsong' or 'Prometheus' is it?" And I was terribly flattered. In another of these early poems, I expressed my fear of, and attraction to, "Death"; while the aggressive address "To the Poets" as liars conveyed both a self-criticism and a distrust of all who merely feign feelings in a literary manner. "Defense" (inspired by a

Nietzsche poem) dramatized as my very own a pathos of truth or veracity which I believed in and liked to flaunt, then as later on.

It seems, however, that with all this productivity went also an increasing sense of isolation and *"Yearning for mother"* (p. 193), which, if A.F.'s impression could be trusted, I felt particularly during an Easter vacation (in 1931?) spent as a guest of the Burlinghams. And even though I have reason to doubt A.F.'s diagnosis on this particular occasion when, I think, I was much in love with Tinky, it is surely true that the negative feelings which I later developed against Dorothy as my mother-in-law were also related to an attempt to ward off an earlier, positive attachment to her. To my own astonishment, I found myself once, as an older man, standing outside the illuminated windows of the Freud house in Maresfield Gardens, London, where A.F. and Dorothy lived at the time, tears running down my cheeks. It was due, possibly, to some wine I had drunk, but certainly also to a sense of self-imposed alienation, the deep regret at the loss of relationships which had been infinitely dear to me, and which I brought about largely by my own will and decision. I was, and remained for many years, a beneficiary of Dorothy Burlingham's unconscious and generous tyranny, and an unresolved vehemence and sense of guilt still point to my early attachment to this "blameless" substitute mother whom I blamed for provoking an invidious comparison with my own "guilty" mother.

Moreover, an analogous consideration also applies to Thesi (p. 195), whose concern when I felt hurt, made me cry with self-pity and think: "If only Mem were like this!"

The frequently semifraudulent, doctored petty-cash accounts of mine (p. 195) belong likewise in a context of negligence and self-destructiveness germane to a sense of isolation or disillusionment. Combined with my sloppiness, they contributed to my father's lifelong and irrevocable distrust of all my dealings in matters of money. Not entirely without reason, he never thought I had any capabilities in this field and hardly taught me anything about it; while I developed, as mentioned before, an excessive and somewhat insincere aversion to anything connected with money, including business or commerce, in keeping with my mother's similarly "reactive" disdain, designed to repress a positive appreciation or rather the worship of money pervasive in our background and society at large. Moreover, the notion that money and its power were my father's prerogative and preserve reinforced an innocuous, but awkward and embarrassing carelessness and persistent mismanagement of money on my part; and it took decades before a reluctant and intermittent, though fairly considerable concern and relish for money, property, and material advantages slowly began to assert themselves against this myth of incompetence. To be sure, the basic decision not to make material profit the aim of my life played its part in all this. However, the preference for intellectual, artistic, or spiritual concerns does not require a man to act the idiot with regard to material interests.

Finally (p. 195; p. 194, footnote 39), the long sought-after "vision" emerges, inasmuch as it could be elicited. Yet the relevant, hastily scribbled sketch remains somewhat unconvincing. For from the crib, standing alongside the wall, one could not see the parents' double bed, situated on the same side in the adjacent room, but only the armoires with mirrors on the inside of their doors; and these were, in turn, visible only when the armoires were opened. Conceivably, I could have looked from the crib across into the dark mirrors to watch the reflection of half-raised, pale thighs and, oddly enough, my father's face, which could not have been turned toward me unless he had turned around toward the mirror, with a bluish tint on his unshaven cheeks, angry eyes flashing at me, because I, or rather the observer's image in the mirror, had been discovered from the other side. How much of this scene, the struggle with thighs, the perspiring, contorted face, may be mere fantasy or made to order, I shall never know. On the reverse of the above-mentioned sketch (see p. 194, footnote 39), there is a drawing of a crude map showing the road to Alland, home of my first governess and to Klausen-Leopoldsdorf, the hunting lodge of my grandfather. On a further sheet, a castrating goddess of fate, the Parca with scissors, appears to "cut" ("circumcise," "cutoff"?) a series of men, or their umbilical lifeline.

The chapter on disillusionment ends in an elegiac mood: Nothing endures but art (see p. 196, footnote 41), an idea I took to heart even while I was getting more and more negligent and sloppy; much as the writing of poetry also proved a consolation.

III. Open End

Perhaps it is due to weariness with the work of memory, if the only denominator for the last part of this story appears to me to be my mourning over the separation from my mother.

Spending the summer of 1931 (p. 197) with her and her Austrian friend brought no solution either. He said about me to Menga: "Why does the boy talk Jewish jargon? He must keep bad company." And this very recollection suggests that, even in memory, I am still jealous of him and angry at him.

The dream of taking leave of Menga (p. 199) brings back memories of my incapacity to reconcile my feelings for her with those I had for A.F., much as, later on, and also as a result of her thoroughly negative attitude, with my feelings for my first, and for my second, wife. And connected with the conflict between Menga and A.F. is also the depreciation of A.F. as "nun."

Anxiety now increased again, as I was increasingly abandoned by both parents, with the main "Frightening Places" in the apartment (p. 199; Figure 2.8B) being located along the hallway where the hovering ghost child might pursue me; at the apartment door leading to the stairway where the burglar would enter; and in the bathroom and the toilets, especially the dark one for the cat and the servants where forbidden thrills might allure and threaten. The broad, squashed "anxiety man" (Figure 2.8C) who is, at the same time, an insect with sharp mandibles, may represent both penis and castration. But worse than that, he proved a danger A.F. warned me about, namely the provocation of strife instigated to bring about the repetition of traumatic abandonment. "I . . . stress in particular how he will spoil and ruin his life with quarrels and repetition" (p. 209); that is, with quarrels designed to serve the reenactment of what I imagined to have been the original scene in which I was left and abandoned as punishment for my own transgression or sin. Anna Freud was right about this!

The poems on "Drives" and "Rage" (p. 271) elaborate ideas and motifs pervasive in Freudian circles. In others, such as "Life," befitting the approach of puberty, the kitsch component and the posturing increase, while the verse ascribed to some Easter vacation (pp. 271ff) (out of place in terms of chronological sequence) recall authentically an elegiacally cheerful mood, the precipitate of my acute and total infatuation with Tinky. Lying in the grass, with swaying stalks appearing large near my eyes, sighing, looking up into the high trees stirred by the wind, I indulged exuberantly in succulently poetic and tenderly yearning emotions. (And it occurs to me now how stupid grown-ups are after all in such matters, for in her observations on my spring vacation with the Burlingham children, A.F. noted only an elegiac sadness in my relationship to Dorothy ("yearning for his mother," pp. 193, 195) but overlooked my being in love. The *Poems about "Nothingness,"* with A.F.'s note: "Hunting trip with father" (pp. 273ff), bring back the memory of a snipe we found shot dead, rigid among reeds, with glazed, dull eyes. This frightened me, or rather, gave me pause, and I have never wanted do any hunting of my own since then.

The dream involving "The Ship of the Dead," following a slight recurrence of *screaming attacks* (p. 211) is again interpreted as a complaint of mine against my bad parents for abandoning me: "How come," I ask Thesi, "that you, who had a *good* mother, are on this ship of the expatriated, the homeless, the friendless!?" (see p. 211). But then this criticism has to be taken back or mitigated: I need to hear, *not* because I believe it, but to silence my own doubts: "Your parents are not bad; it is just that they also want a life of their own."

The avoidance of criticism of my parents, in particular of my mother, was for a long time one of my major objectives. It had a stupefying effect and proceeded less from a need to spare my loved ones than from the need to protect myself from my own criticism of them. The debate about the degree to which a mother should "sacrifice herself" for her child in which some emancipated minds of the twenties were engaged, served to stimulate reproaches leveled by me and others at the egocentric unmotherly mother. It also played its role in A.F.'s criticism of Menga, or at least in criticism which Menga imputed to A.F., and to which, in turn, she reacted by accusing her of being frigid. (I remember now how indignant she was when A.F. told her she should not let me touch her breasts.) And yet I surely also stylized this complex of questions in a male and/or egocentric manner, as conflict between one who gives herself fully to her sexual life and another who denies herself the gratification of her sexual impulses, or between dully faithful and excitingly "bad" or unfaithful women. For my mother herself would claim later on that she herself had always been "semifrigid."

Concerning "The Ship of the Dead" it occurs to me that seven years later the expatriation which is, of course, interpreted here in sexual terms, became a reality for us, somewhat in accordance with Traven's novel. The book, incidentally, got my cousin and me into trouble when we were about to cross the German border into France, because the SS guards at the border objected to a copy of it in my cousin's trunk as forbidden literature, and threatened to send us to a concentration camp when I answered them somewhat impertinently. However, they only had us sweep the floor of the stationhouse and then told us "Jewish pigs" to walk across the border on foot with our bundles on our back, "the same way you sneaked into our country in the first place." And again with regard to the "Death Ship" of the emigrés, I missed such a boat only by a fairly narrow margin. For in 1940 when I was interned in Britain by the British as an "enemy alien," I very nearly got on the *Arandora Star*, a sister ship of our own, which was also to transport "enemy aliens" to Canada, crossing the Atlantic without convoy, but was sunk by a German submarine, with its cargo of both genuine "enemy aliens" and a good many refugees like myself.

One way to overcome the loss of my mother *and* the loss of A.F. in view of the approaching end of analysis was to make them unnecessary by internalizing them so as to *become* those from whom one would be separated. And this would be, it seems, according to A.F., "the mechanism of homosexuality" (p. 213). Instead of staying with mother and A.F., I might play the female role myself, become a "woman" and turn toward men.

And apparently, I also would become the analyst. For in the following, I am "treating" my younger cousin and play the analyst by enlightening him about sexual matters (p. 213). Even later on I retained that patronizing attitude toward cousin Tommy, and suppressed my self-reproaches on that account as I did already when A.F. reprimanded me. For after decades, when we met again, he gave me an unsolicited account of a Swedish cinema where masturbation was provided, and how dull this was. And he still spoke with resentful scorn of my former role as his preadolescent "educator" in matters of sex, which must have been quite absurd. I challenged him to ask me any question at all, and I would know the answer, just as if I was some universal sage. Yet I did help him as he was grieving at the same time over his mother's fatal illness, and the ensuing breakup of his family.

Such role-playing did not change anything in the fundamental situation, the hopelessness of which seems to be confirmed again by the gloomy ending of the planned novella in which neither the poor nor the rich boy wins a contest for leadership, but both are superseded by an indifferent third party (p. 215).

The "dream of Sigurd and Nurmi" (Sigurd was a big boy at the B-R

School; p. 215) is interpreted by A.F. all too positively in terms of my impatience to become a masturbating big boy myself. For wild Sigurd, who always had to fight everyone, including himself, and ended up by committing suicide while still at our school, is presented here in a hopeless struggle against the Olympic champion Nurmi, the speediest of all sprinters.

As another way of freeing myself from those who left me, there appears now the increasing criticism of Menga (p. 211), but, according to A.F., I am compelled to extend this criticism to others, and, generically, in a critical essay on this subject, to *my own* generation (see p. 261). In this essay I drew on the opinions expressed by those around me, notably by disciples of Karl Kraus who were close to my father, who himself inveighed, above all, against journalists. For precisely these superjournalists, like Kraus himself or my father who was to collaborate on journals like the left-wing *Wiener Weltbühne*, saw in the press and the media, in propaganda, and in advertising their most powerful or favorite antagonist.

This new, liberating, critical, and satirical turn, which was to become dominant in me later on, soon came to a climax in the one and only high point of public appearance of my childhood, the speech of the circus director (p. 274) at the B-R school show in December '31. I appeared in a tuxedo as a master of ceremonies, and perhaps even "with a parchment scroll covering my whole body." The generally admired piece of acting was characterized by an ironic twist or refraction. It contained both a satire on the exploiter, the evil father with the whip, and the identification with his role. In derision and in triumph I myself assumed the posture of the scornful tyrant. In this way, my part became analogous to my father's position as a left-wing industrialist and reluctant capitalist, and so allowed for both moral indignation and enjoyment of a sense of power provided by the very role which was the object of my indignation. This sounds all too complicated. But perhaps the dubious integration of contradictory perspectives permitted an illusory synthesis of opposing tendencies, and thus the circus director's "brilliant performance." Obviously, I could not grant myself a second success of that kind. For then, as later on, it seemed to me that moments of success too greatly enjoyed were quite alarming, a challenge activating that negative power within me, which always managed to impede me even if it did not fully control me. In the following year, when beautiful Anne Nederhoud sang the

"Raggle Taggle Gypsies Oh" in her delicate high voice, Vicki and I played two Yuletide clowns; but I was so joyless in the performance of my part and so drearily garrulous that my mother commented on my decline in comparison to the previous occasion; and thus the pitiful balance was reestablished. Though angry and hurt, I also felt somehow safe under the cover of negative criticism. For I was not, I thought, supposed to be better than my parents, and I feared that, as a punishment for success, I would incur my father's and my mother's jealousy, proving myself thereby both an envious dog in the manger and a child that had been made very insecure.

The following dreams and discussions deal again with a quadrangle: Hans/second man/Menga/I, with jealousy in all directions, and the effort to love Menga unconditionally (p. 217). And in all this it is striking to what extent my own excitement and agitation as a child reflected the excitement and agitation of my parents about their "liberated" behavior, their own programmatic enactment of their love affairs, and their inability—a kind of narcissistic incontinence—to refrain from involving people who should have been kept out of their affairs. This was particularly true of my mother in her compulsive exhibitionism and her attempt to oppose established boundaries; though, later on, also of Inge in her nonchalantly undisciplined way; and only to a lesser degree of my father. For in his natural reticence he had to make an effort to align himself with the avant-garde spirits of the time who rather valued "courageous honesty" (meaning: a dramatization of the very realms of experience which were taboo to the compact philistine majority). Yet he made up for his restraint in verbalizing his self-involvement by a life-style and hypochondria which, in turn, imposed his continuous concern with himself on those around him.

The same theme of contamination of my own experience as a child through the way in which the adults experienced their lives, is also implicit in the "dream of Janne and Gabi" (p. 219), for it brings back to me the memory of my "bad" mother crying as she listened to the record of Sophie Tucker's song in praise of "A Yiddishe Mamme," overcome, as she was, by her own helpless sense of tragedy and guilt about her separation from her child. And the interpretation of this same dream also raises once more the issue of the reduction to the sexual, or the preference for the sexual as the symbolic realm into which all problems could be translated. For the adults around me in this milieu of the late twenties and early thirties all seemed to share, in one sense or another, this tendency. Though it was far more compelling than a mere fashion to be indulged at will, and exerted a lasting influence on me, the tendency was certainly far from bringing about the revelation of the transhistorical, all-important fundament which it was thought to be at the time. According to A.F., I wanted to have my fear about my penis more forcefully refuted than she had done. I wanted to hear that I would lose this fear; while A.F.'s remark: "as long as he has doubts about his penis, he will have to drown them in competing" (p. 217) was, in fact, so little reassuring that even now, in reading it, I find myself thinking (somewhat illogically): "So this is how it will always be. For how could competition ever end?" And motifs of this kind certainly continued to play their part even in a phase when "competition" itself had long superseded concerns about my penis as dominant factor.

According to A.F.'s interpretation of the dream, the bad, faithless, and frivolous mother does "gymnastics" with other men, thus forcing me to go to public toilets; while the good one who raises and pampers her little darling in an idyllic garden is elevated upon a throne. In retrospective, however, the dream conveys to me a "neither-nor," a rejection of both aunts of mine in keeping with my mother's judgment. She despised pretty Gabi as a whore, and the plump and good-natured Janne as a dummy (though at the time of the dream the latter was, in reality, already ill, immobilized, impaired in speech and thought by multiple sclerosis). And so the dream would also seem to say that while my mother might herself not amount to all that much, these two were worth less than she. Indeed, the dreamer, Peter, does leave also good mother Janne's garden again to "cross the street." (However, this series of retrograde associations appears questionable, in turn, as it also reflects my present thoughts on what happened to the children involved in the dream later in their lives. For apparently both Janne's well-treated little darling "monkey"-boy and Gabi's neglected daughter, were destined to become severely self-destructive.)

Why have father and mother left me, I asked again and again. My response, according to A.F.'s interpretation of the "dream of the car ride", was now: I am not abandoned because I am a pig, but I have become a pig because I have been abandoned. I have no other choice than "regression to the anal" (p. 221). Retrospectively I can imagine other interpretations; for instance the opposite—I am finer than, superior to, all the others. Walter, son of the author of *Wayward Youth*, is himself a wayward, delinquent youth. Basti, in Laxenburg, is notoriously lazy, a pig; Thesi and Eula, "domestics," get upset that a "dirty boy" has touched me, the fine one. Above all, the great Erik Homburger-Erikson, my teacher, is here demoted: He should have thanked *me*, not "my" chauffeur, for the ride in "my" car. And even now I still think: "I liked him much better than he liked me; and perhaps I was jealous of him, or he of me, because we were both in analysis with A.F." In the dream he joins the chauffeur whom he had thanked the previous day. So, in some ways, he too belongs only among the "servants." He too served, after all, as a kind of private tutor. The elegant people, however, who belong together, are on the highest plane of the social caste system—the *gnädige Frau* (or lady of the house) who is met and taken away by her lover—and I. Another memory of myself shouting at a rightfully angry peasant: "Do you know who I am?" as if my name entitled me to special privileges, associates itself to the episode with Erik, illustrating the same arrogance and presumption of the son of a "captain of industry," which surfaced only rarely and intermittently, together with and in spite of my explicit devaluation of capitalism and industrialists. Anna Freud's interpretation "degrades," my counterinterpretation "elevates" me in reading the dream as imaginary revenge of the privileged and envied, who wants to consider himself above all others. (And I often did feel at the time that some children envied me for being "rich" and/or for being bright or "gifted.") However, both interpretations—A.F.'s in which I am but a poor pig and mine in which I am snobbishly superior—do fit together like prince and pauper, or "above" and "below."

To a lower, earlier netherworld also belongs a memory going far back, possibly to my fourth year, and the frightening dark toilet of the cat and the servants, when Lilli K. (Eula) beat me and locked me in there (p. 223). I remember the hot feel of crying, the fear of the dark, the strong acrid smell of the sawdust litterbox used by the sawdust colored cat (though she later on learned to use the toilet itself). Everything was dark, including the seat of dark wood, unlike the lacquered white one in the family toilet. However, I do not recall "anal stimulation" while being beaten, though later such stimulation as well as play in a sadistic vein did enter into my sexual experience. Perhaps this too was construed hypothetically by A.F. in connection with the postulated "vision," since, according to the child's understanding, the primal scene was interpreted as a fight, a beating, which might, to be sure, occasionally also be part of the real event. And this, in turn, makes me think of the sadistic component in my father's sexuality, the associations of sexual desire with abasement of the object, a sadistic contempt and inclination toward "brutal sex" which I can well understand. I recall a short story of his with the episode of a rape in a setting of war and combat as well as allusions to his difficulties caused by the fact that sexual attraction and esteem for a woman tended to exclude one another. Enough! Like the child in analysis, of whom A.F. notes that he is afraid "something else" or more of the same might still come to light, I am afraid of, and bar at this point in my retrospective, the emergence of further associations.

Anna Freud was right in noting "crooked thinking" (pp. 225–227) and in fostering an "attempt at honest thinking" (p. 223). Resorting to the stereotypical answer that I loved both parents *equally*, I merely covered up my conflict. But as she goes on to compare this "protection against anxiety" with my—comforting—thoughts about "life after death" (p. 225), devaluating the latter likewise as mere subterfuge, I wonder if she doesn't make things too easy for herself. Intensive thinking about one subject frequently, perhaps always, entails avoidance or neglect of thinking about another. The "absent-minded" scholar retreats from concerns with daily "realities," the practical "realist" from riddles of the uncommon or ultimate and unfamiliar. "Insight and blindness" go together. Anna Freud is not entirely wrong. My thoughts about the afterlife as well as my criticism that the Burlinghams didn't "think enough about politics" (p. 225) may have been "subterfuges" among other things; but she omits the "other things" and thus reduces and devaluates these thoughts. My criticism of an escape from politics, in particular, she dismissed too glibly, perhaps because it was, in fact, addressed not merely to the Burlinghams, but to the Freudians of A.F.'s circle and observance in general.

The criticism of the B.'s raised by my politicized mother (p. 225) thus seemed not entirely unjustified to me. Though they were rather fragile children of American patricians rather than of the true and tough aristocracy which has survived the centuries in tenacious arrogance,

Menga thought of them as anemic nobility. She accused me for always going along with these "others," and never being independent enough to be truly myself. She resented my veneration of the blond children and their elegantly simple ways, though she herself stylized the men she chose in the direction of Aryan aristocracy, as in the case of the architect and, later on, of her "fragile" and "delicate" second husband of "ancient, patrician stock." It is, at any rate, inaccurate to say that I created or imagined the opposition between Menga and the B.'s. Like the other oppositions (Menga–father, Menga–A.F.) it was quite real and pronounced. Nor did I simply love Menga most; I also wanted or needed to love her most in order to suppress my reproaches against her. For I also thought of my going to the B.'s as treason against Menga, just because there was a great readiness in me to betray her and also to betray her in favor of Hans.

And yet it is true enough that my assertion and conviction: "I like both equally" (p. 225), repeated compulsively for some years, served an avoidance of conflict, and that even the occasional pretence of a preference for my father was a device to establish a kind of balance; if only a euphemistic, palliative, false one. Perhaps even this present book, which is relatively protective of my father but most explicit in the criticism of my mother, may perpetuate something of this state of affairs. At any rate, a constraint vis-à-vis my parents persisted for a long time, and made me avoid some judgments, initiatives, actions, and achievements lest I antagonize either of them, but especially my father.

The above digression also confirms the charge of "crooked thinking" (p. 227). According to A.F.'s notes, I asked about lesbian marriages or whether the piano teacher (who always used strong perfume) had a venereal disease, whether the actress Sybille, my father's ex-lover, was sterile, and whether A.F. was having an affair with her own father, merely in order not to ask a direct question about my own father and his current lover. However, the following uncensored, uncontrolled *associations* do come to mind: Anna and Sigmund? Anna with Sigmund? Did he not analyze her? Did he not describe her as his Antigone? An incestuous relationship between Anna Freud and her father was certainly "imaginable" for me as a boy in love with her, and as such it was actually of the highest, independent, and quite "uncrooked" and straightforward interest. Regarding crooked thinking, denials, and so on, I might add that my denial of my father's sexual relations with Inge simultaneously evokes the image of the two together on a trip in a sleeping compartment of a train; and now connects up with the later image of such a compartment lit up brightly with an open dark window and two triumphant lovers making love on the upper berth while the train speeds through the night.

My associations to the "anxiety dream of Eva Johannsen" (p. 227), and the "anxiety man" who is "a prostitute" conjure up the unsolicited memory of a woman with a clitoris almost the size of a penis, which I found repulsive, impressive, somewhat gruesome. "No need for shame and fear with her." The blue-gray eyes also fit this encounter. Odd. Could make one superstitious. A woman with a penis—perhaps this is akin to my mother's occasional ambition "to be like a man." This is at any rate how I, as a man, saw it. Here as elsewhere I try again to solve the dilemma of being "between man and woman," which happens also currently to be the topic of a study of mine about the controversy on bisexuality involving Freud, Fliess, and Weininger.

"Artificial in Menga's defense" (p. 229): The passage illustrates a compulsion directed above all against my own inner criticism and leading to multiple complications and contortions. I wanted A.F. to say in defense of Mem that only *my* imitation of Menga was phony, not Mem's own manner of speaking. But actually I often did think that she was talking too much and in a precious, affected, faddish way, including, possibly, the all too readily used remark that someone "needs to be in analysis," which, however, would have been quite justified in the case of Tilly, who was frightfully high-strung. Analysis might have been good for her. Yet I was also conscious of the fact, which I heard discussed, that the less privileged, such as chamber-maids, could not afford analysis.

Work Projects (p. 231): These would seem to be more productive than getting caught up in conflicts, quandaries, speculations about my parents, and my dilemmas with them. Anna Freud stresses that in one of these projects I intended to pit one great man (Marx) against another (Freud)—probably in the hope that I myself might prove to be the greatest. She also appreciates that the synthesis of Marx and Freud, attempted at the time by Bernfeld as well as Reich, represented our—Mumi's and my—faith and credo.[5]

Intellectual and Physical Exhibitionism: Associations: To be sure, even in the kind of work which later determined my life and became its main content, the problematic of "intellectual and physical exhibitionism" (p. 231) continued to manifest itself. Anna Freud interprets: "Wants to show his penis as he has shown his novella." Is this then, the affective background which accounts also for the compulsive component? And as it reaches a certain threshold and threatens to turn into real exhibitionism, the arousing element in self-exhibition mobilizes also a sense of guilt and the sense of one's own smallness? Whom or what does this exhibitionism imitate? Father? Mother? Both? I have a fleeting memory of my father speaking about what it feels like to walk by windows of well-lit rooms and wanting to look in.

As the reflections and interpretations about the "dream of the two directions" (p. 233) suggest, the intellectual, ideological conflicts and solutions (analysis vs. politics; Freud vs. Marx) merge with personal and sexual problems (Hans vs. Menga). The solution: "the parents can come together again if he gives up his claims on both, castrates himself," is the negative counterpart to the all-encompassing solution of bisexuality.

Associations: Again my characteristic wavering between "neither-nor" and "as well as": The drawing of the two directions looks like a penis with two arms, or a vagina distorted into a pair of tongs, depending on whether one looks at the semisphere as protuberance or cavity. And yet, I ask myself, whether such continuity in associations proves the identity of the subject, or whether the need to establish a continuous identity may not be a primary motif for the present endeavor.

---

[5]The best-known work of Siegfried Bernfeld (1892–1953) dating from his earlier period, is *Sisyphos oder die Grenzen der Erziehung* (Sisyphos or the Limits of Education) (Wien: Internationaler Psychoanalytischer Verlag, 1925; reprinted: Suhrkamp Verlag: Frankfurt am Main, 1967). For Bernfeld's other works up to the early thirties, see Siegfried Bernfeld, *Antiautoritäre Erziehung und Psychoanalyse* (Antiauthoritarian Education and Psychoanalysis), 3 volumes, edited by Lutz von Werder and Reinhart Wolff [Frankfurt: Ullstein, 1974 (Frankfurt: März Verlag; 1969–1971)], which includes a complete bibliography (in volume 3). For Wilhelm Reich see, for example, *The Sexual Revolution* (New York: Farrar, Straus and Giroux, 1974; translation of *Die Sexualität im Kulturkampf*, 2nd ed., 1936).

"Dream of Capitalism" and "Dream of the Lahngang Lakes" (pp. 233–235): Associations: In the latter these translucent Alpine lakes situated high above Grundlsee at the foot of the "Dead Mountains" do not appear at all. In my thirties, in another dream about them, I am on my way up with Herbert, my childhood friend. The landscape, however, is fantastic, far more rounded than the severe, stony Lahngang region. In the larger of these lakes were huge golden-brown trout which one could see from the high slope above. Hans caught a few with a baiting system laid out across the lake. Much of this is unclear to me. In the dream of March 1 (pp. 233–235), and somehow befitting dream logic, it seems plausible that a cleaver should represent capitalism, hence, a castrator. It is equally plausible that changing train carriages (i.e., vehicles of intercourse) should stand for changing one's man or woman; that is, sexual partners. I think about my first, broken marriage as if that had been a jumping off the train which had shocked the B.'s. Only it was not I who jumped off, nor were they shocked. In all this apparent confusion, it becomes clear that the issue is *comparing ways of life*: of man and woman, the capitalist father and the mother who changed her men. And this is also confirmed by the later dream about fishing with Herbert in the Lahngang region. As a boy I once stayed for a week with him and Hans in a mountain hut on the larger lake: three men by themselves. All this, and the thought of my adolescent attraction to Herbert with whom I am fishing in the imaginary landscape with a round pond, point to the "male" or homosexual option. And so does the context in which I had the later dream, namely at an early point in my marriage, after a visit from Herbert in Grundlsee, when he invited me to join him in a sauna and revived the memory of that other alternative.

The entries before Easter 1932 (p. 235) still deal with the two directions, pro and contra homosexuality, pro and contra my emancipation from my father, pro and contra my mother whose affectation (p. 237) I imitated although it made me angry and jealous to boot, as it always appeared when she turned on her seductive "art of conversation." Thus I took over from her precisely what bothered me in her, identified myself precisely with what I found hateful, with the enemy, so to speak, and I did so, at least in part, in order to take the edge off my own criticism of her.

Yet my trip to Berlin at Easter to visit her (pp. 237–239) was a positive, exciting event and an experience of new freedom, as soon as my father had ceased to run alongside the train as it slowly got going. For now I made myself comfortable in the sleeping compartment, with the pleasant sense of being an elegant and privileged young gentleman (accompanied though this was by a tinge of bad conscience), and a notion of adventure, as I was for once outside our sheltered sphere.

My "turning away from Menga" (p. 239) after my return from Berlin reconfirmed, however, the old unsolved conflicts. What had she done? She had taken me to a silly cabaret, staged by an acquaintance of hers, and it impressed me greatly on account of its indecency (there were half-naked girls pointing at themselves and warbling something about "hair here, hair there"). But then I subjected this experience to a kind of moral censorship and found she should not have taken me along to a performance of this kind. Even attending the less offensive show at the Scala now seemed to me to have been inappropriate or in poor taste. And hence A.F. noted that, after my return from Berlin, I was "ashamed about the cabaret," but did not dare to love anyone, "in order not to hurt Menga." And what follows thereafter also concerns my maneuvering and wavering between criticism of my mother and faithfulness to her, and taking revenge on the world by doing badly in school.

Even so, in the "dream of the waiting room" (p. 239) the stage of prepuberty is reached, including waiting for the "holy she-devil" for whom "men drop their pants." What I couldn't wait for was being grown-up. The attempt to force ejaculation was like a game, a pressing, motivated by a sort of frantic "urethral" ambition in the hope of not just wetting the bed but instead being able to produce the sticky fluid which was said to arrive with a pleasantly tingling sensation when you rubbed the penis, as it later did happen at night, accompanied by almost painful shivers of lust and a big yellow moon outside my window.

And here, with the anticipation of virility, the treatment breaks off, or, at any rate, the notes come to an end, to be followed only by some writings of mine, such as poems about waiting and time, and a polemical essay about the public secondary school (the *Realgymnasium*) into which I was finally accepted after considerable private tutoring by the wise and humorous Bernard Taglicht. As mentioned above, the Burlingham-Rosenfeld School had guided and spoiled us happy or unhappy few by simplicity, exemplary clarity of spirit or

375

taste, and a lack of firm scholastic requirements. Much as it went against my grain, I was now forced to cram systematically for tests and examinations in a setting which was both rugged and more pedantic, more vulgar and more restrictive, but provided a major context also for my friendships and flirtations or love affairs until my eighteenth year. At that time, after Austria's enthusiastic *Anschluss*, we Jews had to transfer to a *Realgymnasium* in Vienna's former ghetto district where, although addressed by our Aryan teachers as "scum of the earth," we were still permitted to graduate, which I managed to do in the late spring of 1938, just before my emigration to England as both a Jewish refugee and an "enemy alien."

INDEX

(See also Index of Persons and Places: xix–xx)

Adelaide (playmate of P.): 7
Adi (playmate of P.): 293
Aichhorn, August (city councillor; psychoanalyst; taught at B–R School): xi, xxix–xxx, 369
Aichhorn, Walter (son of August; pupil at B–R School): *see* Walter Aichhorn
Ann Nederhoud (foster child living at Rosenfelds): xxix, 366–367
Anne Heller (daughter of P. and Tinky): 303, 308
Anthony, Saint: 156, 353
Antinous: 312
Aphrodite: 306
Appendix: contents: 243 (*see also* A.F.)
Avenarius, F. [editor of *Hausbuch deutscher Lyrik* (anthology of German poetry)]: 360

B–R School (= Burlingham–Rosenfeld School): x, xxviii–xxxii, 301, 366, 375
Bacchus: 312
Baer, Basti, Sigurd: *see* Basti Baer; Sigurd Baer
Basti Baer (playmate and schoolmate of P. at B–R School): xxix, xxx, 11, 23, 25, 143, 157, 169, 188–191, 194, 207–209, 219, 221, 227, 359, 369
Beethoven, Ludwig van (Emperor Concerto): 269
Bella (Hellers' Great Dane): 112, 179, 285, 294
Bergmann, Thesi: *see* Thesi Bergmann
Bernfeld, Siegfried ("Brassi"; psychoanalyst; pedagogue): xi, 126, 127, 142, 337, 340–342, 344, 351, 373
Bernfeld-Viertel, Liesl (actress): 341
Bernhardt, Kurt (Curtis Bernhard; movie director): xxxvi, xlii, 290
Bethge, Hans (poet-translator): *see Chinese Flute,The*
Binder, Sybille (actress): xl, 227, 371
Bittner, Günther (professor of pedagogy; psychoanalyst): ix, 352
Blos, Peter (teacher-director at B–R School; later, psychoanalyst): *see* Peter Blos
Bob Burlingham (oldest child of Dorothy): xxiii–xxv, xxix, 72, 131, 157, 296
Bondy (directed progressive boarding school in Germany): 234–235
Bornstein, Bertl (psychoanalyst): 340
Brom, Mrs. (manicure): 283
Buffalo Bill (pulp magazine): 360
Buresch (gym teacher at B–R School): xxx, 27, 29
Burlingham: family: xxiii–xxv, xxix, 13, 73, 92, 97, 107, 141, 183, 193–197, 211, 223–225, 229, 235, 241, 310, 314–318, 361, 370–371. *For individual members, children, and "Mother" (Dorothy), see* Bob, Dorothy, Mabbie, Mikey, Tinky
Burnett, Frances Hodgson (author of *Little Lord Fauntleroy*): 28, 304

Chaplin, Charlie: 25, 27
Chevalier, Maurice (actor): 290
Chinese Flute, The (anthology of Chinese poetry, trans. H. Bethge): 8, 9, 13, 33, 41, 119, 296
Chris Menzel Heller (married to P.): 298, 302, 324
Christ: 293
Christmas Carol, A (by Charles Dickens): 91
Claudius, Matthias (German poet): 11, 297

Crébillon (writer): 291

David and Goliath: 19, 21, 25, 27, 33, 87, 298, 301–302, 320
Daxelhofer, Jeanpierre (2nd husband of P's mother): xlii, 347
De Sica (film director; actor): xxxvii, xlii
Dietrich, Marlene (actress): 337
Diomedes (Homeric warrior): 189
Dorothy Burlingham ("Mother"): x, xxii–xxv, xxvii, xxviii, 67, 193–195, 211, 314–317, 356, 361, 364
Dreams: 3, 7–33 passim, 43–47, 67, 81–83, 85–89, 93, 101, 103, 107–109, 111–115, 119–123, 131–161 passim, 169–181, 189–193, 199, 207–211, 215, 219–221, 227, 230–235, 239, 281, 283, 286–288, 293–295, 297–304, 312–314, 319–328, 333–335, 344–348, 351–359, 363–369, 372–375
Pavor Nocturnus: 3, 281–283
Dührauer, Friedrich (piano teacher): 284
Dumas, Alexandre (author of *The Count of Monte Cristo*): 126, 131, 338

Ekstein, Rudolph (psychoanalyst): *see* Preface (especially ix–xii)
Elisabeth (Queen of England): 169, 177, 356
Elisabeth Iona (pupil at B–R School): xxix, 155
Erik Homburger Erikson (psychoanalyst; teacher at B–R School; then in training with A.F.): x, xxv, xxviii–xxx, 72, 175, 181, 207, 221, 248, 355, 369
Erikson, Joan (teacher at B–R School; psychologist): xxx
Ernst, Dr. (art historian): 340
Ernst(i) (Ernstl; Halberstadt Freud = psychoanalyst W. Ernest Freud; grandson of S. Freud; pupil at B–R School): xxv, xxx, 47, 72, 99, 121, 296, 313, 351, 362, 369
Eugene, Prince of Savoy (Austrian hero): 282

Eula (Lilli K.; P's first governess): 161, 183, 194, 223, 293, 305–307, 351, 362, 369
Eva (pupil at B–R School): 181, 195–197
Eva Johannsen (dream of): 227, 372
Eva Rosenfeld (mother of Victor; co-founder of B–R School): *see* Rosenfeld, Eva

Fellerer, Max (architect; lover of P.'s mother): xl, xlii, 215, 222, 293, 338, 363
Flaubert G. (writer): 288
Francis Joseph, Emperor: 352
Frank, Karl ("revolutionary"; lover of P.'s mother): xlii, xliii, 124–127, 131–135, 141–142, 151, 161, 338–339, 342–344, 347–348, 350–351
Franzl (playmate of P.): 7, 221
Freischütz, Der ("Schreifritz"): 335
Freud, Anna: *see* A.F.
Freud, Sigmund: xxi–xxv, xxviii, xlix–1, 47, 73, 127, 138–139, 143, 156, 227, 231–233, 313, 318, 351, 354, 357, 371–373

Gabi Steiner (mother of Mädi; P.'s aunt): 11, 13–15, 219, 289, 292, 298–299, 367–368
Garger, Ernst von (art historian; friend of P.'s parents): 137, 161, 181
Goethe (poet): 25, 47, 101, 313 (Prometheus), 316, 348, 360
Goldscheider (taught at B–R School): 3, 286
Grieg (composer): 97
Grillparzer (poet; author of *Die Ahnfrau*): 174–175

Hans Heller (industrialist; P.'s father): ix–x, xii, xxxiii–xxxvi, xxxix, xl–xlii, xliv, xlvi, liv, 4, 5, 11, 17, 20–29 passim, 35, 47, 67, 83–89, 95, 113–115, 119–121, 124, 127, 131–133, 137, 139, 140–143, 149–151, 155–157, 161, 174–183, 188–